The Zouave Officer

The Zouave Officer

Reminiscences of an Officer of Zouaves—
The 2nd Zouaves of the Second Empire on
Campaign in North Africa and the Crimean War

Jean Joseph Gustave Cler

LEONAUR

The Zouave Officer
Reminiscences of an Officer of Zouaves—
The 2nd Zouaves of the Second Empire
on Campaign in North Africa
and the Crimean War
by Jean Joseph Gustave Cler

First published under the title
Reminiscences
of an Officer
of Zouaves

Leonaur is an imprint
of Oakpast Ltd

ISBN: 978-1-84677-918-3 (hardcover)
ISBN: 978-1-84677-917-6 (softcover)

http://www.leonaur.com

Publisher's Notes

In the interests of authenticity, the spellings, grammar and place names used have been retained from the original editions.

The opinions of the authors represent a view of events in which he was a participant related from his own perspective, as such the text is relevant as an historical document.

The views expressed in this book are not necessarily those of the publisher.

Contents

NOTE.—THE DEFINITIONS OF ARAB WORDS,
GIVEN BY THE UNDERSIGNED,
HAVE BEEN FOR THE MOST PART
TAKEN FROM
GENERAL DAUMAS' WORKS.

TRANSLATOR

(From the report of the U. S. Military
Commission sent to Europe in 1855-'56.

The *Zouaves* are all French; they are selected from among
the old campaigners, for their fine physique and tried
courage, and have certainly proved that they are, what
their appearance would indicate, the most reckless, self-
reliant, and complete infantry that Europe can produce,
With his graceful dress, soldierly hewing, and vigilant attitude, the *Zouave* at an outpost is the *beau ideal* of a soldier.

They neglect no opportunity of adding to their personal comforts; if there is a stream in the vicinity, the party
marching on picket is sure to be amply supplied with
fishing-rods, &c.; if anything is to be had, the *Zouaves* are
quite certain to obtain it.

Their movements are the most light and graceful I have
ever seen; the stride is long, but the foot seems scarcely
to touch the ground, and the march is apparently made
without effort or fatigue.

The *Zouaves* have, combined with all the activity and energy of the others, (the famous *Chasseurs*,) that solid en-
semble, and reckless, dare-devil individuality, which would
render them alike formidable, when attacking in mass, or
in defending a position, in the most desperate hand to
hand encounter. Of all the troops that I have ever seen, I
should esteem it the greatest honour to assist in defeating
the *Zouaves*.

George B. McClellan,
Captain 1st Cavalry,

Introduction

1

The *Reminiscences of an Officer of the 2nd Regiment of Zouaves* are compiled from notes, taken daily and with much care, by one of the most eminent officers of the corps.[1]

The 2nd regiment of *Zouaves*, from the day of its organization in Oran, up to that of this publication,—which treats of it in the double point of view, of the historical and the picturesque—has scarcely for a moment ceased to find itself in the presence of an enemy.

In the southern portion of our African colony—in the Kabylia of the Babors,—in the east—and, still more recently, in the greater Kabylia[2]—this regiment has been invariably associated with every expedition, and almost every feat of arms of the last few years.

"Of all the soldiers in the world, the *Zouaves* are the first and bravest," said the Marshal de St, Arnaud, on the eve of the battle of the Alma. These words have sown the seeds of a noble pride in the heart of every individual member of the corps.

There is a question which the non-professional reader may

---

1. The late General Cler, who was killed at the battle of Magenta.—T.
2. The last few pages, describing their services in the greater Kabylia, have been omitted in the translation, for the reason that they cannot justly come under the head of *Personal Reminiscences*, since General Cler, from whose notes this little work is compiled, was not engaged in these campaigns. Consisting of nothing more than a meagre historical sketch, of the two expeditions made by the French into that country in 1858 and 1857;—and devoid of all personal incident—they possess no sort of interest for the general reader.—T.

ask, and which we have often heard asked, ourselves; "How is it that regiments, which are recruited of the same material which enters into the composition of the other regiments of our army, should often seem to possess a certain superiority over other corps? Why should they be considered among ourselves as *corps d'élite*, and by our enemies as among their most formidable opponents?"

A reply to this double question may perhaps be found in a brief glance, at the organization, the method of recruiting, the *esprit de corps*, and the original formation of the regiments of *Zouaves*.

Shortly after the taking of Algiers, our government, wishing to avail itself, in the interests of our new colony, of the services which might he expected from some of the natives, who showed a disposition to enter into the ranks of our army, organized a battalion of infantry, of which the companies, though commanded by French officers, were almost entirely recruited from among the natives of the country. These new soldiers, whose oriental costume was preserved, took the name of *Zouaves*; a name given by the Turks to the native foot-soldiers, whom the *Dey* of Algiers was in the habit of recruiting from one of the great tribes of the Kabylia.

This battalion soon proved to be extremely serviceable in the war of detachments carried on against the native tribes. And it was, therefore, decided to raise a new battalion, and to form the two into a regiment. The command of this new regiment was given to Colonel de Lamoricière, whose name soon became one of the most famous in our African army.[3] The natives of the country were still admitted to serve in the regiment; but the French element was already predominant.

In 1843, after the first few years of occupation, and in consequence of the important services rendered by these two battalions, chiefly during the campaigns of 1840 and 1841, the regiment was increased, and made to consist of three battalions, of nine companies each; one of which constituted the *depôt*. It was

---

3. The same now in command of the little army of the Church.—T.

10

at this epoch, that the native soldiers almost entirely disappeared from the regiment. To be admitted into its ranks was already an object of emulation among the best, the bravest, and the most vigorous soldiers of the African army. The uniform,—the manner of life,—the greater liberty, there enjoyed, than in the garrisons of France, or even of Algeria,—the certainty of being present wherever a musket shot was to be fired,—the glory to be acquired,—were, all of them, considerations well calculated to attract into our ranks the descendants of those Gauls, our forefathers; whose proud saying it was, that, *were the heavens themselves to fall, they would yet bear them up on the steel of their lances.*

Besides the conditions of success resulting from the nature of their original organization, we should add, that it was subsequently decided, with much good sense, to give to the *Zouaves,* who were destined to light as skirmishers, the same tactics and armament already adopted for the *Chasseurs à pied.*

The system of recruiting, too, contributed not a little to the reputation which the *Zouaves* so rapidly acquired. We have already exposed some of the reasons which caused this arm to be sought in preference to others. We may add, that the soldiers of these regiments are usually admitted into them upon, their own application. Many of them are *enfans de Paris,* or of our other large cities.[4] Most of them, whose original entry into. the service had been as volunteers, or free substitutes,—having already served one term—are thus inured to the soldier's life, and thoroughly seasoned to the hardships which they gaily support, to the fatigues which they despise, and to the dangers of battle, of which they but make sport.

They are proud of their uniform, which resembles that of no other corps; proud of their name, of an origin so singular and mysterious; proud of the daring acts of gallantry, with which they are constantly enriching the history of their corps;

---

4. The unsuspicious stranger, inquiring of a Zouave from what tribe he hailed, has often been gravely answered, "From the tribe of the *Beni-Pantins,* or that of the *Beni-Mouffetards.*" (Equivalent to replying, that they belonged to the clan of the McPantins or to the *sept* of the O'Mouffetards—Pantin and Mouffetard being two important streets in the Faubourg St. Marceau of Paris.—T

and happy in the freedom which is permitted them, whether in garrison or on the march It is said that the *Zouave* is fond of wine; 'tis true but that which he seeks in the flowing bowl, is the excitement of pleasure and not that brutal oblivion of himself, induced by drunkenness.

These regiments number in their ranks—disbanded officers who, weary of an idle life, prefer to such the musket and the *chéchia*;[5] non-commissioned officers who have served out a first term, but who glowing with a courage sometimes bordering upon rashness, cannot rest long before they again seek to win from the risks of battle, their stripes and an honourable position or else a glorious death—ex officers of the *garde mobile*;—discharged sailors, strong and broad shouldered, who laugh at the cannon as at the storm—and finally young men of good family, who wish to replace, by the red ribbon of the Legion of Honour,—a ribbon bought with their best blood upon some field of battle,—the fortune which they had squandered away in the streets of Paris

No wonder, then, if with such elements, the regiments of *Zouaves* should make a brilliant show, in presence of an enemy! *Should war break out, we will show our Zouaves to the enemy* is the remark said to have escaped an eminent person, himself a competent judge in the matter of course, and a keen appreciator of military merit, just before the opening of the Eastern Campaign. The Russians saw them, in fact, saw them face to face; and in the course of this narrative we shall see whether, or not, they learned to appreciate these heroic soldiers.

The officers are usually selected from those belonging to regiments of the line, and always from among the number of those possessed of the most vigorous constitutions, both moral and physical. Full of energy, carrying their attachment to the flag to its last limits, ever ready to confront death, and courting danger, they are more ambitious of glory than of promotion. Like all their comrades in the army, indeed, they understand

---

5. more properly *chachia*, a cap—the red undress cap worn by the *Zouaves*, round which the turban is rolled when in full dress.—T.

12

that, in their noble profession, fortune is the very last thing, to be thought of.

To be the foremost among their gallant soldiers, and to set them an example of every military virtue,—this is their only thought. Our ancestors used to say, *Noblesse oblige*. They willingly adopt this noble motto. Their nobility, however, consists not in old family parchments,—but in the uniform, which they wear, and in that title of officer of the *Zouaves*, of which they are so proud.

The *esprit de corps*, that religion of the soldier, is carried to the highest point among the *Zouaves*. Many a simple private in these regiments would refuse to exchange his turban against even the stripes of a non-commissioned officer in any other corps. There exists, in fact, among the officers and soldiers of this corps, a spirit of military brotherhood, which, far from proving injurious, is found, on the contrary, to be the most solid bond of discipline. The officer, instead of an inferior, sees in the soldier only the companion of his dangers, and of his glory. Penetrated with the idea, that the "stomach's gratitude" [6] is by no means an unmeaning expression, he is constantly solicitous to spare his men every privation, which can be avoided.

In countries where there is danger that the necessaries of life may fail, or be not easily procurable, he does not hesitate to come to the aid of his soldiers, with all the means at his disposal. He lends them his own beasts of burthen; he advances money to their mess. The soldier, in return, exhibits the liveliest gratitude; he ever gives proof of the utmost devotion to his officer, and feels for him even a sort of filial respect.

Although the discipline is very strict, he never murmurs against the punishments which are inflicted on him. In the hour of battle, he never abandons his officer—but watches over him; to protect him, will incur death, himself,—and never suffers him to fall into the hands of the enemy, if wounded. At the bivouac, he

---

6. Were this "stomach's gratitude" a little more thought of and attended to in our army, we should not have one-third of the number of deserters which now annually exhausts its strength.—T

attends to his fire,—takes care of his horse or mule. If he comes across any fruit or game, he brings it to him. Convinced of the desire of their officers to see them well-fed on an expedition, the *Zouaves* often ask, that a part of their pocket-money should be employed in the purchase of provisions for the tribe.[7]

The colonel of a regiment of *Zouaves* is held usually in as much veneration, by his soldiers, as the father of a family. Not one among them but feels proud of his success, but rejoices at having contributed to his glory or advancement. Commands, which proceed directly from him, are sure to be executed with the utmost punctuality. "Since the Father has said so," they repeat to one another, "we must obey. The *Father* knows what he is about. He wants to do as much for us as possible."

In a critical emergency, the colonel may even resort to a Draconian discipline, without having to fear the disapprobation of his men.

Such are some of the considerations, which have seemed to us of a nature, to explain the brilliant reputation, which the *Zouaves* have won for themselves. We will now commence our narrative of the military existence of the 2nd regiment; an existence, which probably bears a striking analogy to that of the two other regiments of the same arm, and, we will add, to that also of the other regiments of our glorious army.

2

CREATION OF THE REGIMENT

Marshal de St. Arnaud, Minister of War, had earned his promotion in Algeria. Having often come in contact there with the regiments of native, or rather special troops, organized for service in the colony, he had, on many occasions, been enabled to appreciate their rare usefulness. As soon, therefore, as he had as-

---

7. According to a fashion borrowed from the Arabs, which exists in our African army, those soldiers who are in the habit of messing together, are said to belong to the same "tribe." Each individual of a tribe has usually his allotted functions, being those for which he has a special aptitude; one looks after the wood and the fire, another after the water and the cooking, a third makes the coffee, a fourth pitches the tents and so on.

sumed the portfolio, and as the solidity of the new government had begun to give promise of a more stable era, he began to think of increasing the permanent portion of our African army. In February, 1852, he addressed to the President of the republic a report, in which he set forth the advantages likely to accrue from such a measure.

The Prince President, taking into consideration the reasons urged in this report of the Minister of War, decreed on the 13th of the same month, the formation of three regiments of *Zouaves*, out of the elements composing the single regiment of that arm, then in existence.

Each of the three battalions of the latter, became thus the nucleus of a new regiment.

The 1st was organized at Blidah; the 2nd at Oran; the 3rd at Constantine. The basis of the decree of September 8, 1841, was that, adopted for their organization. And, contrary to that of the 16th of March, 1838, it was decided: 1st, that officers of the regiments of infantry might be admitted, with the same grade, into the three regiments of *Zouaves*, upon the designation of the Minister; 2nd, that the rank and file might be taken, in about equal proportions, from all the regiments of that arm.

As soon as the decree for the formation of these three regiments, was promulgated, there spread throughout the whole army, an emulous desire of being incorporated into them. Officers and soldiers who had already served in Africa, claimed that this service entitled them to. a preference; those in a different category, claimed, for that very reason, a right to this opportunity of making a campaign. All were eager to be allowed to wear a uniform, already illustrated by feats of arms, which, even in the brief space of its young existence,—that scarcely could date back as far as the first years of our conquest of Algeria,—had already won for the corps an imperishable renown for bravery.

Marshal de St. Arnaud, an admirable judge of the qualities which should distinguish the *Zouaves*, selected for the three regiments men of a vigorous temperament, both in a moral and physical point of view. Of the officers selected', nearly all had already given proofs of their soldierly qualities; whilst the non-commissioned officers and privates had all seen several years of service. It must be added, also, that many corporals, and no inconsiderable number even of sergeants, among those belonging to regiments stationed in France, voluntarily renounced their stripes for the sake of being included in the detachments ordered to join the new corps in Africa.

The 2nd regiment of *Zouaves*, organized at Oran, received, as its nucleus, the 1,400 *Zouaves* who constituted the 2nd battalion of the original regiment. These were marched from Blidah under the orders of Major Morand. The ranks were then filled up with 2,400 men, partly drawn from regiments in France, and partly from those stationed in the province of Oran; so that the effective strength of the regiment was, from the beginning, of not less than 3,800 veteran soldiers.

The new *fusil à tige* was given to the men; the same, which had been placed, for trial, by the Board of Artillery, in the hands of the men of the original regiment of *Zouaves*. A captain of Artillery was detailed to superintend the experiments, which were directed to be made with this new arm. Instead of the decree of the 4th March, 1831, regulating the tactics for infantry, that of the 22nd July 1845, laying down the tactics for the *Chasseurs à pied*, was the one adopted for the *Zouaves*.

All that has been just said of the 2nd regiment, applies equally to the other two; so that there was thus quickly raised a body of not less than 10,000 experienced soldiers, in the prime of life, well armed and instructed, brave, fearing nothing, and who could justly be considered a picked and chosen troop, ready and fit for anything. And most nobly were the high expectations then deservedly formed of it, to be subsequently realized in the Crimea.

Colonel Vinoy, (now General of Division,) then commanding the 54th of the line, an officer who combined with great firmness of character, a peculiar aptitude for the command of the special corps raised for African service, received the command of the 2nd Zouaves. To second him, he had Lieutenant-

Colonel Cler (now Brigadier-General in the Guard). The other field-officers were; the Commissary, Blaise; Majors Fraboulet de Kerléadec, Morand, and Malafosse; all of whom had, by long service in Africa, acquired all the experience and qualifications necessary, for the command of such troops as the *Zouaves*.

The regiment was organized under the eyes, as well as under the inflexible direction of General Pélissier, then commanding the province of Oran. At the end of three months, the 2nd Zouaves was uniformed, drilled, and ready to take the field. This result was due to two causes—the zeal of the officers, and the concentration, upon a single point, of all the elements which were designed to contribute to its formation.

Towards the end of April, the lieutenant-colonel, with two officers, six sergeants, corporals and privates, embarked for France, with the mission of receiving in Paris, from the hands of the Chief of the State, the eagle, which they were so soon, and at such close quarters, to display to the enemy.

In September of the same year, 1852, the 1st battalion was ordered to take up its station at Tlemcen, Certain companies of the other battalions were detailed for work upon the roads.

Two months later, came the order to prepare for an expedition. Great was the joy among the *Zouaves* of the 2nd regiment, on the receipt of this good news. The lieutenant-colonel was then in command of the regiment; grave family interests having recently called the colonel to France.

Book 1 - Laghouat

1

In the early part of November, 1852, General Pélissier received orders from the Governor General, to assume command of the different columns appointed to operate against Mohammed-Ben-Abd-Allah, Scheriff of Ouargla; who had been for some time trying to get up a revolt among the Saharian tribes of the provinces of Oran and Algiers. These columns, to the number of six, were organized at the military stations in the Tell.[1] Those ordered to operate in the south-east, had their points of departure fixed at Bouçada, Médéah, and Boghar. They were, after concentrating, to push on and form a junction with General Yusuf[2] The three others, under the immediate command of General Pélissier, were assembled at Sidi-bel-Abbès, Saïda, and Oran, The infantry portion of this second column was made up of the 2nd Zouaves.

The points of concentration of each of the various parts of this little army, were fixed upon the high plateaus; at Djeffa, for

1. Algeria, from the sea to the Desert, with reference both to its soil and to the character of its inhabitants, may be considered as divided into two great belts, the Tell and the Sahara, each widely differing from the other; the Tell, an arable and tolerably well-watered country, has a width, reckoning from the sea, of from 40 to 70 leagues. The dividing line of the waters is just beyond; and then comes the Sahara,—the Algerian Sahara—a region of oases, which, in its nature, forms the transition between lands that, without being cultivable, still produce certain plants—and the arid, bare, and seemingly illimitable wastes of the desert. Laghouat in the centre, Géryville to the west, and Biskra to the east, mark the limits of the Algerian Sahara.
2. A native chief, who has been for nearly 30 years in the service of France. He is the creator of the famous *Spahi* regiments.—T.

the eastern column—at El-Biod and El-Aricha, for the western.

On the 4th November, the 2nd Zouaves received its orders to make up two expeditionary battalions, of 600 men each. Companies of the 2nd and 3rd battalions were at once called in from Oran, Mers-el-Kébir, Arzew, and other places; and of these, two battalions, each of five companies, of 125 men each, were promptly formed. The sick were sent to Oran, so that none remained, but such as were in a condition to take the field at once. Lieutenant-Colonel Cler took the command, having under him Majors Morand and Malafosse, commanding battalions; Adjutants (with the rank of Captain) Abatucci and de Lignerolles, and Assistant Surgeon Canteloube.

Before entering upon a detailed description of the part played by the regiment in this trying expedition, we deem it useful to present a brief sketch of the events which had preceded it, as well as of the objects which it was intended to effect.

In the beginning of the year 1852, both our influence in the south, and the establishments, which we had attempted to create in the oases, were alike threatened with destruction, by the intrigues and fanatical preaching of the Scheriff of Ouargla, Mohammed-Ben-Abd-Allah. The tribes of the Sahara were beginning to waver in their allegiance to us. The insurrection, swelled by fragments of the great tribe of Arba, had attained the most alarming proportions in the neighbourhood of Mezab.[3] The attraction exercised by this focus of revolt over the wandering tribes of the Sahara, in the provinces of Oran and Algiers, finally inspired the commandant of the subdivision of Médéah with serious uneasiness; and to put a stop to the desertion of the nomads, he finally established himself among them with a column of troops, and spent the whole summer in the environs of Laghouat, Ksar-el-Aïran, and Tadjerouna.[4]

It was for us an object of the utmost importance, to isolate the

---

3. An oasis to the south of Laghouat, on the borders of the Algerian Sahara of the province of Oran.

4. Ksar-el-Aïran is near, and a. little to the east of Laghouat Tadjerouna, about 16 leagues to the south-west of Laghouat.

insurrection, both of the tribes of the sub-division of Médéah, and of those of the division of Oran. The Scheriff Mohammed still exercised a very great influence over the tribes bordering upon Morocco. And the fidelity of these last was already considerably shaken by the embarrassments which had been occasioned us by the tribe of the Beni-Sassen of the Riff.[5]

The Laghouat of the Ksel,[6] the Ouled-Sidi-Cheikh, and a part of the Maknas, all living to the south-west of the town of Laghouat, seemed, by the advanced position of their cantonments, to have been gained over to the Scheriff's party, and to be ready to furnish him with a new base of operations in the west. They were, in fact, occupying the Oued-Zergoum, about twenty leagues above Tadjerouna; and Mohammed, accompanied by powerful *goums*,[7] had been there to visit them.

Towards the end of March, a light, small column of French troops had moved from Mascara among these tribes for the purpose of compelling them to draw back, and return to the north of their *ksours*.[8] This operation was effected, without any resistance being offered to our troops, thanks to the position beforehand taken in advance of Tadjerouna, by the column of the general in command of the Médéah subdivision.

Before retracing its steps, this small column arrested the chief of the Ouled-Sidi-Cheikh, Si-Hamza; whose presence as a hostage at Oran, was calculated to repress any outbreak of hostile spirit among the adjoining tribes.

The general commanding at Médéah having returned to his head-quarters, the Saharian tribes of the two provinces found

---

5. The name of Riff is given to all that mountainous country on the frontiers of Morocco, extending from the sea to the neighbourhood of Ouchda, a town situated about 40 kilom. from the Mediterranean, near the eastern frontier of Morocco.
6. The Ksel is that mountainous country in the west, lying between the country of the Chotts (great pools of water, usually dried up); between the high levels (on the dividing ridge of the water-courses), and between the Sahara of Algeria.
7. The irregular cavalry of a tribe; also any band of horsemen armed and equipped for war.—T.
8. *ksours* are villages frequently surrounded by gardens, sometimes enclosed by walls of stones or brick, in which the tribes of the Sahara are accustomed to store the grain which they purchase in the Tell.

themselves, by reason of the steps which had been taken for that purpose, cut off from all communication with the insurrection. They spent the summer in malting their purchases of grain, apparently without dabbling in any plots; but, hardly had their purchases of grain been completed, and all their stores laid up, before it began to be noticed at Médéah, that Laghouat was fast becoming a market for the insurrection.

The grains of the Tell, brought thither in the name and on account of the subject tribes, were being sold to the refractory ones. The consequence was, that all the measures which had been taken, with a view to starving the insurgents into submission, were thus completely eluded. These last were drawing near to Laghouat with their flocks and tents, both to open a return trade with the different parts of the Tell, and to (quarter themselves by force upon the loyal tribes of the high table lands.

Matters had got to such a point, that General Yusuf was again compelled to leave Médéah in the month of October, in order to prevent, if still possible, the outbreak which now seemed imminent. He established a post at Djeffa, 80 kilom. to the north-east of Laghouat, for the double purpose of controlling the Ouled-Naïls, who occupied the country lying between Laghouat and Djeffa, and of facilitating the operations of the columns about to move into that part of the table-lands.

For, these table-lands, in addition to being destitute of natural resources, were so far removed, besides, from our advanced posts in the Tell, that it was almost impossible to give to an expedition, passing through them, that character of persistence, which could, alone, render it effective. On the approach of General Yusuf, the insurgents fell back several days' march in rear of Laghouat.

The French column pushed on as far as the oasis, and was well received by its inhabitants. General Yusuf made no stay there, but returned to Djeffa, leaving in Laghouat an officer of native *spahis*, with about twenty troopers of the Magzem,[9] with directions to maintain good order, keep up a strict police, and

---

9. Maghzem, or Makhzem, cavaliers, a band of horsemen—usually the mounted guard of some native potentate.—T.

do all in his power to restore and confirm the authority of our agents there.

On returning to Djeffa, the General learned that large numbers of the insurgents, crossing the country of the Makna, and spreading alarm and confusion throughout the whole Ksel, had thrown themselves into the Djebel-Amour; a chain of mountains which, with a direction from south-west to north-east, separates the oasis of Laghouat from the high plains of Cheliff. He was told, besides, that a band of their scouts had pushed on still further. Obliged to remain in Djeffa, for the sake of hastening the completion of the works undertaken at that post, Yusuf lost no time in reporting to the Governor General all that was transpiring, and meantime, while awaiting his orders, kept his eye upon the surrounding tribes.

When the news of these events had spread through-out the Sahara of Oran, it excited there a considerable fermentation. The tribes of the Djebel-Amour passed into the country of the Harrars, and these fast, in much disorder, flung themselves upon the Chott-el Chergui [10] The Laghouat of the Ksel also came down into the basin of the same *Chott* and planted their tents there pell-mell with those of the Harrars.

This state of things, skilfully improved for their own purposes by the Scheriff's agents and the discontented of both provinces appeared of sufficient consequence to General Pélissier then commanding the province of Oran to induce him to ask permission of the Governor General to move toward the south, in order to be in readiness to act promptly should matters assume a more threatening aspect. It was moreover become indispensible to restore confidence to the inhabitants of the Sahara to settle them again in then own country, and to arrest the growing influence of the Scheriff.

General Pélissier's propositions having been approved, three columns were immediately assembled at Oran, Mascara, and Sidi-Bel-Abbès, and thence moved on Frenda, Saïda, and El-

---

10. A large pond lying parallel to the limits of the Tell, on the high levels of the Sahara of Oran.

Aricha;[11] having passed which, they were to operate around El-Biod, on the outer borders of the country of the Harrars and the Hamians, and in the midst of that of the Laghouats of the Ksel.

We are now in possession of the events which preceded the expedition, in which the 2nd Zouaves took such a glorious part. And, therefore, leaving at this point the general operations, we shall in future confine ourselves to those of the column which set out from Oran, on the 6th November, and to which were attached the two field battalions of the regiment, whose history we desire to trace.

2

The 2nd Zouaves started from. Oran on the 6th November, bivouacked the same day on the Oued-Tlelat, (28 kilom.);[12] the next day, on the Oued-Sig, (32 kil.); the third, on the Oued-el-Hamman, (24 kil.); the fourth at Mascara, (24 kil.) During the first three days, the column had been exposed to heavy rains.[13] It had crossed the plain of Oran, and the forest of Muley-Ismäel, which stands in a slightly undulating and somewhat marshy *Sahel*, celebrated for the action in which Colonel Oudinot was killed.

Ascending the valleys of the Sig and of the Habra, along the course of the Oued-el-Hamman, the *Zouaves* had crossed the spurs of the mountain range, which divides the plain of Oran from that of Eghis; a range, covered with undergrowth and clumps of trees, and the scene of many combats with the Arabs during the war against Abd-el-Kader. On the opposite slope of these mountains is situated Mascara, overlooking the plain of Eghis.

---

11. Towns and an encampment in the province of Oran, situated (from east to west) on the confines of the Tell and of the high table lands.

12. A kilometre is 0.6313 of a mile.—T.

13. The nomad tribes of our Algerian colony shift their camping places almost daily, being wanderers over, rather than occupants of its territory. Good water with them, as with us, is the consideration which determines the selection of every stopping place; and thus our columns always bivouac on the banks of rivers (*Oueds*), or close to fountains and running brooks. (Which the Arabs render by the word *Ain*, so frequently prefixed to names of places.—T.)

Continuing their march on the 10th, the 2nd Zouaves halted for the night at Cacheron, in the plain of Eghis, 24 kil. distant; the 11th, on the Oued-el-Abd, 32 kil. further; the 12th, at Muley-Abd-el-Kader, (29 kil.); and the 13th, in advance of Frenda, a distance of 17 kil. During the latter half of the march, the column, after descending that side of the mountains, on which is Mascara, had, whilst crossing the plain, passed the night under the magnificent shade trees of Cacheron; and had plunged, the next morning, into an apparently interminable succession of mountains, separated one from the other by wide and beautiful valleys.

The Arabs seldom cultivate these valleys; it is true that they are in great part covered with woods. The column soon struck the mule path to Frenda, which it followed as far as the little Arab town of that name, built upon the highest point of the last acclivities, and just at the base of the table-lands.

From the 14th to the 19th of November, the two battalions successively halted at Aïn-sidi-Aïssa, Guétifa, Haoudji, Mekam-sidi-Chikz, Aïn-Krechal, and, finally, at El-Biod. They had marched over more than forty leagues, chiefly upon the table lands, and in the country of the *Chotts*,[14]—a vast, uncultivated solitude throughout; one long, dead, almost unbroken level, without trees, or any vegetation, and offering nothing to relieve the eye, but a few strips of meagre pasture land, and some pools of brackish water, the only remains of the *Oueds*, which, taking their rise in these regions, soon lose themselves in the sands, and are running streams, only during the season of the heavy rains.

From the 26th to the 39th November, the column tarried at El-Biod; and the *Zouaves* were employed in raising from its ruins the little Arab *Ksour*, once standing there; whose situation at the spring of a rivulet, gave a promise of advantages, which were subsequently realized. For, under the name of Géryville, this post became afterward the central point in our military organisation of that country.

On the 22nd, the 2nd Zouaves was overtaken by the col-

---

14. *Chotts* are immense ponds dried up during a portion of the year.

umn from Saïda, commanded by General Bouscarrin, (formerly Colonel of the 3rd Spahis.) General Pélissier being informed, the same day, that General Yusuf's column had left Djeffa, and was marching upon the insurgents, who were encamped around Laghouat, and in the neighbourhood of Ksar-el-Aïran, became immediately satisfied that the enemy would soon fall back upon Berram, which was the base of operations of the tribes then at war with us.

Berram is an oasis, lying to the east and somewhat without the boundaries of the Mezab. Acting at once upon these supposed intentions of the enemy, the general-in-chief gave orders for the assembling of the *goums* and footmen of the tribes still loyal to us, by the 25th of the month. His plan was to send the *goums* to attack the enemy on his retreat towards Berram, whilst he, himself, would support this movement of our native auxiliaries, by moving with his column in advance of Tadjerouna, on the Oued-Zergoum.

On the 25th November, accordingly, 700 horsemen of the southern *goums*, with 600 footmen, assembled at El-Biod, to start, the next morning, for the oasis of the Mezab. The movement of these *goums*, at this particular juncture, acquired great importance from the fact, that Genera! Yusuf had succeeded in overtaking, near Ksar-el-Aïran, a portion of the rebellious tribes. He had razed to the ground several *douairs*;[15] and what remained of the L'Arba, and such of the Ouled-Naïls, as still held out, had fallen back on Berram, just as General Pélissier had foreseen. In this position, throwing out scouts to the north, and with their west flank protected by immense wastes, by natural obstacles deemed insurmountable, and by the sands of the desert, they imagined themselves safe from any attack by us.

The *goums*, however, continued to advance towards the southeast. The warriors of the tribe of Hamian-Cheraga, turning out in mass, in aid of our object, were marching to the south. In or-

---

15. *Arabicè, Douar*—a collection of tents, the encampment of a tribe or family; so called, from the fact of the tents being pitched in circular form, around an open centre.—T.

der to protect these faithful and generous tribes, and to preserve their thus defenceless families and flocks from any attempted *razzia* of the enemy, General Pélissier sent orders to the eastern column, then at El-Arich, to move forward, and establish itself at Fekarine. It thus, at the same time, covered our lines of communication, and the tents of the Hamian-Cheragas.

On the 26th, learning that General Yusuf had been obliged to halt at the head waters, in front of the oasis, the general-in-chief resolved to march at once upon Laghouat. The troops with him were accordingly directed to set out the next morning.

The 27th, the 2nd Zouaves marched 25 kil., and encamped upon the southern declivity of the Ksel, near Stiten. The 28th, the regiment went 40 kil., and passed the night upon the Oued-Mekenza; the 29th, bivouacked upon the Khreneg-el-Malah, near the ruined *ksour* of Macta, (36 kil.;) the 30th, at the *ksour* of the Ouled-Yagoub, near Tadjerouna, (36 kil.;) the 1st December, at El-Aouita, at the *ksour* of the Mekralil, (36 kil.)

Laghouat being only a few leagues distant, General Pélissier's column was divided into two portions, to each of which a different direction was given. The convoy and greater part of the troops, under the orders of General Bouscarrin, went on for the night as for as Recheg, on the Oued-Mzi, 28 kil. beyond. The other portion, consisting of cavalry, artillery, and a picked battalion of the 2nd Zouaves, with the eagle of the regiment, marched straight upon Laghouat, under the immediate orders of the general-in-chief.

This part of the column halted, on the 2nd of December, a few leagues short of the city, in order to receive a convoy of water sent to it by General Yusuf; and, immediately after having received this supply, *débouched* into the plain lying to the south of Laghouat, by the Teniet-Erremel. Before entering upon the description of the assault and capture of this Arab city, we will first give a rapid sketch of the singular country passed over by the 2nd Zouaves from El-Biod to the oasis of Laghouat,

After quitting El-Biod, the regiment took a south-easterly direction, and soon, turning off from the channel of the Oued-

Sidi-Nasseur, began to climb the mountains of the Ksel, The country through which it was then passing, is seldom ever cultivated; indeed, scarce trodden by any other feet than those of the nomads, who come there for the purpose of depositing the grains, purchased from the Tell, in their *ksours*—a species of villages, with narrow and dirty streets, and of a most desolate aspect. These *ksours* are scattered here and there along the roads, or, to call them more correctly, the paths, followed by the tribes.

Towards the end of the second day's march, the column reached the southern point of the Djebel-Amour, ail extensive range of mountains, having a direction from south-east to north-west; and within, which are enclosed elevated plains, watered by a few scanty threads of water, that disappear from the eye, at every moment, in the sands, with which the soil is overlaid. Nothing can he more unusual, than the mountain shapes which here meet the eye.

On every side, arose cones, pyramids, truncated pyramids, all sorts of regular figures—representing, sometimes, a succession of redoubts rising one behind the other, and again, a series of diadems, or colossal tiaras, whoso rocky parts are of a yellowish colour. Their sides have, for the most part, a declivity of 45°, and are separated from one another by belts of sand and gravel, of about the same thickness.

One of the loftiest chains, that of the Khreneg-el-Malah, is the one most distinguished, also, by the singularity of its forms. It consists of three gigantic truncated pyramids, towering high above all the other summits of the range; and which, from its base upwards, is composed of layers of pure salt, porphyry and puzzolana Its summits are extinct craters; its sides, abrupt and seamed with ravines, are covered with volcanic remains and the debris of the different aggregations which have contributed to make up the primitive skeleton of the mountain.

The Oued-el-Malah which winds around its base following the course of a defile which is sometimes quite dry, becomes, at others and with but a few hours' rain, a raging, and utterly impassable torrent.

The 2nd Zouaves effected its dangerous passage on the 30th November, at the very moment that a frightful storm was bursting over the Tell and the table lands fortunately, much of the violence of the storm was already spent, before it reached them

On the fourth day's march the column emerged from the defile of the Oued-el-Malah into a region of sands and oases. No signs of cultivation here;—nothing but vast solitudes, relieved of their monotonous uniformity only by slight irregularities of the ground occurring at long intervals and by a few rocky and cragged elevations. The dividing ridge of the waters of Northern Africa lies hereabouts

The few *ksours*, which are met with, in this foreground of the desert are poor and of inconsiderable extent. They serve as granaries to the tribes of the Sahara, who, on their return from the Tell make a temporary deposit of their grain here. They are occasionally surrounded by gardens, in which may be seen a few scattered palm-trees; hut, upon the whole, are undeserving of the name of oasis. The first oasis, entitled to the name, which is met with towards the south, in these first stages of the desert, is that of Laghouat.

3

As before said, on the 2nd of December, towards three o'clock of the afternoon, General Pélissier's light column came suddenly out upon an immense plain. To the left, and two leagues away to the north, the eye discerned, stretching well across the horizon, a long and dark green line, slightly indented here and there, by the branches of a lofty forest of palm-trees. Rising above this line of verdure, were to be seen the blackened turrets of a city, and the white minarets of a mosque.

At sight of this scene, the beautiful and picturesque effect of which was something new to their eyes, the *Zouaves* were not slow in understanding that the goal of their long and weary journey was nearly attained. And there flashed through their minds an instantaneous presentiment of the admirable creation, which would soon burst, in all its splendour, upon, their sight—giving testimony, even in the midst of the desert, to the omnipotence of God, and to His infinite bounty, thus so lavishly bestowed even upon those who are doomed to dwell amid these fearful wastes of burning sand.

The oasis and the city of Laghouat were, in truth before them.

Situated 110 leagues to the south of Algiers, Laghouat is built in the shape of a double amphitheatre, upon the inner sides of two opposite hills, slanting from north-west to south-east. With a rocky and precipitous ascent from the outer plain, these hills stretch gently down towards each other, imparting in this way to the city, the appearance of an open fan. The two parts of this quaint-looking town are separated by the artificial channel of a small stream, the Oued-Mzi, on the banks of which the 2nd Zouaves had encamped the night before. Only a few years previously, and the oasis, alone, occupied this intervening space.

Laghouat, at the period of General Pélissier's arrival before its walls, covered an area of 2,000 metres in length, and contained 700 houses. With its low portal and wailed court, each one of these was entirely independent of the neighbouring houses. Built of sun-dried bricks, without any aid from lime, they were all of a uniform brown colour, which threw something of an air of mourning over the whole town.

The most noticeable edifice was the Casbah of Ben-Salem, in the south-western part. It consisted of four large, quadrangular houses, each of two stories high, and communicating one with the other; the upper terraces of which overlooked a part of the city, and were defiladed by a parapet, which caused the whole to be used as a citadel. Four gates, let into the walls, at the outer base of the hills, gave admittance into the town.

The two southern gates were connected by a long street, which ran through the whole length of the town, cutting it in two. The defences of the place consisted of a wall, four metres in height, which entirely surrounded it, and along which, at regular intervals, were towers, from eight to ten metres in height, constructed of sun-dried bricks, and having the appearance of broad-bottomed obelisks. To the north and south, that is to say at either end, were extensive gardens, which served the purpose of advanced works, and, indeed, of very excellent ones; for being intersected in every direction by numerous and high partition walls, they completely blocked all access to the town.

The total superficies of these gardens was from about 1,000 to 2,000 hectares;[16] their greatest width was of 3,000 metres. It thus appears that, after having reached the edge of the oasis, and before arriving within cannon-shot of the town, the columns of attack would still have to cross an extent of garden space near 1,200 metres in length, and which, if resolutely defended, could with difficulty he taken from the enemy.

The oasis of Laghouat teems with the richest and most luxuriant vegetation of which it is possible to conceive. The vine, the fig tree the pomegranate, and all the fruit-trees peculiar to the south of France, are equally at home there But the indisputable monarch of all is the palm tree—with its lofty bearing slender and elegant shape and evergreen foliage There were, in the oasis when the French column penetrated into it, not less than 25 000 of these valuable trees—which have been so justly denominated the "kings of the desert."

For, it would be certainly difficult to exaggerate the value of the palm-tree. Not only is it most valuable in itself;—its fruit, one of the principal articles of food among the tribes of the Sahara;—itself, their great staple, and the most undoubted source of their wealth: but it is also the friend and the protector of other trees. Under its green and compact dome, are to be found growing the most delicate plants; which, but for that shelter, would assuredly perish under the scorching rays of a sun, which spares nothing but its own dense foliage. There can be no question, that but for the camel, the barb, and the palm tree, man would be unable to traverse the arid plains of the Sahara, or breathe long in its stifling atmosphere.

The population of Laghouat amounted, at this time, to about 4000 souls. As we have before remarked, the town was made up

---

16. A hectare is equal to 2.47 acres—T.

of two pretty equal parts, connected together by rather a wide *plaza* which had been reclaimed from the oasis, and was still ornamented by a few palm-trees. These two quarters of the town, only separated from each other by an old gate, were inhabited by two distinct populations,—two different tribes, having each its own mosque, and its own separate civil administration,—and known, respectively, as the *Hallaf*, and the *Serin*.

It may be easily conjectured, that civil dissensions would frequently break out between two populations living in such close vicinity to each other, yet having different chiefs, and few interests in common. And, so, in fact, it was, for the Hallaf and the Serin were frequently at war with each other; but it was not their custom to call in strangers, either in the capacity of auxiliaries, or as arbiters to regulate their differences. Whichever party happened to be the most active, enterprising, and vigilant, succeeded in obtaining command of the stream by which the town was supplied, and was then enabled to dictate its own conditions to the other; for, the other party finding itself without water, was naturally at its mercy. Taken altogether, the relative independence of these two quarters of the same city was a most singular fact, not to be paralleled, perhaps, in the history of any other people.

Such was the town of Laghouat and its oasis, and such were its inhabitants, when General Pélissier made his appearance before the place, upon the Oued-Mzi on the 2nd of December. The commander of the French army lost no time in comparing notes with General Yusuf, for the purpose of getting a general idea of the condition of things, and of thoroughly acquainting himself with all the occurrences which had taken place before his arrival. He thus learned, that General Yusuf had already despatched several ineffectual summons to the inhabitants and *Scheriff*,—that his envoys had been beheaded,—that his propositions had only provoked an outburst of fanaticism,—and, that the *Scheriff's* only reply to them consisted of idle boasts and menaces. (*See note following.*)

Note:—As an indispensible complement to the above

description, we shall make no excuse for subjoining the following brief historical and political sketch of the town:—

Laghouat is a place of no inconsiderable antiquity. Where now stands a single city, were formerly to be seen two; close neighbours, and consequently great rivals, and each under the government of a powerful family—the Hallaf commanding in the northern, the Serin, in the southern town. There came at length a time, however, when one of these two families had become strong enough to seize upon the sole authority, to unite the two cities and rule over both oases. This family was that of the Ben-Salem, descendants from that of the Serin.

The old Ben-Salem wishing, in 1844, to strengthen himself against the power of Abd-el-Kader, asked to receive an official investiture of his principality from the French government, with the title of Khalifat. This was readily granted, and a column of troops was immediately sent thither under command of General Marey, and under the guidance of Ben-Salem himself

When he died, in 1850, the Hallaf, who had never relinquished the hope of one day resuming their power, and who saw that the sons of Ben-Salem were but little fitted to maintain their influence in the oasis, began to excite trouble in the town. The general commanding the sub-division of Médéah, thereupon came over to Laghouat for the purpose of confirming the authority of the Ben-Salem, who were our own partisans; and, on his departure, left an officer of *spahis* and some troopers, with that view, behind him. Scarcely had the general, however, returned to Médéah, when the Hallaf, calling in to their assistance the Scheriff of Ouargla, introduced him and his negroes into the place. The children of Ben-Salem, being forced to fly, sought a refuge, accompanied by our *spahis*, with General Yusuf, at Médéah. And the *Scheriff*, in the meantime, caused to be arrested as hostages, and kept as close prison-

33

ers, all the members of the Smalah of the Ben-Salem, with as many of their leading partisans, as had been unable to escape by flight.

So that when General Pélissier made himself master of Laghouat, the town was in the hands of the Scheriff of Ouargla, the Ben-Salem and their followers were in General Yusuf's camp, and the women, children, and servants of these unfortunates were shut up in the fortified house, called the Khalifat's house, and guarded by negroes. These last, whilst trying to defend themselves, had nearly occasioned the massacre, by our troops, of these guiltless and unfortunate victims of war—our own friends—but who were not known to be such by our soldiers at the time.

The next day, 3rd of December, at seven in the morning, General Pélissier made his arrangements to take a turn around the oasis and the town, that he might personally acquaint himself with the difficulties, which he would have to encounter in the attack. The reconnoitring force was chiefly composed of the cavalry of the two columns and of the friendly *goums*. On its arriving within view of a lofty eminence which went by the name of Sidi-el-Hadj-Aissa, and near which was built a *marabout*,[17] called by the same name, the natives turned out in force, lining the comb of the mountain which extended between these two points. The companies of the 1st Zouaves were instantly ordered to repulse this sortie; which they succeeded in doing, though not without severe loss, nor until after having been compelled once to fall back.

They were supported by a company of the 2nd Zouaves, commanded by Captain de Fresne, and assisted by a company of the 60th of the line, and one of the *tirailleurs indigènes*.[18] This

---

17. The term *Marabout* has various significations. It is, in the first place, the name of a fanatical class of Arabs in each tribe, who are distinguished above all the others by their excessive and bigoted zeal in the cause of Mahometanism. It is also the name given to the small solitary temples, or shrines of that faith, which are to be found scattered through the country, and which are usually built over the tomb of some *dervish*, reputed more than commonly holy. And finally, it is applied to the Mahometan priest, who has charge of one of these out of the way temples.—T.

affair over, and the general having completed his reconnaissance of the approaches to the town, and particularly of that part of it which he designed attacking, the troops were sent back to camp;—just as they reached it, the head of General Bouscarrin's column was seen *débouching* on the Oued-Mzi, through the Ras-el-Aïoun.

The same day, an hour before dark, Lieutenant Colonel Cler set out from General Pélissier's camp, accompanied by General Bouscarrin, to go and invest the place on the south, and at the distance of about 1,000 metres from it, in front and to the right of the *marabout* of Sidi-Aïssa. The troops placed under the lieutenant-colonel's orders for this purpose were the two battalions of the 3rd Zouaves, a battalion of the 1st Zouaves, and a small battalion, made up of three companies of *Zephyrs*,[19] and one of the *tirailleurs indigènes*. Just as he was quitting the bivouac, General Pélissier came up and, pressing his hand, said to him, "Recollect, Cler—that I must have you to breakfast with me, before noon tomorrow, on the highest terrace of the Casbah of Ben-Salem,"

When the advanced guard of this column had arrived within view of the *marabout*, and about 200 metres from the southernmost point of the oasis, 500 Arabs came out to meet it, uttering their accustomed yells—the column instantly halted and threw itself into order of battle;—but the enemy, remarking, doubtless, that it was strong both in numbers and position, again retired into the town, or behind his advanced posts. And, in a few moments more, both town and oasis had relapsed into that mournful silence, so characteristic of the cities of the desert, and which makes them resemble, for all the world, some vast necropolis.

By nightfall, the preparations for the bivouac had been completed; and by eight o'clock, two small hills, whose rocky summits were on a line with the prolongation of the southern part of the city, had been occupied by three companies of *Zouaves*,

18. A corps of native African sharp shooters in the service of France, the same so distinguished recently in Italy, under the nickname of "*Turcos*."—T.
19. The nickname given to the soldiers of the special corps, known as *bataillons d'Afrique*.—T.

(one of the 1st, and two of the 2nd regiment.) When this had been effected, all that separated the head of our advanced positions from the town, was the lofty hill, on which stood the *marabout* of Sidi-Aïssa, and against which we were about to direct our principal attack.

At ten o'clock, the two field-pieces were moved up to within thirty paces of the enemy's outposts, and ten balls and shells were fired from the greatest elevation of these pieces into the lower town, for the purpose of exciting confusion among the inhabitants,[20] and of misleading the garrison as to our true object. At eleven o'clock a column, composed of two companies of the 2nd Zouaves and one of the *bataillon d'Afrique*, with two sections of engineer workmen, all under the command of Major Morand of the 2nd Zouaves, was sent against the marabout and the hill, with orders to take them by main force, and thus perfect the head of our attack.

The operation promised to be one of no ordinary difficulty; for not only was the enemy there in force, but the positions to be taken were naturally of great strength, and to be carried only by a vigorous *coup de main*. Strict orders were given to make no reply to the fire of the Arabs; and these and the other necessary recommendations having been addressed to the men by the lieutenant-colonel himself, the little column set out in silence, thoroughly resolved upon the accomplishment of its perilous task.

The next ten minutes were moments of exceeding anxiety at the bivouac, for, everyone felt that the slightest hesitation might fatally compromise the success of the expedition; which, however, was one of the very last importance, since its issue, if favourable, was almost certain to insure our getting possession of the town.

But the confidence which his chief had placed in him was fully justified by Major Morand; he earned the enemy's works at

---

20. At the second discharge there arose a great clamour from the lower city, the cause of which, as ascertained after our capture of the city, was the sight of one of our balls falling within the court of the Khalifat, where was confined the family of Ben-Salem.

the point of the bayonet and so sudden was his attack, and such the impetuosity with which it was made, that it only cost him one man killed, and three wounded. Once master of the hill, he lost no time in occupying the *marabout* nor in commencing the construction of a breaching battery, and of another called the magpie's nest, destined to support it. The *marabout* was pierced through in two places to receive the 8 pr.: and a sandbag parapet was thrown up on its right, for the protection of the howitzer. Meantime, another company was hard at work to the rear and on the northern declivity of the hill, constructing a ramp for the passage of the pieces.

At one o'clock in the morning, when these different preparations had been in part completed, the two cannon, under command of Lieutenant Caremel of the artillery, and escorted by two companies of the 2nd Zouaves, set out from the bivouac. Nothing could exceed the promptness and resolution with which all these various duties were performed, though carried on under an uninterrupted cross-fire from the gardens on the right, and from the towers on the front of attack.

Fortunately, the night was very dark, which rendered the aim of the besieged so uncertain, that they only succeeded in wounding two of our men. After having set up the pieces in the breaching battery, the two companies, which had escorted them thither, returned to camp.

The remainder of the night was employed in completing the battery; an operation which the enemy scarcely attempted to molest. At break of day, every tiling was ready. At eight o'clock. General Pélissier, who had just reached the battery, gave the order for it, and the fire both of our two pieces of artillery and of our sharp-shooters was immediately opened on the town. At the same hour, Lieutenant-Colonel Cler received directions to prepare a column of assault, and conduct it to a place in rear of our attack, between the first and second hill. Four companies of the First and Five of the Second Zouaves were accordingly organized into two small battalions, and marched to the post assigned them.

On their way thither, the enemy threw a few round shot [21] at them, which passed over the head and front of the column, but, fortunately, without injuring anyone.

Hardly had Lieutenant-Colonel Cler reached his post, however, before he received orders to go and take command of the troops, in place of General Bouscarrin, who had just been severely wounded, whilst accompanying the general-in-chief to the battery. To reach this advanced point of our attack, it was necessary to proceed for some distance along a bare and rocky ridge, which was completely swept by the fire of the enemy, both in flank and front. Whilst doing so, his orderly, a trumpeter of *spahis*, was killed at his side, in the very same spot where, a few minutes previously, General Bouscarrin, and the general-in-chief's trumpeter, had. been wounded. The lieutenant-colonel himself, however, and the adjutant on duty with him, succeeded in reaching the battery uninjured.

The fire of our two pieces, aided for a moment by that of a mountain howitzer, was kept up for about three hours. Two sections of the 2nd regiment of Zouaves, under command of Captains Banon and Lauer, were then detailed for the defence of the battery, and with directions to keep in check the feeble fire of the place. The men of these two sections being sheltered behind sand-bags from the enemy's balls, had no losses to deplore. The walls of the *marabout*, indeed, were beaten down, and second Lieutenant Arnaud was wounded in the head by a stone; but there was no serious casualty. Meanwhile, a supply of. ammunition was brought up to the battery, and a signal pyre [22] was built to indicate the moment for the assault, and give notice of it to General Yusuf—who was, at the same time, to attack the town from the north. Soon, everything was in readiness for this last attack.

---

21. These balls were fired from a Dutch 6-pounder, which was carried by hand from one point of the walls to another, so as to create an impression that the Arabs were possessed of several pieces of artillery.
22. The two first *Zouaves*, set to construct this pyre, were killed. Corporal Vincendon, who succeeded them, was more fortunate. He is now a captain in the regiment, and a Knight of the Legion of Honour.

On the 4th of December, 1852, at eleven o'clock in the morning, General Pélissier, having satisfied himself that the breaches, made in the two curtains, were at length practicable, gave orders for the immediate formation of the three battalions, which were to make the assault. Four companies of the 1st, and eight of the 3rd Zouaves, were formed at once; the first-named four, under command of their major, (Major Barois, of the 1st,) were to attack on the right; the 3rd Battalion of the 2nd regiment, commanded by Major Malafosse, on the left, whilst the 2nd Battalion of the same regiment, under the orders of Major Morand, was to constitute a reserve, but with orders specially to support the right attack. To this last column, principally made up of the men who had been on guard at the battery, was intrusted the eagle of the regiment, A section of engineer workmen, commanded by Captain Brunon, of the engineers, accompanied these columns.

Upon the appearance of the signal agreed on, which was at length seen shooting up from the breaching battery, the bugles sounded the *Zouaves'* own march. And, whilst General Yusuf, admonished by the glare of the signal-fire, prepared to commence the attack on the north side of the town, the assaulting columns on the south, also, received at length the ardently desired command to advance.

There are few moments more solemn, than those which precede an assault. With silent lips, but eyes and ears eagerly on the watch to catch, and, if possible, anticipate the signal, each man of those who soon are to mount the deadly breach, fairly longs for that moment to arrive. Nor is a less impatience felt by those, who, following close upon the forlorn hope, expect shortly to have to take the places of their friends and companions, slain by the enemy's hands, or buried beneath the crumbling ruins.

There is, perhaps, not one among all these soldiers, who would not gladly know himself to be twenty-four hours older; not one, however brave he may be, whose past life and past sins do not rise up suddenly before him, or who does not once more, in imagination, take a last tender leave of friends, of family, of one perhaps dearer to his heart,—and yet, among them all, not one—who, in spite of the danger which overshadows him, does not feel proud, and esteem himself most happy, to form, one of the storming party. For, should he escape from death, how proudly will he not he yet able to say, some evening at the bivouac-fire, or later, perhaps, over his own family hearthstone, "I, too, was present at such a siege: I was even the first to mount the breach!"

In fancy he can already see his colonel, stopping as he goes by, to call him, and say, "Ah! it is you, my friend; you were with me at such an assault, and well do I remember how daringly you behaved on that occasion."

Should he fall, still chiefs and comrades will say of him, "Poor ——, what a gallant fellow he was!"

And then the cross,—the hope of gaining the cross of the Legion of Honour—that cross, sublime creation, which has produced so many heroes in our beautiful land, how much is it not in the thoughts of both soldiers and officers! Shall not the cross, perhaps, be the reward of his courage? To return home, decorated, at the end of the campaign! what a delightful thought! With inducements such as these, and by working on those chivalric feelings, which are still natural to the hearts of Frenchmen, and glow so brightly in those of our soldiers, one may accomplish with them almost anything,—one might, I had almost said, attempt the impossible.

On the 4th of December, 1852, then, twelve splendid companies of our old African campaigners,—1,200 of those *Zouaves*, whom as yet nothing had been able to resist, were impatiently awaiting near the breaching battery of Laghouat, the signal from their bugles. And they were shortly gratified; for, yet a moment more,—and there arose, pealing upon the air, the stirring notes of the *marche des Zouaves*—that warlike march, which had sounded already for the storming of Constantine, as well as before the redoubts of Teniah, of Mouzaïa, and at Zaatcha!

At the first sound of this well-known blast, the right battalion, (1st Zouaves,) bounding forward at a run, so rapidly clears the interval which separates it from the foot of the rocky slope, beyond which lies the breach, as scarcely to suffer any loss. The left battalion, (2nd Zouaves,) preceded by a forlorn hope, composed of one of its own sections, dashes simultaneously across the rough and rocky space which extends from the outer edge of the oasis as far as the lower city; but, exposed to a cross fire, which sweeps every foot of the ground it has to pass over, reaches the foot of the hill with a loss of not less than eighteen men.

The reserve, (2nd Zouaves,) following close on the heels of the right attacking column, arrives in its turn, and with but slight loss, at the foot of the declivity, on top of which stands the breached and battered wall of the curtain.

At the same instant, General Pélissier, followed by the officers of his staff, by the lieutenant-colonel of the 2nd Zouaves, and by a section of the guard of the trenches, advances also to the breach for the purpose of superintending in person, and, himself directing the general assault upon the town

The twelve companies of *Zouaves*, as before remarked had already reached the foot of the hill, which constitutes the natural *glacis* of the town. Once arrived at that point these brave soldiers dash forward at a run and climbing over all obstacles or crossing with the help of short ladders the gaps made by our cannon in the walls and putting to the sword all who make any effort at resistance, they with that *furia francese*, so dreaded by our enemies, burst like a sudden whirlwind into the upper part of the town

Intimidated by the rapid progress of the storming columns, the Laghouat hastily abandon their defence of the upper town, and precipitate themselves by the hill slopes, to the right and left, into the lower town. The Arabs also, who had been posted m the gardens, fearing lest then retreat should otherwise be cut off, abandon likewise then positions, on the outer borders of the oasis, and fall back within the safe cover afforded by the perplexing labyrinth of the palm groves

And thus, in consequence of the vigour of our attack, the upper city soon falls entirely into our hands. Quickly following up this happy result, General Pélissier gives orders to the reserve column to throw itself rapidly to the left, and to the left column to march straight upon the Casbah of Ben-Salem, whilst he directs Lieutenant-Colonel Cler, at the head of some companies, taken from the three battalions, to move also upon that citadel, and attack it both in flank and

The Casbah is unable to hold out against this combined attack. Captain Fernier and his *Zouaves*, accompanied by Lieutenant-Colonel de Ligny, Superintendent of Arab affairs in the province of Oran, bursting open the door, rush headlong into the interior of this species of fortress. Its defenders are driven, at the point of the bayonet, into the court, the upper stories, even upon the terraces above. Just then, bethinking himself suddenly of General Pélissier's remark to him the day before, the lieutenant-colonel of the 2nd Zouaves hoists the eagle of his regiment upon the dome of the minaret, at the very moment that the chief of the negroes to whom the *Scheriff* had intrusted the defence of the place, falls dead at his feet, pierced through and through by the balls of those who composed the guard of the French flag.

The city was ours, but the 2nd Zouaves had to pay dearly for this brilliant feat of arms. It cost them the blood of no less than sixty of their number, who had been either killed or wounded; without including Major Morand, who had been mortally wounded, whilst leading on his column against the Casbah. Though a glorious, it was yet a bloody baptism for the eagle of the new regiment.

We shall be excused, we trust, for devoting a few lines, here, to the brave Morand. This intrepid officer, one of the bravest in his regiment, was endowed with a singularly chivalric spirit. A passionate admirer of the heroes of the first empire, and with some reason to be so, since he was, himself, the son of one of those men of bronze, who had contributed so much to the glory of the great Napoleon.

Morand, on the eve of the storming of Laghouat, had requested permission from his commanding officer, to wear on that occasion a light-coloured, gray overcoat over his uniform, for the express purpose of being, thus, the more easily recognized by his own soldiers, and the Arabs. As he was just in the act of mounting the breach, he sounded, himself, the *marche des Zouaves* upon a small bugle, which he had been in the habit of carrying with him into action—ever since he had been a captain in the *chasseurs à pied*.

As they were bearing him to the rear, mortally wounded, he chanced to be carried before two of the picked companies of the 50th of the line. These brave soldiers eagerly hastened to pay him all the honours due to his rank. Touched by this mark of respect, Morand, making an heroic effort to overcome his weakness, turned to them, and half rising, said, "*Voltigeurs* of the 50th, I thank you; may you meet with a better fortune than myself, for, my career as a soldier is here ended." Nor was he in this deceived; as it was thought necessary to amputate his leg at the thigh, and he shortly after died. His brother, Louis, a lieutenant, was wounded on the same day, whilst fighting at the head of his section.[23]

It was not long before General Pélissier himself arrived upon the terraces of the Casbah of Ben-Salem. He gave immediate orders to the commanding officer of the 2nd Zouaves, to rally the scattered fragments of his regiment and complete the capture of the place, by stretching out a hand to the assistance of General Yusuf; who, at the head of his column, had also penetrated into the town, by escalading the walls on the north side. Colonel Cler was also directed, after effecting this junction, to clear the town of every Arab who should continue to resist, and to pursue them even as far as the gardens of the oasis.

The instructions of the general in chief were carried out to the letter. The open square of the Moorish Baths, in the centre

---

23. There were four of these brothers Morand is the 2nd regiment of Zouaves— they are the sons of that heroic general, who bore the brunt of Davoust's terrible battle of Auerstadt, in which 60,000 of the flower of the Prussian army were beaten by 30,000 French. Louie Morand, the lieutenant here mentioned, was, at the opening of the Italian war, a major, having for a while been orderly officer to the Emperor.—T.

of the city, was in this way taken possession of. On reaching which. Colonel Cler got sight, to his left, of an Arab, upborne on either side by two Mzab, who was making for one of the gates opening into the oasis, and just about to pass through it. He had him instantly pursued; but the group succeeded in escaping under cover of the thickets in the gardens.

This Arab turned out to be no less a personage than the *Scheriff* himself—not in the least, wounded, but so overwhelmed by his defeat, as to be unable to walk without assistance. Indeed, if what the Arabs of the Tell—those especially, living in the western part of the province of Oran, and who are well acquainted with him—say of the *Scheriff*, be true, he is, though a man of great political abilities, most sadly wanting in the courage of a soldier.

The *Zouaves*, after marching through a series of narrow and tortuous streets, many of which were completely overshadowed by the projecting upper stories of the houses on either side, succeeded at length in coming up with General Yusuf's column, and, forming head of column to the left, took possession of the buildings communicating with the gardens. This part of the city, however, was but feebly defended.

As the column was retracing its steps to the Casbah of Ben-Salem, the attention of the soldiers was attracted by shouts and screams proceeding from a fortified house, in which a large number of persons seemed to have taken refuge.

This house, which had been the property of the Ben-Salem, and was for that reason called the house of the Khalifat, was, at the moment, filled with the families of those, who had been the chief partisans of the former chief of Laghouat, and whom the *Scheriff* of Ouargla had retained there as hostages, as we have before related. The Mzab, to whom the *Scheriff* had confided the guard of these unfortunates, having fired upon our troops, while these were engaged in the attack upon the Casbah, had drawn upon themselves, first the attention, and, subsequently, the vengeance of the assailants.

For, as soon as the Casbah had fallen into our hands, our men precipitated themselves with the utmost fury upon the house of the Khalifat. The first court was quickly carried; and the garrison, still continuing to fire, had retreated into a large, interior court, surrounded by terraces, and apartments filled with Jews, women, children, and old men.

Just at this moment, the Lieutenant Colonel of the 2nd Zouaves, having effected an entrance through a small back door, which he had forced open for this purpose, made his appearance in the innermost part of the house, accompanied by a few of his officers and *Zouaves*, and saw at a glance what was passing. But, being recognized as a chief by his uniform, he was instantly surrounded by the unfortunate Laghouat, the poor victims of this war, who, flocking around him and his officers, in the hope of thereby escaping the fury of their assailants, so hung upon their vestments and clung to their limbs, as almost to pin them to the spot.

Half suffocated by this frantic embrace, and completely separated from their soldiers by this living wall of human flesh, the officers of the 2nd Zouaves had the utmost difficulty in disengaging themselves—in making themselves known to the conquerors—and in putting a stop to the carnage which was going on. However, thanks to their energetic efforts, they succeeded at length in saving the lives of no less than three hundred Laghouat, belonging to the highest aristocracy of the town; and who were at once transferred to the great Casbah. Hither were also carried five flags, which had been taken in the house of the Khalifat. The *Zouave*, Labalme, who had captured one of them was, on the spot, promoted by his colonel into the first class.

It was, now, two in the afternoon, and the city of Laghouat was in the quiet possession of our troops. Even as, on the previous day, he had announced that he would, General Pélissier had penetrated into the city before noon. Nor did he forget to remind Colonel Cler—who, after the taking of the house of the Khalifat and the deliverance of the hostages, had rejoined him—of his promise to breakfast with him on the highest terrace of the great Casbah. And, there, amid the bloody relics of the fight, surrounded by captured standards, seated upon rich Arabian carpets—overlooking the whole oasis, as well as the almost boundless horizon of the desert—an essentially military repast was served up to the general-in-chief and to General Yusuf, who had just arrived at the Casbah.

There were, no doubt, many things wanting to it. For instance, in lieu of silver, the guests were obliged to content themselves with the knives of the Sappers of the 2nd Zouaves, which those brave soldiers were kind enough to lend to their chiefs. The coffee, too, was prepared in their camp kettles. Yet this improvised breakfast, seasoned as it was by the appetite which results from three hours' hard fighting, and from the rejoicing inspired by a splendid victory, was thought delicious by all who partook of it.

In the evening, a little before nightfall, the children of Ben-Salem and such of their principal officers and partisans, as had taken refuge in General Yusuf's camp, hearing of the miraculous escape of their wives and families, came eagerly forward to reclaim them. Colonel Cler, who had been appointed by General Pélissier commandant of the town, was not a little gratified at being relieved of this fair, feminine population, whose presence in the midst of his troops, still beside themselves with the excitement of victory, might not have been unattended with inconvenience to say the least, if not with danger.

Indeed, some of these women, the Jewesses especially, with their biblical costume in such sad disarray, with their great black eyes, their magnificent hair, and their complexion of such a pale, delicate white, presented a type of beauty seldom to be met with elsewhere than in the East, or, as here, in the desert. Each of these fair unfortunates, on quitting the great Casbah, to which they had been removed after the fall of the town, testified her gratitude to the French officers, by kissing their hands and even their garments.

One of the battalions of the 2nd Zouaves passed the night in the house of the Khalifat, amidst the wreck of furniture and the confused remains of provisions, clothes, and spoils of every sort, with which the courts were littered. Such of the *Zouaves* as the enemy's balls had spared, gathering around the bivouac fire, exultingly related their feats during the day—full of pride and joy at having thus again added a new lustre to their uniform.

The next day, the second battalion went out to join the first at the camp on the Oued-Mzi, distant about a league from the city; and there remained until the 16th of December. The garrison of Laghouat, meanwhile, was employed under the orders of Colonel Cler, in clearing out and burning to ashes the numerous dead bodies, with which the streets and houses were everywhere heaped, and whose decomposition threatened to become a source of pestilential disease.

On the 9th of December, the army fulfilled the sad and solemn duty of paying the last funeral honours to the remains of Major Morand and of three other officers, killed during the siege; all of whom were buried on the breach, as had been the brave Colonel Combes, at Constantine, some few years before.

On the 16th, the regiment commenced its return march for Oran. The 2nd Zouaves set out on its journey north, in company with the column under General Pélissier's command. It made its noon-halt, the first day, at Reched, and established its bivouac that night at the *ksour* of Tadjerouna, 23 kil. from Laghouat. The next day, it went as far as Aïn-Madhy, 24 kil. further.

Aïn-Madhy is a little town, which was the theatre of important events during the first few years of the religious and political history of Abd-el-Kader. And it had still for its chief, in 1852, the principal actor in these, a *marabout* of ancient lineage,—himself a chief of great renown,—the old Tedjini.

After having been many times besieged, this little town, situated just at the commencement of the Sahara of Algiers, had, thanks to the energy of the Tedjini family, succeeded in making itself independent. It paid no tribute to the Turk, and was at peace with all the world,—when, in 1838, Abd-el-Kader, who was meditating a renewal of his religious war against us, cast his eyes on Aïn-Madhy, and resolved to establish his *depôt* there. It was there that he proposed to himself to leave his Smalah and his treasures, in the event of our getting possession of the establishments which he had created in the Tell.

To give some colour of a pretext, however, to the quarrel which he meant to pick with the Scheriff Tedjini, Abd-el-Kader publicly declared, that, as the *Scheriff* of Aïn-Madhy had failed to make his appearance at an assembly, specially convoked with a view to another holy war against the Christians, and at which all the other Mahometan chiefs had been present, he was unworthy of remaining any longer at the head of a population of Mussulmen and thereupon he came with some cannon and a body of his regulars and laid siege, to the place

All the neighbouring tribes declared themselves for the brave and venerable *Scheriff* of Aïn-Madhy. And the latter after sending away all who were not capable of bearing arms, shut himself up in his town with 350 of the best marksmen of the Sahara and during eight successive months had the glory of success fully resisting the utmost efforts of the *Emir* , who was at length compelled to abandon his original project though not before he had ravaged the gardens, cut off the waters, and committed the most cruel acts if devastation.[24] A single mutilated palm tree was the only thing left standing in the gardens; for which old relic of the war, the Arabs of the desert profess even to this day, the greatest veneration.

However, before retiring altogether from before the place, the *Emir*, who was but little in the habit of stopping at any means, whether honourable or the contrary, which promised to secure him his ends, had first recourse to an infamous stratagem for the purpose of gaining possession of Aïn-Madhy, and of at least wreaking his vengeance on those who had just so signally defeated him. He, therefore, in virtue of a vow which he pretended to have made many years before, begged permission to remain five days in the town, to say his prayers at the mosque.

Such a request, addressed by one *marabout* to another would, he felt sure, never be refused:—nor was it The brave and loyal-

---

24. These details are taken from General Daumas' curious and instructive work upon the Sahara of Algiers.

hearted old Tedjini admitted him at once into the place, and even retired himself to Laghouat, that he might leave his fellow *marabout* more liberty in the fulfilment of his vow. But no sooner had Abd-el-Kader secured his object, than he, like a very chief of brigands, in violation of al! faith and of all law, and although he had sworn upon the Koran to observe the treaty which had been just before concluded, had the walls and every house in Aïn-Madhy razed to the ground, sparing only that, in which he had taken up his own lodgings, and which had been the dwelling of the Scheriff.

This revolting action, which would alone suffice to fix an odious stain upon the life of Abd-el-Kader, aroused the populations of all the neighbouring tribes and *ksours* against him. When, recalled to the north by the course of events in that direction, he at length withdrew from Aïn-Madhy, they fell upon his convoys, massacred his escorts, and did him all the harm in their power. Tedjini subsequently returned to his town, and having rebuilt its walls and houses, continued thereafter to govern it undisturbed, with a reputation for holiness and courage, which caused him to be greatly revered by all the inhabitants of the desert.

It was reported of him, that he had taken an oath never to look upon the face of a sultan; and he had, in fact, refused to see Abd-el-Kader in 1838; whilst in 1844, though he had given orders for the sumptuous entertainment of the officers of General Marey's column, then proceeding under the guidance of Ben-Salem to Laghouat, he had yet declined to make his own appearance before them.

As all of these particulars were well known to the officers, and even to many of the *Zouaves* of the 2nd regiment, so was it not without, a sensation of profound amazement, that the French column saw coming out to meet it, no less a person than the *Scheriff* himself, at the head of his followers. It was certainly the very first time that the venerable Tedjini had ever condescended to face a *Kébir*.[25] He, however, politely invited General Pélissier to honour him by a visit to his house, and by accepting

---

25. *Kébir*, means great, powerful.—T.

of a *diffa* there.[26]

At length, for the first time, were the streets of this as yet unconquered city to be trod by Christian feet. But there is every reason to believe, that the *Scheriff* was greatly more influenced, on this occasion, by the apprehensions excited in him by the presence of a powerful French army, than by any very sincere desire, which he may have entertained, of drawing more closely together the bonds of his alliance with our colony.

It was in the library of his Casbah, that Tedjini received General Pélissier and his officers. And, on his giving orders to that effect, the *diffa* soon made its appearance. Each one seated himself, after the eastern fashion, around a large carpet on which were set out the various dishes, of which the repast was composed. A steward from Tunis presided over a host of servants, who waited upon the guests.

There can be few more curious spectacles, than that exhibited by one of these *pantagruelic* repasts, which the Arab chiefs are occasionally in the habit of offering to our generals. Precisely as in the amusing vaudeville, entitled, *Vatel, or, the grandson of a great man*, one scullion, after another, makes his appearance on the scene—with this difference, however, that, in the vaudeville, there are not more than from eight to ten, all of them wearing the usual prosaic, white jacket, and covered with the still more prosaic, cotton cap—and their evolutions, too, are there limited to the narrow space of only a few square metres.

Whereas, in Africa, the scullions appear to the number of hundreds, each carrying upon a wooden platter, some preparation more astonishing, if possible, in its nature, than those which had preceded it. Some of them are barefoot; the only garment worn by others is a woollen shirt, confined at the waist by a camel's-hair rope; others, again, rejoice in the possession of an old *burnous*,[27]—which once, perhaps, was white.

Their large, black, speaking eyes, their thin and bony bodies,

26 *Diffa* has the various significations of gift, repast, hospitality in general—T
27. *Burnous* is the name of the long woollen cloak with a hood to it, which is universally worn by the Arabs and Kabyles.—T..

their long, hooked noses, their limbs blackened by constant exposure to a burning sun, the calmness of their mien, the invariable silence which they observe, the gravity with which, one after a they come in and set down before you, their *couscaws*, their *pilaws*, their mutton, their eggs, their griddle-cakes, &c.,—all these various features of an almost patriarchal ceremony, impress it with a character of originality, which is not devoid of charm.

It must be admitted, however, that the *diffa* offered to the French column by the *Marabout* of Aïn-Madhy, differed in one respect wholly, from other similar entertainments,—that is to say, by the greatly superior style and appearance of the attending menials.

For, many of old Tedjini's servants belonged to the first families of the town—yet, withal, were proud of forming a part of his domestic retinue. All of this description were quite richly dressed. In fact, everything about the house, or rather palace of this little prince of the Sahara, was characteristic of the sedentary habits of the master.

Such contrasts are frequently met with in the various parts of our colony. For, whilst with those who dwell in tents, everything is always in a sort of mere provisory condition, each man being bound to hold himself in constant readiness to follow his tribe or his *douar*, wherever they may go, and to transport his wives, his children and his flocks, from one point to another at a moment's warning,—with the Kabyles, on the contrary, or those who live in *ksours*, everything bears the impress of stability,

For us Frenchmen, there will be always wanting at such repasts the one thing, most needful—wine, that is to say, and cordials. Still, it must be acknowledged that, in these latter times, there have been known a few *caïds*, who have had the good taste to offer us at their *diffas*,—in addition to the viands peculiar to the desert—some bottles of rare old Bordeaux, Burgundy, or Champagne, which they had managed to procure. Heaven only knows how or why, but which were none the less acceptable to their guests.

The following is the bill of fare of the *diffa*, offered by the

Scheriff of Aïn-Madhy to General Pélissier's column on the 17th of December, 1852:

1° Dates—fresh, excellent, and in abundance.

2° Camel's milk—served up in little silver kettles, which circled round among the guests, each one taking a drink himself, and then passing on the bowl to his neighbour. Of this ceremony, it may be observed that, however redolent it may seem of fraternal charity, and the simplicity of a more primitive age,, it is yet, to the stranger unaccustomed to it, anything but agreeable.

The milk of camels is far richer than that of our best cows it is held in high repute by the people of the desert and the Arab chiefs of the Tell are even quite chary of it.

3° An endless variety of *fricassees*—composed of chickens and rice, and seasoned with such a profusion of red pepper and pimento, as to make one's hair fairly stand on end.

4° The *couscoussou*—a standing dish on all such occasion The *conscoussou* is a very excellent and a very acceptable dish, even to French palates, when prepared after a French fashion; and, in this way, it is often served up at the tables of our officers. But, with such a dosing of red pepper and other similar ingredients, as that of the pious Scheriff had undergone, it must be confessed that it is rather difficult to make it sit lightly on a European stomach.

5° A succession of sheep roasted whole, with accompaniment of kidneys, cooked in their own grease. We are bound to speak respectfully of these, for there are few roasts which could presume to compare with them. So much, indeed, do the Arab cooks excel in the art of roasting, that it is really difficult to comprehend, why the millionaires of Paris do not send their *chefs de cuisine* down into the Tell and the Sahara, to take a few lessons in this art.

6° A great heap of fritters and of cakes made with honey—the study of which would, we think, hardly repay the culinary artists of France, for making the above-mentioned journey.

All of the above was served up in great profusion; but the

only drink offered with it, was water—perfectly fresh, indeed, but, alas! scented with rose and jessamine! In default of wine, good wine, a Frenchman is undoubtedly able to content himself with pure water—but perfumed water! ...

At the conclusion of this Homeric repast, which, we are bound to say, produced two very opposite effects upon the Scheriff's guests,—effects on which we deem it unnecessary to dwell, however,—coffee was handed round,—the Moorish coffee, prepared as all coffee is in Algeria, and therefore delicious, both as to savour and perfume.

Unfortunately, they are in the habit of serving it to you in cups, which, in point of capacity, have a much closer analogy with either a thimble or a nutshell, than with the reasonable proportions of our pretty china cups of English or Sèvres porcelain. This is evidently a great mistake, of which the Arabs should certainly endeavour to correct themselves.

Finally, as the complement to this banquet of the desert, came the long pipe, and Tunis tobacco.

On the 18th of December, the 2nd Zouaves moved as far as the Oued-Monilch; the 19th, to El-Kadra (a *ksour* in the Djebel-Amour); the 20th; to the Oued-Mekrenza, which flows between two lofty chains of mountains; the 21st, to Aïn-Krechale the 22nd without having made its noonday halt, to the Oued-el-Nadjel; a bivouac, at which it remained another day, to await the arrival of the convoy from El-Biod The distance marched by the column during this first part of its journey, was of about 200 kilometres.

The regiment having resumed its movement on the 24th, encamped that same evening at the Mekam of the Sidi-Chikr, after a march of 49 kil.[28] The next day, it had another long and difficult march to make, of 36 kil., and a noon-halt without wa-

---

28. From the 22nd to the 24th December, the sky became overcast with clouds, and the weather freezing, with a violent west wind, which excited serious apprehensions of one of those snowstorms which are so terrible during the winter season in the region of the high table lands of Africa. Luckily for the column, however the clouds disappeared on the 25th, and the 2nd Zouaves was enabled to reach the Tell without having had to encounter a storm.

ter. It passed that night at the well of Askoura; that of the 26th, at Guetifa; of the 27th, at Medrissa; of the 28th, at Ardjetoum; and of the 29th, at Tiaret, 28 kil. above the cascades of the Mina.

On the 30th, the regiment lay in camp.

During this second part of its itinerary, the 2nd Zouaves had got over another 200 kil. But the country passed through, being almost the same over which it had marched on its way to Laghouat, we deem it unnecessary to repeat the description before given of that; especially as all the principal localities in the Sahara of Algiers, have been admirably depictured in the work of General Daumas.

On the 31st December, the regiment again took up its line of march and, seven days after, reached Oran, passing through Kaf-Lereeg, Zamora, Relizan, Bou-Guivat, Aïn-Nouissi, and Mefessour (188 kil.).

The column, during this last stage of its journey, had to cross a chain of high mountains,—descending after that into wide valleys, where, for the first time, some promising plantations were met with; though wood and water were as yet scarce. The third day, it entered upon the country of the Flittas, a wooded, cultivated, and inhabited district, of irregular aspect and difficult approach; next, traversed the fertile and beautiful plain of the Mina, and crossed that river at Relizan, just a little above its bar. Passing then through the country inhabited by the tribe of the Borgia, on a line with, and at about the same distance from the coast, as Mostaganem and Arzew, it finally reached Oran— where the inhabitants were awaiting it, ready to give it a triumphal reception.(*See note following*)

Note:—The expedition to Laghouat was productive of two very important results, the one moral, the other material; the latter, in that it firmly established our supremacy in the south, so firmly indeed, that there has since been no attempt to disturb it;—the former, in that it showed the Saharians, that there were no distances, which we would not surmount, and no sands, nor any deserts, which could stop us, or shelter our enemies from the chastisement which they might have justly provoked from us.

The Scheriff Mohammed-Ben-Abd-Allah, who had succeeded in effecting his escape from Laghouat, hid himself among the Beni-Mzab, at Ouargha, seven days' journey to the south-east. Instead of trying to be there forgotten, however, he must needs again attempt in 1853, to levy war upon the tribes which were subject to us.

But his punishment was not long delayed; the governor-general at once sent orders to the *goums*, and Arab contingents of the three provinces to take the field, followed at long distances by our own columns, Si-Hamza, our Khalifat of the Ouled-Sidi-Scheikh, attacks the *Scheriff*, beats him after an obstinate fight, destroys his prestige in the eyes of the Beni-Mzab; and such is the impression produced on these people by material force, that all the tribes immediately hasten to call in our columns, and pay them tribute—whilst Mohammed, tracked from town to town, driven out of Metlili, out of Nyoussa, and even out of Ouargla, is at length compelled to take refuge in the oases belonging to the regency of Tunis, in the direction of Nefta.

Many rewards were distributed in the 2nd regiment of Zouaves, in consequence of this expedition to Laghouat. Lieutenant-Colonel Cler and Major Malafosse were promoted to be Officers in the Legion of Honour; Captains Fernier and Abatucci, Lieutenant Kléber,[29] Assistant Surgeon Canteloube, Orderly Sergeant Bouchard, Corporal Moreau, and the *Zouaves* Rogel, Beicas and Giboteau, were appointed knights in the same order.

Besides which, seven military medals were granted to the following named, *viz.*, Sergeants Verneur, Girardot, Wiedembach, de Chalot,[30] and Catelan, and Corporals Ehrard and Beignard.

29. Lieutenant Kléber is said to have been the first to mount the breach at Laghouat. At the opening of the Italian campaign, he was a captain in the *chasseurs à pied*.—T'
30. Subsequently promoted to a lieutenancy, and killed at the attack on the villages of the Beni-Menguillen, during the campaign of 1857, against the mountaineers of the Djurjura,—T..

Finally, Captain de Fresne was promoted to be major in the 14th regiment of the line; First Lieutenant Morand, to be captain in the regiment; Second Lieutenant Arnaud, to be first lieutenant; Sergeant Major Castan, and Orderly Sergeants Seriot and Breugnot, to be second lieutenants.

Book 2 - The Babors

1

Whilst the 2nd and 3rd Battalions of the 2nd regiment of Zouaves were engaged in the expedition to Laghouat, the 1st Battalion, which had been on detached service in the subdivision of Tlemeen, was also in the field, as part of a column sent into the high table-lands, to occupy the advanced positions of Aïn-Tekarin and El-Aricha; and which was charged with keeping in check the discontented tribes in the West, as well as with watching the roving and independent tribes dwelling on the frontiers of Morocco, This battalion had no encounter with the Arabs, but suffered greatly from the cold. In the last days of December, 1852, it returned to Tlemeen; where, at the end of January, it was replaced by the 2nd battalion.

During the winter, some companies detached from Oran, were employed in repairing the roads through the province.

In the month of January, 1852, the Governor General, foreseeing the necessity of sending shortly an expedition into the greater Kabylia, issued orders to all the troops composing the army of Africa, to prepare for taking the field, by resuming their practice in target-firing and their military marches: all of which was strictly complied with in the 2nd regiment of Zouaves.

About the middle of March, accordingly, the regiment got orders to put two of its battalions on a war footing; which done, these battalions were to hold themselves in readiness for embarkation, on the 10th of April, with Bougie for their proximate destination. But, in order to break in the men to fatigue, to get them in good wind, and, also, to give the officers a chance of taking all their sumpter mules along, the day of departure, thus fixed, was by permission anticipated; and the two battalions, instead of going round by sea, marched from Oran to Algiers overland.

The six companies in the 1st, and six in the 2nd Battalion, which were the first to march, constituted the two war battalions. The companies of the 2nd Battalion, which were then at Tlemeen, having been recalled to Oran, the regiment set out, the day succeeding their arrival, for Algiers, under command of Colonel Vinoy, seconded by Lieutenant-Colonel Cler, and by Majors Fraboulet de Kerléadec, and Malafosse.

The effective strength of each company, at the moment of its departure, was of 123 men, present and under arms, so that the total aggregate of both battalions, inclusive of the staff, amounted to 43 officers, and 1,533 men.

The regiment took the road to Mostaganem, along the low valleys of the Mina, of the Rioü, of the Cheliff touched at Orleansville, crossed the Cheliff at the Bridge of El-Kantara, arrived at Milianeh, after following up the course of the Oued-Boutan and then going down that of the Oued-Geer, passed by Blidah, crossed the Mitidja and the Sahel, and finally reached Algiers on the 14th of April, after a twenty days' march, during which it had to leave only one man behind, and for which Colonel Vinoy was accordingly complimented by the governor-general.

The 2nd Zouaves received a hearty welcome in the capital of our new colony, and remained there from the 14th to the 25th of April. Quartered ill the great Orleans barracks, it did garrison duty during its stay, and the conduct of its men was excellent.

On the 25th of April the regiment left Algiers, under orders to proceed to Setif, by the way of Aumale, and thus traversed the great plains of Mustapha and the Mitidja; the former of which is covered all over with rich plantations, whilst the latter, skilfully cultivated, is destined yet to become the great kitchen garden of France, and to supply, by means of railroads, all the great towns of the mother country with fruits and early vegetables, both during winter and spring.

In order to get to Aumale, the *Zouaves* had to cross the mountain chain, which connects the lesser Atlas with Cape Matifoux. This chain, which is of great height, is intersected by numerous and deep valleys, lying quite close to each other, sometimes parallel, and sometimes perpendicular to the summits. Its sides, rugged and arid, are frequently difficult, sometimes impracticable to the traveller. The Arabs have, in their figurative language, given names to these defiles, which are perfectly characteristic. Here, 'tis an elevated peak, exposed to the East, which they have named *the gate of the Sun*;—a little further on, 'tis a long, narrow, choked-up, and almost impervious ravine, which they have nicknamed, *Cat's gorge*;—probably, because that animal, which contrives to work itself through the smallest apertures, is the only one likely to get through it.

Cat's gorge takes its rise in a deep and funnel shaped glen, with ravined sides, into which the sun's rays seldom ever penetrate, even during the longest days of the year. This wild and savage hole is called *Sack of the damned*; in consequence, perhaps, of the Arab traditions having in earlier times located there the abode of the doomed. During eight months of the year, these high regions, being exposed to all the winds from the sea, are visited by the most furious storms and hurricanes.

Convoys on the march, which are so unlucky as to be caught by these, have great difficulty ill extricating themselves, frequently, men, horses, mules, are all swept into the deep pits which beset the path, and disappear from the sight in a mass of snow. Could a few such shelters for travellers, as are those hospitable houses, which we meet with in the passes of the Alps, be erected here, they would be of incalculable service.

The Arabs relate that, in the year 1847, a convoy of 17 men, belonging to the *train d'équipages*, were thus buried alive by one of these terrible hurricanes, and that, when their dead bodies were at length got out, there was found among them a mother,—hiding in her bosom the head of a child,—whose feet the quartermaster sergeant, in command of the detachment, had also tried to keep warm, by pressing them against his own naked breast.

Beyond Aumale, the march lay through a savage country, the haunt of wild beasts, and only visited by tribes which had not yet been fully reduced to submission.

On the 3rd of May the regiment planted its bivouac just below the town of Mansourah (protecting place,) which is built on the top of a low peak, shaped like a truncated cone, one of the lesser spurs of the range of mounting, which separates the Tell from the upper table-lands. The village looks down, upon a considerable valley opening to the north-west. From the terraces of its houses, the eye takes in the whole country of the Djurjura, of the Oued-Sahel, and of the Bibans.

Its houses are built of schistose stones, of a yellowish colour, which, in their natural shape, that of a rectangular cube, are found scattered in great abundance over the surface of the ground. The roofs, which are slightly inclined, are supported by stout frameworks of pine and larch, and are covered with a layer of earth. Within the houses are subterranean granaries, of a singular construction; being a species of vases, resembling huge jars, whose sides, adorned with rough sculpture, are made up of a composition of earth and dung, mixed with chopped straw. Grain keeps admirably in these great vases,—which are a very tolerable imitation of the ancient pottery of the Carthaginians and Numidians.

Just at the foot of the conical hill, on the summit of which stands the village, are the sparkling fountains, whence flow two separate rivulets, each one of which turns with its rapid stream, the wheels of a mill of simple construction and machinery. The two streamlets serve next to irrigate an oasis planted with fruit trees, olive trees, and vines. Yet this luxuriant vegetation stands but as a single green spot on the face of the southern slope of this great valley; which everywhere else is rocky, uncultivated, and barely dotted here and there, in its upper portions, with a few scattered clumps of stunted pines.

Under the guidance of the *caïd*, who, with the gracious politeness peculiar to the Kabyles, did them the honours of his capital, the officers of the regiment contrived to climb up to the rustic peristyle of the *djemma* (place of assembly, city hall) of Mansourah.

From this elevated point, the delighted eye ranged over a vast and magnificent panorama;—embracing, on the first level, not far from the village, the beginning and serpentine course of two ravines, whose waters, scattering freshness through the oasis, wound close by the bivouac of the *Zouaves*, lower down,—on the second level, to the north-west, immense valleys, stretching away up to the very last offshoots of the Djurjura,—closing up the view in this direction, the mighty range of the Djurjura, itself, with its long wall of snow, at a distance to the north of the picturesque village, of some 15 or 20 leagues,—and, finally, great level plains, uprising from the borders of which, one saw the serrated peaks and slender crest of the chain of the Oued-Sahel,—whilst still, in the lower part of this grand landscape, stretching away from, and quite isolated from the chain of the Bibans, were to be discerned the two great masses of lava, which form the sides of the deep and narrow gorge, known as the *Gates of Iron*, so celebrated since the adventurous expedition of the Duke of Orleans.

The day had been very warm. The air sultry, and charged with electricity, gave warning of an approaching storm; the coming of which seemed to be also announced by the great masses of black clouds, piled up against the horizon, and by the low mutterings of distant thunder. Every one could read in these signs the prelude to one of those mighty tempests, which are occasionally witnessed in the early spring-time, in the mountainous regions near the sun. It seemed to be brewing just over the summits of the Djurjura.

Soon, the black clouds began to mount and spread themselves over the whole sky, and then dividing again, fell back into a regular order of deep columns, which, shooting upwards from each mountain-peak, gradually faded away in the immensity of the heavens. These belts of cloud,—separated from each other by bands of ruddy light, reflected from the last rays of the setting sun,—then began to draw near with giant strides, leaping from the Djurjura over to the Oued-Sahel, from the Oued-Sahel to the Gates of Iron, and thence to the Bibans. Their approach was heralded by magnificent flashes of vertical lightning, and by terrific thunder-peals; of which the prolonged and hollow reverberation, as mountain echoed them back to mountain, filled the soul with a vague, mysterious terror. In less time than it has taken to describe it, this great cataclysm of the heavens had traversed a distance of no less than twenty leagues.

The officers of the 2nd Zouaves, when they saw the storm coming on, began to think of getting back among their men. Mounting their horses, then, they rode at full speed to the bivouac; which the rain had soon converted into an immense morass, out of which the men went floundering, the next morning, with the mud half way up their legs.

The weather, unsettled by this storm, which lasted for eighteen hours, continued bad until the arrival of the column at Setif, on the 8th of May. The temperature m these elevated regions (the Medjada is 1200 metres above the level of the sea, and Setif 1100 metres) often becomes icy cold after one of these storms Such was the case now flurries of snow, and cold, drizzling rains, rendered the bivouacs both chilly and damp The march, both over mountain and plain, was frequently interrupted by great ponds of mud and water, by rivers which had overflowed then banks, and by quagmires. Under the Borj-Bou-Ariridj, the column was even obliged to bivouac in a marsh, and the men found it impossible to light fires, by which to make their soup

The Medjana, a high and fertile plain, is well cultivated, as well as admirably adapted to the cultivation of cereals. The undulating plateau, which extends between Setif and this plain, has a striking resemblance to that of La Beauce;[1] whilst the Roman ruins, scattered over its surface, prove the former opulence of this ancient province, which was then deservedly styled the granary of Rome. The site of Setif is literally heaped with ruins;

1. One of the most fertile in France.—T.

and the walls of the old citadel, hastily constructed out of *débris* of every sort, still attest the desperate resistance made by the Lieutenant of Belisarius, at the moment when the old, tottering Roman world was everywhere beginning to give way under the efforts of the Barbarians.

During these days of storm, and snow, and mud, the *Zouaves* displayed an admirable courage. More heavily laden than ever were even the Roman soldiers, wet to the skin, obliged to wade through torrents, to climb steep and slippery acclivities, to biv-ouac in water, and without wood, yet did their cheerfulness nev-er abandon them, and the gay, national spirit coming to their aid, enabled them to make light of their misfortunes. Singing when-ever there was a gleam of sunshine, laughing like schoolboys, whenever one of their comrades happened to lose his shoe, his gaiter, or his legging in some muddy rat, or when, slipping and falling upon the miry soil, he arose, transformed into the mud statue of a *Zouave*,—these gallant fellows were never ones heard to mutter a single complaint.

On the 8th of May, the regiment arrived at Setif and pitched its camp to the north of the city,—on a site, which was soon to be occupied by the troops of the whole expeditionary army.

The governor-general, having set out from Algiers on the 9th, disembarked at Bougie on the 10th of May, and arrived at Setif on the 13th.

The different corps, detailed to take part in the expedition, were arranged into two divisions; of which one was command-ed by General Bosquet, under the immediate direction of the governor-general, and the other by General de MacMahon; and which, consisting each of two brigades of infantry, with a suit-able pro-portion of the other arms of service, were intended to act together, or separately, as circumstances might require. The number of battalions was 14, and the aggregate effective strength of the army, of 13,000 men.

The 2nd Zouaves, under its Lieutenant-Colonel Cler, was placed in the 1st brigade of General Bosquet's division, which brigade was commanded by its own Colonel, Vinoy. On the

13th of May, the whole army was reviewed by the governor-general. The appearance of the infantry was very imposing; for, all of the battalions war-worn troops, and, among them, a battalions of *Zouaves*.

During the time thus spent by the three regiments of *Zouaves* at Setif, they had many pleasant reunions, all in the most fraternal spirit. It was the first time since their organisation, that all three regiments had been brought together, and upon the same expedition; so that all belonging to them, officers, non-commissioned officers and soldiers, eagerly conspires to make the most of the opportunity thus afforded. All wished to show, too, that they were animated by the same *esprit de corps*, and that, as members of the same family, they were desirous of remaining united by the same sentiments of glory and emulation, without ever seeking to become rivals of one another.

On the 19th of May, the governor-general's column, leaving Setif, and moving northward, planted its bivouac five leagues farther, on the right of the road to Bougie, and upon the banks of the Oued-Chilkan. General de MacMahon's division, inclining to the east, marched in the direction, of the Oued-Berd, at the foot of the southern slope of the Babors.

On the 19th, the division to which belonged the 2nd Zouaves, marched 20 kil, and bivouacked on the Oued-Draouats,[2] which runs parallel to, and to the south of the Babors range of mountains. But, hardly had they got settled in their bivouac, before the three first companies of the 1st battalion, under Major Fraboulet de Kerléadec, were sent without knapsacks, and in company with two battalions of the 2nd Brigade, to attack the Kabyle tribe of the Djermounah, who had not yet come to ask the *aman*.[3]

This little column succeeded in driving the enemy out of deep and rocky ravines, in which it was no easy matter to get at him, and in burning the villages of his tribe, there situated. The

2. Called also the Oued-Merkad, it is one of the most principal affluents on the left of the Oued-Berd.

3. That is to say, to make their submission. *Aman* signifies, according to the manner in which it is used, safe conduct, confidence, forgetfulness of the past, or forgiveness.—T

Kabyles made no very great resistance; though from the top of their mountains they rolled down upon their assailants large rocks, by the fragments of which several men were wounded. Unfortunately, this little operation, the opening one of the campaign, cost the regiment the life of a meritorious officer. Second Lieutenant Liabœuf,—a brave and veteran soldier, who fell, smitten by apoplexy, just as he was in the act of leading on his section, to the assault of one of the enemy's positions.

During the 20th, the column remained in its bivouac on the Oued-Draouats. In the course of the day, however, eight companies of the regiment, accompanied by some other troops, set out under command of General Bosquet to reduce a fragment of the tribe of the Beni-Rhamin, which still continued to hold out against us.

On arriving at their villages, General Bosquet directed the eight companies of *Zouaves*, divided into two separate columns, under the respective orders of Colonel Vinoy and Lieutenant-Colonel Cler, to attack and make themselves masters of the lofty positions and precipitous rock of the Takoucht,[4] where the Kabyles had secreted their wives and children. This assault, executed with the most determined vigour, was attended with complete success. The heights, though bristling with difficulties, were carried, one after the other, and soon the whole rocky semicircle, which enclosed the villages, was in the possession of the *Zouave*.

The two columns, after reuniting on the conclusion of their *razzia*, again separated, retiring each to the villages below by the same path, by which it had climbed to the attack. The various positions taken, were then successively and slowly evacuated, under the continued fire of the Kabyles; who, pouring down in swarms after the descending columns, and giving the men no respite, were yet kept steadily at bay, and occasionally severely punished, by a sudden resumption of the offensive.[5] Having at

---

4. This point is 1,004 metres above the level of the sea.
5. The troops were disposed for this purpose into *échelons* of sections, or half-sections, according to the usual custom in such cases, so as to be able to cross their fire over every point that they abandoned.

65

length come up with the reserve, which was awaiting them at the bottom of the valley, the two small columns returned to camp, without being further molested. Their progress down the hill had been marked by one of those traits of reckless daring, on the part of Colonel de La Tour-du-Pin, an officer of the staff, for which that officer's reputation was so well established.

Colonel de La Tour-du-Pin, to whom we shall again devote a few lines in our narrative of the expedition to the Crimea, was a man of an antique type of character. Surnamed by the officers of the army "the *La Tour d'Auvergne* of our day" he was well known to everyone in Africa, but especially to the *Zouaves*, whom he was in the habit of accompanying, as an amateur, on all their expeditions. Having been put on the retired list on account of excessive deafness, de La Tour-du-Pin, whose passion for war was perfectly absorbing, never let slip any opportunity of gratifying it; betaking himself for that purpose to any country, which offered him a chance of fighting, dangers, or glory. He had thus served as a volunteer in the Holstein war; and, having recently obtained that which he esteemed as the greatest of favours, the permission to accompany the expedition to the Babors, he was, as a matter of course, present on the occasion of the attack on the Takoucht, with the *Zouaves* of Colonel Cler.

The retreat had been just sounded, and the extreme rear-guard was in the act of falling back upon the reserve, when, turning round to see what the Kabyles were at, Colonel Cler perceived, away off in the distance, a man seated astride of a pinnacle of rock, and who seemed to be exposed, on one aide, to all the fire of the Kabyles, on the other, to that of the French. He at first supposed, that it must be some bold chief of the enemy, who, out of a spirit of bravado, made it a point of honour to be thus the first in arriving at the positions abandoned by the French.

But he was quickly undeceived by hearing a *Zouave* exclaim,—"why, it's the Colonel with the frying-pan!" For, so had the *Zouaves* christened the brave de La Tour-du-Pin, on account of the ear-trumpet which he was compelled to carry with him. And, in fact, on taking a second and more careful look at him, Colonel Cler could no longer doubt, that the individual, thus tranquilly perched aloft, and who appeared to be so earnestly engaged in examining the Kabyles through his telescope, was no other than the veritable colonel with the frying-pan, himself; who, meanwhile, was being made a perfect target of by the mountaineers, and calmly receiving their concentrated fire at the distance of only a few hundred metres.

Of course, immediate orders were given to the *Zouaves*, to turn once more upon the enemy, drive them back, carry out by force if necessary, this reckless observer, and bring him back with them, himself, his horse, his frying-pan, and his telescope.

De la Tour-du-Pin, disturbed in the observations which he was in the act of making on the range of the Kabyle firelocks, was almost vexed at, the interruption; but the orders given to the *Zouaves* were precise and positive, and so, he had to submit with the best grace possible, to the seizure operated by them on his person, and to undergo besides, not only the friendly reproaches of the officers, but the mocking laughter of the *Zouaves*.

On the 21st of May, the governor general broke up his bivouac on the Oued-Draouats, and moving along the dividing ridges between the valleys, thus ascended to the pass of Tizi-ou-Sakka, which lay to the north, and about 13 kil. beyond.

After climbing for an hour along the ridges, the column, finding itself cheeked at length by insurmountable obstacles, was obliged to turn off to the left, into a deep valley inhabited by the subject tribe of the Beni-Slimane, Even here, the road, which follows the windings of a small watercourse, proved to be exceedingly rough,—although it ran through a populated country, thickly interspersed with the Kabyle villages.

At ten o'clock in the morning, the 2nd Zouaves, being at the head of the column, arrived at one extremity of the pass of Tizi-ou-Sakka—and found the confederated Kabyles assembled at the other, prepared to dispute its passage. On coming within sight of the enemy, the 1st Battalion, which was filing out of the pass, man by man, dashed at once across the open space, which separated it from the positions occupied by the Kabyles; and as soon as the companies were re-formed in front of these, they, under the direction of Colonel Vinoy and Major Fraboulet, assaulted and quickly carried the precipitous heights of the Tararist,[6] which the enemy had fortified still farther, by some entrenchments of loose stones. The 1st, 2nd, and 3rd companies, were those chiefly engaged in this attack, which cost the regiment only a few wounded men.[7]

Whilst this was going on, the 2nd Battalion, under the command of Lieutenant Colonel Cler, was employed on the left of the pass, in protecting the retreat of platoon of *Chasseurs-à-pied*, which was engaged at a distance from the camp, in one of the villages of the valley of Irzer-ou-Sakka.

On the 22nd of May, as the Beni-Tizi had as yet sent only a few persons, of inferior consequence, to treat with us, the governor general, to hasten a decision on their part, sent five battalions without knapsacks, to the attack of some of their villages, in the valley of the Irzer-ou-Sakka. Three of these battalions, under the immediate orders of General Bosquet, moved directly down into the valley; whilst the two others, which belonged to the 2nd Zouaves, under the command of Colonel Vinoy, took a circuitous route, and crossing over one of the projections of the Tararist, came round into the same valley at a point about 13 kil. below where it springs from the mountain side, and so as completely to cut off all escape towards the sea, from the population of the threatened villages.

Although Colonel Vinoy had to make his way over frightful roads and by zig-zag mountain paths, this manoeuvre was none the less completely successful. Three large villages were in turn attacked, carried, pillaged, and set on fire; and the Kabyles, with

6. The Tararist is one of the highest points of the chain—one of the ramifications of the—Babors which divides the valley of the Irzer-ou-Sakka, from that of the Agrioun.

7. The terrible effects produced, even at great distances, by the cylindro-conical ball, were verified on this occasion, by the appearance of the Kabyle corpses, which strewed the battle-ground. For, many of these, though struck at a distance varying from 1,000 to 1,200 metres, were yet pierced through and through; whilst the wounds inflicted were as large as if made by grape-shot.

their wives and flocks, were compelled to flee for refuge into the woody covert of their deepest ravines. Becoming panic-stricken, when he saw his retreat cut off, the enemy defended himself but poorly, and fled, throwing away his arms, and abandoning a numerous flock to Lieutenant Colonel Cler; who, with three companies of Major Malafosse's battalion, pursued him for two hours.

Unfortunately, such were the difficulties of the ground to be overcome by this small column, whilst ascending the bed of a mountain stream, interrupted here by rapids, and there by cascades, that it was, little by little, compelled to abandon nearly all of its spoils, and succeeded in bringing back to camp only 120 head, out of all the captured flock.

This vigorous and successful blow at the Beni-Tizi, soon bore its fruits. On the 24th, the headmen and delegates of several tribes assembled at the bivouac of Tizi-ou-Sakka to make their submission to the French, on the terms dictated by the governor-general. The preliminaries having been adjusted, an armistice was concluded,—upon the condition that hostages were to be delivered to us and that our columns should be free to cross the country in any direction, without being molested.

Tizi-ou-Sakka, on the Mordj-Souel, (the beginning of the waters in the prairie of echoes), where the governor general's column remained from the 22nd to the 29th of May is at an altitude of 1000 metres above the level of the Mediterranean Sea It is one of the few passes which break the long continuity of the great Babors chain. The Arabs in their figurative way, have given to these lofty mountains the name of the *Gates of Vapour*; a name which the dreadful weather, to which the column was exposed during the whole of its stay at the bivouac of Tizi-ou-Sakka, would seem most abundantly to have justified.

In fact, the troops may be said, during this time, to have dwelt among the clouds, with the storm for their companion. But the position was one of great military importance; for, commanding from this point the entrance into all the principal valleys, the troops had only to remain a while here, to be sure of obtaining, before long, the submission of all the great tribes, inhabiting this part of the Kabylia.

On the 29th of May, the governor's column descended the northern elope of the Babors mountains, and moved towards the sea. Crossing several salt plains, and leaving the Tararist to its left, it encamped that, night near the Kabyle villages of Aït-Tahissiout, and Aït-Takribt.

On the 31st of May, the Governor moved his bivouac to Aliouen, at the foot of the northern extremity of the last spur projecting from the range, and in full view of the sea. To get to this bivouac, the column was obliged to open a road for itself over the steep and rocky declivity of the Kef-Rida; a road, over which, even when made, it had the utmost difficulty in forcing its way, owing to the precipitous character of the ground.

The progress of the column was also considerably retarded, by the height of the mountains, which it had constantly to cross. Sometimes, it was from eight to ten hours, in getting over a distance of only four kil. Whilst there was such an uninterrupted succession of fogs and rain, that it became necessary to light fires at regular intervals along the road, by way of guiding the march of the rear-guards; who, even with the help of these friendly beacons, rarely ever succeeded in getting into camp before ten and eleven o'clock at night.

Yet, in spite of all the discomforts to which they were thus exposed, the men would no sooner have dried themselves before a good fire, and refreshed themselves with a copious bowl of soup, before they could again be heard indulging in gay and animated conversation; each relating, after his own fashion, his impressions of the day. Among the *Zouaves*, some who had heard it said, that these wild and inaccessible mountains had once served as a refuge to the last of the Vandals in Africa, took it into their heads, that they had actually discovered the burial-place of Gelimer, the last king of the Vandals, in the vicinity of an isolated rock, in a, cavern, the entrance to which they had found choked up with debris of various kinds.

On the 1st of June, the column under the immediate command of the governor general, transferred its bivouac to Sidi-Rehan, on the borders of the sea; on the 2nd of June, to Sidi-Etnin, on the left bank of the Oued-Agrioun. On the 4th, it effected its junction with the division of General de MacMahon; who, since the 18th of May, had succeeded in reducing to subjection, the tribes inhabiting the right bank of the Agrioun and the eastern part of the Babors country.

During this first part of the expedition to the Babors, the 2nd Zouaves had a much greater amount of fatigue to endure, than of dangers to run. Its march lay through a mountainous country, full of tall and craggy peaks, and of valleys of irregular form,—deep intersected with ravines, obstructed at the bottom with trees, rocky and steep near the ridges,—in a word, such a country as compels even the foot-soldier to be careful how he steps along the narrow and difficult path, lest he should tumble headlong over the awful precipices, which line its sides.

From the 1st to the 6th of June, however, the troops attached to the governor-general's column were amply compensated for their fatigues, and the discomfort endured during the preceding days. Making short marches, and reaching their bivouacs thus at an early hour in the day, their halts were invariably made close to the shore of the Mediterranean, in rich prairies, through which flowed streams of sparkling water.

Pleasant shades, cool breezes from the sea, an atmosphere that was fragrant with the thousand odorous scents from flowering meadows and groves in bloom, everything combined to invest these bivouacs with a charm, of which the recollection was likely to impress itself deeply on every mind. Nothing was wanting to the enjoyment of the soldiers. Fresh provisions, brought round by sea; fruits, and even ice, which the newly conquered Kabyles gathered for them in their gardens, or sought for them in the dark fissures of their lofty mountains,—all good things abounded in the camp.

For, such is war . . . habitually full of dangers and privations, occasionally glowing with all the harmonies, and poetry, and pleasures of life,—but at all times attractive to such as are ambitious of honour and glory, to the men of ardent imaginations, to all who detest the monotony of a dull and uneventful life!

On the 5th of June, the governor-general summoned to his bivouac at Sidi-Etnin, a part of the populations lately reduced to obedience, that they might assist at the investiture of their chiefs with the *burnous* of authority. In the centre of an immense square formed by the troops, were accordingly to be seen from 500 to 600 Kabyles, with their wild features, their soiled and sordid garments—the very same men who, only a few days before, had suffered all the ravages of war, but who now came, full of undoubting confidence, in the midst of the very bayonets which had decimated them, to pay their homage to the might of France.

The governor general, having first explained to them the intentions of the mother-country, as well as the advantages which they would find, not only in following the advice given them by the officers entrusted with their affairs, but also in living at peace with their neighbours, next distributed as many as forty red *burnous*, among the chiefs whom he had retained at the head of their tribes and villages. Each chief or *caïd* came forward to receive at the hands of the *spahis* his *burnous*, which was at once thrown over his shoulders; then, after kissing the governor's hand, and receiving his, he resumed his place among the representatives of his tribe.

This striking ceremony, which was accompanied by the utmost military pomp, announced by signal guns, and closed by salvos of artillery, did not fail to produce a deep impression upon the minds of the new chiefs. Yet, on their cold and passionless features could be discerned no sign of their inward emotion!

After the ceremony of the investiture, followed the Holy Sacrifice of the Mass,

Upon an elevated point in the centre of the governor's bivouac, an altar had been erected with the help of drums, cannon, and gun-carriages—an altar, of which the only ornaments were a few simple field flowers, and some trophies of arms. It was surmounted by a rustic cross, constructed of two knotty branches of the cork tree,—just such a cross, no doubt, as that on which the Christ was nailed! Neither walls, nor roof had this improvised chapel,—it stood framed amid the sole beauties of nature. And yet, neither St. Peter's at Rome with its magnificent paintings, the gay Madeleine at Paris with its carpets, its marbles, and gilding, nor the vast Gothic cathedrals of old France with their sculptures, stained glass windows, and dim religious gloom,—could pretend to compare with the grand effect produced by this simple and primitive temple; which, effacing from the memory whole centuries which had intervened, carried one hack to the days of Constantine in the Gauls, of Philip Augustus on the morning of the battle of Bouvines, and of St. Louis among the ruins of Carthage. . . .

On the left, as well as behind the army,—stretching away in the far distance, until blending with, it became wholly lost in the thin and vapoury atmosphere just above the horizon,—lay the immense expanse of the Mediterranean; whose waters,—whether as now, calm and blue as those of some summer lake in Italy, or whether lashed into fury by the storm—still roll incessantly between the shores of beautiful France and those of her young colony.

The Mass was said by Father Regis, the Superior of the convent of La Trappe at Staöuelli; a monk, in whose military instincts and genius for organization, one could detect many gleams of the great and vigorous characters of Urban II., Peter the Hermit, and the illustrious Bishop of Antioch,

The lines of troops encircled the ground; in front of their ranks stood the officers. Behind, upon the hill-slopes, amid groves of the evergreen mastic, and thickets of rose-laurel and myrtle, lay the white tents of the encampment; whilst, still farther back, under beech and olive trees more than a hundred years old, stood groups of Kabyles, silent and wondering spectators—and yet themselves a feature in the scene, and lending a still more strange and picturesque effect to the green arches of this great *basilica*, of which the wild adornments seemed to have been contributed by nature, herself.

During the celebration of the Mass, one of the bands played portions of the *Prophet, Guillaume Tell,* and of the *Lucia.* Perhaps never before had any of the compositions of the great masters awakened echoes as sublime, as those of the Babors and of the valley of the Agrioun! Both officers and soldiers were visibly impressed by this imposing ceremony; but at the moment of the Elevation—when the priest raised on high the Blessed Host, and colours and guidons, with every head of the great multitude present bent low before it, amid the long rolling of drums, and the thunder of cannon,—this first feeling was quickly changed into one of the very deepest emotion. One could almost fancy in that moment, that the Church of France was at length taking solemn possession of this district, now trod by Christian feet for the first time, perhaps, since the days of St. Augustine.

This ceremony, of which the recollection will remain forever engraved on the memories of all who assisted at it, terminated the first part of the governor-general's expedition into eastern Kabylia.

Before describing the second, we beg to be indulged a few succinct observations upon the Kabyles of the Babors.

3

The Kabyles, or inhabitants of the mountains of Algeria, differ in almost every respect from the men of the plains, or Arabs properly so-called. The former, a people of permanent settlements, irrevocably attached to one locality, live in towns and villages, of a greater or less size, and have their houses, their gardens, and their fields. The latter dwell in tents, which they pitch in some new place, almost every day. Wandering along in the direction of the water courses, and within certain fixed bounds, they plant the earth within these, either in whole or part, and sell their harvests as soon as they have gathered them Their summers are thus spent in the Tell, or northern portion of Algeria, but on the approach of winter, they move to the south, into the Sahara, or among the oases.

The manners and customs of these two people, although inhabitants of the same country, are utterly dissimilar; and did not the Mahometan, their common religion, furnish them with a point of contact, and a certain bond of union, no doubt but that they would be greater strangers to each other, than are even the different nations of Europe among one another, or those of the new world.

It will, therefore, not be wholly uninteresting to give some idea of a country, in, which the habits, usages, and morals of the people, are of such a peculiar kind, and to point out, at the same time, some of the considerations which should, and must in the end attach them to France.

The Arabs of the mountains, or inhabitants of the two Kabylias, are almost continually at war with the Arabs of the plains and great valleys The latter look upon the former as a sort of brigands who live altogether by what they can take by force. Now, the inducements which the Kabyles of the Babors had in 1853 to make their peace with the French, were sufficiently apparent. By doing so, by making their submission, by begging the *aman*, they not only secured for themselves pardon, and the oblivion of their many past misdeeds, but, what was of much more importance to them, they thus succeeded in opening many new and lucrative avenues to their trade.

On the other hand, so long as they continued to hold out against us, they were tracked like wild beasts, not only by our own soldiers, but by the *goums* of our subject tribes,—whenever they attempted to come down to the Arab markets, whether on the coast to the north, or in the Medjana to the south; and, not daring to trust one another, they were thus obliged to brave a thousand dangers, in order to obtain a market for their produce.

To feel over them the strong hand of some governing as well as protecting power, was almost a necessity, therefore, for the inhabitants of the Babors; and as they knew us to be not only powerful, but generous and just, they desired no better than to range themselves am.ong the number of our subjects, so soon as powder enough should have been burned between us, to justify,

75

or at least palliate in the eyes of their women and old men, the commission of such a heinous sin, as the sacrifice of their long-inherited independence.

The necessary result of this state of things was, that never, since its arrival in Africa, had our nation obtained such a cordial and sincere adhesion from any of its native subjects, as that which it now received from the Kabyle tribes of these mountains But it must be admitted, that it was perhaps, even more the moral ascendency exercised over them by France, than the power of our arms, which had triumphed over their long resistance, and silenced, at length, their ancient prejudices.

The day on which the armistice was concluded, numerous hostages were brought in and presented to the governor The Kabyles strolled carelessly through our bivouacs, apparently without the slightest apprehension; and the sutlers of the army, on the other hand, travelled through the country which we had just laid waste, not only without being injured, or even insulted, by such of the population as had escaped our *razzias*, but with their friendly assistance, on the contrary, whenever needed. How easy, then, it is to govern these men, when their time-honoured customs are properly respected, must from this fact clearly appear.

The origin of these mountaineers goes back even to the earliest inhabitants of Northern Africa. And, as all the various tribes and races of men, who successively possessed this country, whether conquerors or conquered, ended by becoming thoroughly amalgamated, the Kabyle necessarily inherits the blood, not only of the Berber and Numidian, but of the Carthaginian, the Roman, the Vandal, and the Arab. Both his moral and physical temperament naturally bears the impress of this long and mixed descent—to which the Turk, alone, has contributed nothing.

If, now, what history tells us, be collated with the oral traditions, which are usually so faithfully handed down among a tribal people, there can be no room to doubt, that the last Vandal bands, whom Belisarius drove out of the Roman province, sought refuge among the rocks and caverns of these mountains,—extending from the sea to the great plain of the Medjana. And it was here, that Gelimer, the last king of these savage and restless barbarians, the ruthless destroyers of the old world, kept for so many years at bay the utmost power of his enemies, the Græco-Romans.

The remembrance of this old tradition, and of the disasters experienced by the Turks, at every attempt made by the latter to penetrate into their country, had persuaded the Kabyles that they were unassailable and invincible: and in their figurative style, they were accustomed to say, "we fear naught but the bird of prey." . . . But when they saw, that no obstacles were capable of stopping us, that, even under the hottest fire, our soldiers climbed and drove them off their mountains, occupied their passes, and spread themselves over their valleys, they were obliged to acknowledge, that we were stronger than they; and, when once this idea has been beaten into the head of an Algerian, be he Arab of the mountain, or Arab of the plain, he will no longer think of resisting.

We shall dilate no further upon this topic, which has been treated in a superior manner by General Daumas, in his interesting work upon the greater Kabylia; and as there is no difference between the Kabyles of the Djurjura and those of the Babors, we unhesitatingly refer our readers to that curious and instructive volume.

4

All risks of battle were now at an end; but there still remained many painful marches and laborious works for the troops to execute, and especially for the 2nd Zouaves.

Whilst the division of General Bosquet, under the direction of the governor-general himself, was operating on the left bank of the Agrioun, in the heart of the Western Babors, that of General de MacMahon, on the right bank of the same stream, was effecting the submission of the Kabyles living at the foot of the northernmost Babors.

Both divisions had been united by General Randon at his

bivouac of Sidi-Etnin. He now resolved to scatter his columns again through that portion of the country lying between Milah to the south, and Djijelli to the north; and, after reducing all the tribes inhabiting it, to hurry to completion the road, which had been laid out between these two points, so as that, from Setif to Bougie, and from Djijelli to Milah, the whole of the mountainous quadrangle, known as the Kabylia of the Babors, should find itself under complete subjection.

The 2nd Zouaves accordingly, set out from Sidi-Etnin on the 6th of June and marched to Ziama, on the shore of the sea—crossing the river Agrioun, as well as some high mountains on the way.

The mountain which border the sea between the Agrioun and Ziami though of considerable altitude, are divided by spacious valleys, tilled and inhabited by a very industrious population of Kabyles; the more able-bodied portion of whom are accustomed very often to emigrate to Bougie and Algiers. Like our Auvergnats, these sturdy mountaineers hire themselves to the towns-people, either as domestics, or men of all work; and as they make excellent servants, they are enabled to return to their villages after a few years' absence, with quite a little fortune for them—the fruit of their labour and economy.

The vegetation of these mountains is very luxuriant; the ash and the olive tree are to be found there of as much as two metres in diameter, just above the ground. Their villages are tolerably well built, usually upon the sides and close to the summit of the mountains; and around them are gardens and orchards; well watered by the streams which flow from numerous springs, and producing both the fruits and the vegetables of Southern Europe, in great abundance.

On penetrating a little further into the mountains, one meets at every step with streams of water, rushing through narrow gorges,—with waterfalls, green prairies, and rich virgin forests; whilst veins of iron and copper ore, which the Kabyles smelt in primitive furnaces of their own construction, are found upon their sides.

While Bosquet's division was making this movement parallel to, and at only the distance of a few kilometres from the coast, MacMahon's, with which the governor-general was now marching, was moving on the same point, by another road.

Ziama is an old Roman post, well situated, in a military point of view, at the mouth of a small river, some thirty-two miles west of Djijelli, A miserable Kabyle village, some walls, a few ruined fragments of the old towers, which flanked at intervals the Roman *enceinte* of the place, are all that now remain of this little city.

The two divisions, reuniting once more at Ziama, remained in their bivouacs, among the wooded valleys in its vicinity, until the 10th of June, exposed to the most dreadful weather. The rains having at length ceased, though on the 10th, General Bosquet's column, separating for the third time from MacMahon's, changed its bivouac to Tsarouden, among the Beni-Marmi. During this first day's march, it moved directly east. The next day, continuing to advance in the same direction, it crossed the small stream of the Oued-Dardouet, and established itself at Aïn-Bou-Kekacb:—it was now in the country of the Beni-Four'hal.

Beyond this bivouac of Aïn-Bou-Kekacb, the country became so exceedingly broken and irregular, that General Bosquet found himself obliged to divide his column into two parts, and to send one of them on in advance, to open a double track, of sufficient width for the passage of the infantry and the pack-train.

Accordingly, in virtue of orders received the preceding day, the lieutenant colonel of the 2nd Zouaves, with six companies of his 1st Battalion, and all the engineer troops, had to set out on the morning of the 12th, for the purpose of opening this road. He bivouacked that night at the pass of Selma; on the 14th, at Azera-Tzou; and on the 15th, at Tiburluc, where he awaited the rest of the division, which came up the next day (16th).

During these four days, the little column had, by its energetic efforts, succeeded in fully accomplishing the duty assigned to it, although it had to work in a stony and mountainous country, of very uneven surface, and which was scarcely inhabited. By means of this road, General Bosquet was enabled to penetrate into the country of the Beni-Adjir.

On the 16th of June, the division, thus reunited, encamped at Tibatren. On the 17th, it moved to Bou-Azza, after marching for some leagues along the ridges,—winding partly round the series of peaks, which divide the waters of the Oued-Djindjen and Oued-Nil, to the north, from those of the Oued-Kebir, to the south. On the 18th, it lay in camp, and received, that day, the visit of the chiefs of the Beni-Afer and Beni-Idir, who, on their return from tendering their submission to the governor-general, had thought proper to assure General Bosquet, also, of their friendly dispositions.

On the 19th, striking off in a northeasterly direction, instead of pushing farther to the south, as it had been latterly doing, the column got into the country of the Beni-Afer, after crossing some very high and difficult mountains. It encamped upon the Fedj-el-Arba,—the highest point of the pass, through which was to pass the projected carriage road between Djijelli and Milah. The next, ten mortal days, the troops were kept at work upon this road, and finished as much as 14 kilometres of it.

Finally, on the 29th, after having taken an active part in, and borne its full share of the fatigues of this expedition into the Babors, in which there was far more of marching and working, than of fighting to do, the 3rd Zouaves was dismissed, and took its leave of the governor-general. The next day, taking its leave also of its general of division, and of the other troops, it set out for Djijelli, where it was to embark, and thence go round by sea to the province of Oran.

Following the new road which it had helped to make, it encamped that Bight upon the Oued-Nil; the next evening, upon the Oued-Djindjen; which it crossed the following day (July 3rd), and pushing on, it arrived by eleven of the morning at Djijelli. During this last day's march, the regiment passed over the rich plain, which, covered with fine olive trees, extends from the Oued-Nil to Djijelli.

A few hours afterward, the vessels which it was expecting, steamed into the little harbour; and by dawn of the next morning (July 4th), the whole regiment had taken passage on the *Tanger*, the *Titan*, and the *Berthollet*, and after a run of thirty-six hours, reached Mors-el-Kebir in the night.

For the services rendered by it during this expedition, the regiment received, at the subsequent distribution of rewards, four decorations of the Legion of Honour, for Captains Blanchet and Lavirotte, Lieutenant Doux, and Sergeant Lalanne, and four military medals, for Sergeants Bertrand and Hervier, Corporal Berger, and the *Zouave* Squiban,

Colonel Vinoy was promoted to the general of brigade, and Lieutenant Colonel Cler to be colonel of the regiment; of which he assumed the command with feelings of unfeigned gratification.

It was about the end of August, that Colonel Vinoy, who had been appointed general by a decree dated the 10th of the same month, took leave of the noble regiment which he had formed,—of which he had been the first colonel,—and in which he had succeeded in gaining not only the esteem, but the respectful affection of all who belonged to it, whether officers, non-commissioned officers, or simple soldiers.

When the moment had arrived for him to embark, he was accompanied to the vessel, which was to take him back to France, by all his officers, and a large number of his *Zouaves,* And their final adieux were there exchanged, attended on both sides with sincere emotion, and the most lively regrets. And yet they were soon to meet again,—and on the same fields of battle, too,—he and his gallant regiment;—though in a foreign and a far distant land.[8]

The remainder of the year 1853, and beginning of 1854, were spent by the 2nd Zouaves in working at the road between

8. General Vinoy (now General of division,) was, by his parents, destined for the ecclesiastical life; but feeling a stronger vocation for that of arms, he preferred to follow the latter. It was recently remarked of him by a French writer, that "*il n'est pas certain, qu'il fût devenu Cardinal; mais il est bien près, aujourdhui, les Autrichiens aidant, du Maréchalat.*"—T.

Oran and Tlemcen. But, as France had, about that time, decided to take part in the great struggle, which had grown out of the complication of affairs in the East, the 2nd Zouaves threw away the pick, to resume the knapsack and the musket of the soldier —and, returning to Oran, began to organize its war battalions, prepared to cast on the French side of the future scale of battles, the experience of its chiefs and officers, and the daring courage of its men, with the resolute will and indefatigable activity of both.

Book 3 - The East—1854

When, in the early part of February, 1854, orders arrived in Africa for forming, in the 2nd Zouaves, two war battalions, destined for service in the East, great was the embarrassment thereby occasioned. For, every man of the 98 officers and 3,700 men belonging to the regiment, became at once clamorous for permission to accompany the expedition;—and yet, the number of those who were to compose this first draft, had been irrevocably fixed at not more than 56 officers and 2,206 men.

The eagerness, so universally exhibited throughout every corps of our army, to share either in a campaign, if there be talk of one, or in any service which promises danger or excitement, is notorious. And yet, that this feeling should, if possible, be even stronger among the *Zouaves*, was not only not unnatural, but might even have been expected; especially, when it is considered, that the regiments of this arm were created with a permanent view to war.

But here, there was still another reason for it. For, the very suggestion of the East, that land of the rising sun, over whose history, and around whose name, floats such a perpetual halo of mysterious interest, sufficed to set all imaginations on fire! Each one burned with the desire, not merely of tailing part in a war conducted upon a grand scale, and of assisting at great battles, such as those of the first Empire, but quite as much with the yearning wish to make one of those long and picturesque voyages,—one of those great and romantic expeditions, such as were the crusades in the days of Godfrey de Bouillon and

St. Louis,—the campaigns of Egypt and Syria, under General Bonaparte,—or even the Russian war of 1813, when the star of Napoleon first began to pale.

In the minds of many of the young officers, too, there was associated with the natural ambition of winning distinction and advancement at the risk of their lives, an actual craving, besides, to become acquainted with dangers,—not greater, in reality, than those which had attended their service in Africa,—their combats with the Arabs, and their encounters with the Kabyles,—but of more colossal proportions, and greater importance in the eyes of the world.

They were impatient to learn if it were true, as they had sometimes heard it whispered around them, that the species of warfare which they had been carrying on in Africa, was of a nature to disqualify them for the grander operations of a European war. Many a gallant soldier was there among them, who, during the last twelve or fifteen years, had fought just as many campaigns, had seen every variety of service in Africa, had braved the bullets of its natives, and the more appalling dangers of its climate,—and yet had never been a mark for the cannon-hall or the shell. In the face of the Russian batteries, now, how would these troops acquit themselves, for whom the thunder of an enemy's cannon, and the crashing of his bombs through the air, were things as yet unknown?

All of these different causes, operating all together upon the lively imaginations of individuals of every rank, produced such an excitement in the regiment, that every man set himself to work to invent some excuse, or devise some means, of getting himself attached to the first draft which should quit this land of Africa, once so dear to him,—but now so thoroughly depoetized by the mysterious prestige, which clung round that magic name, "*the East.*" . . . .

The colonel, taking a skilful advantage of the enthusiasm thus manifested, announced in orders, that "every man convicted of a serious breach of discipline, should positively be deprived of the honour of making the Eastern campaign."

This was enough. From that day, during the whole of the three consecutive months of February, March, and April, which the regiment passed at Oran and Algiers, in company with the various other troops destined for the expedition, the 2nd Zouaves set an example of virtue, we had almost said, for which it had certainly never got the credit before.

On the 12th of April, the war battalions embarked for Algiers, whence they were to take their final departure for the East.

The unfortunate companies, whose hard fate it was to remain behind, saw the others set out, with feelings of indescribable bitterness. Many officers and soldiers were even unable to restrain their tears; and the greatest vigilance and even severity had to be exercised, to prevent many of the *Zouaves*, from privately smuggling themselves on board the transports, which were to carry off their more favoured companions.

Even old Marie, the venerable *cantinière* of the regiment, who, during twenty years, had accompanied the original regiment of *Zouaves* upon all its campaigns, but who, on account of her age and infirmities, was now to be left in *depôt*,—unable to submit to such a hard decree, disguised herself as a soldier, in the hope of slipping off, in this guise. Recognized, however, just as the battalions were disembarking at Algiers, she was complimented upon her spirit by the colonel, but compelled to return to Oran. Not without great difficulty, however; for her heart was set upon going, and the colonel had need of all his authority to prevail upon her to change her purpose.

This worthy woman, known to the old *Zouaves* only as *la belle Marie*, but latterly as old Marie, had got to be one of the *chronicles* of the bivouac. Often, during the watches of the night,—by the fireside,—under the tent, or in the trenches, might some of the older soldiers of the regiment be heard relating of her traits and incidents, which were always full of interest for their auditors. One, among other things that they were in the habit of telling of her, was, that Marie,—whose beauty had been quite proverbial at one time,—had formerly occupied a most distinguished place in society; but that, having become a widow, and not wishing her children, who were living in affluence in France, to have to blush for her, she had profited by the irregularities, incident to the first attempts to establish a civil organization in Algeria, to make a legal death.

Whatever be the merits of this story of our *Zouaves*, for the truth of which we shall not undertake to vouch, there is yet every reason to believe, that the past history of *la belle Marie*, (we prefer to call her still by that name) does, in fact, conceal all the mysterious elements of a romance.

On the 1st of May, the 1st battalion, with the field and staff of the regiment, received on board of the *Montezuma*, as she lay in the harbour of Algiers, the last *adieus* and kind good wishes of General Randon, the governor general of the colony. Five days afterward, the 2nd battalion embarked from the same port, on board the *Cacique*.

On the morning of the 8th, the *Montezuma* put into the harbour of Malta, and remained there until the 9th, for the purpose of taking in coal.

The rode which constitutes this island, is extremely arid, and but slightly elevated above the level of the sea. So great, indeed, is the absence of vegetable soil, that the inhabitants frequently send to Sicily for it; and every year, at the close of the rainy season, they may be seen carrying back upon the heights, that which had been washed away from them into the gullies below.

Owing to this, the aspect of the island is dreary and unpromising; the trees are few and usually of stunted growth; and the surface of the ground, only occasionally relieved by a few patches of sombre *verdure*, has a uniform grayish colour, which, at sea, makes it quite undistinguishable from the houses which are built upon, it. The island is 28 kil. long, by 13 wide, and having a, population of 123,000, is, consequently, one of the most densely inhabited portions of the globe.

The city is built in the form of an amphitheatre, upon the sides of five detached hills, between and around which, the sea makes up in long deep inlets, forming safe and commodious harbours, which admirably adapt Malta to be the *entrepôt* of that trade between the East and West, to which it is indebted for all its prosperity.

The streets are laid out at right angles, with great regularity. The houses are generally of cut stone, surmounted by terraces, and with latticed balconies in front, which are daily thronged by the fair and indolent inhabitants of this warm climate, at the hour when the evening breeze sets in from the sea.

In the principal quarter of the city, that of Valetta (La Vallette), are yet to be seen the vast and sumptuous palace of the Grand Masters, now inhabited by the English Governor—the immense hotels in which the knights of the different nations were accustomed to take up their quarters, when they came to perform their tour of service on the island—together with churches, and numerous chapels, of an Italian architecture, beneath whose rich mosaics repose the remains of the knights, in whose honour they were erected The formidable fortifications which protect the city, rise in terraces, one above the other, crowned occasionally with gardens or *porticos*, of a Babylonian fashion.

These various relics of a grandeur and a power, now passed away, incessantly remind the stranger, that this city was founded and inhabited by an order of nobles, half monks, half knights, who were wealthy, powerful, and most warlike.

At each step, too, one meets with reminiscences of France; paintings, furniture, carpets, monuments—the name borne by the principal quarter of the town,—the tombs of those, who were the greatest among the Grand Masters, Villiers de l'Isle Adam, de La Vallette, de Vignancourt;—in a word, everything in this, now English isle, recalls the well-known fact, that the knights of the three French *languages*[1] stood in the foremost rank of these highborn and gallant spirits,—who so long were the outpost and bulwark, we might almost add the saviours, of Western Europe;—and who so often hurled back from its threatened kingdoms, the constantly succeeding waves of the fierce Osmanli invasions!

---

1 There were, in all, eight languages, *viz.*; Provence, Auvergne, France, Italy, Aragon, Germany, Castile,—and, down, to the time of Henry VIII., England.—T.

At the present time, Malta with a population of 45,000 souls, has a silent and listless appearance. Sicilian languor and British phlegm have replaced the warlike bustle of other days.

Yet, to the credit of the English it must be admitted, that they have had the good sense to meddle as little as possible, with either the manners, the customs, or even, the civil administration of the people. The result is, that much apparent harmony exists between the two populations.

Two days after quitting Malta, the frigate was ploughing her way through the waters of Greece, and within close view of the barren and naked coast of the Morea, as we ran down the western side of that peninsula. During the day, the rock of Ithaca, the islands of Sapienza and Esparteria, the gulfs of Navarino and Koroni, were dimly seen, off to our left. Towards evening. Cape Matapan was doubled, and the frigate shot through the narrow strait, which separates the Peloponnesus from the island of Cythera, now Cerigo.

During this period of the voyage, the thoughts of all were busy with that olden world, of which so many vivid memories were suggested by every isle and headland that we passed. The very band, as it played on the quarter-deck, seemed bent on awakening the echoes of Cythera, and, if possible, arousing the shades of the once fair priestesses of Amathonte, by the deliciously appropriate symphonies which it selected, from *Haidee* and *La Favorite*.

Soon, the sun went down behind the mountains, which border the gulf of Calamata, and the higher peaks of Mount Taygetus, still glistening with their winter's coat of snow; and the mind, amid the thickening darkness, insensibly lost itself in reveries, as airy and fitful, as the evening mists, which began to settle upon the plains,—reveries, in which, lazily floating over a sea of thoughts, it yet lingered chiefly upon the ruined site of Sparta, lying but a short distance inland, and upon the mountains of Cythera close by,—within whose ancient groves, even where now stand but arid rocks, were once celebrated those hidden mysteries in honour of the queen of love, from which the uninitiated were so carefully excluded.

But, as the frigate rounded the Cape of St. Angelo, with what a tide of intoxicating memories was not the imagination flooded! Even the shadows of the night, seemed gradually to resolve themselves, into dim outlines of the beautiful goddesses of the Greek mythology. In the soft sighing of the wind, and the low, gentle murmur of the waves, the spell-bound ear seemed listening once more to the song of the Syrens, or the choral chanting of the Nereids. the very air, was that once breathed by Themistocles,—by Pericles,—by Alcibiades, and Phidias; the same, which had kissed the fair cheek of Lais,—and wantoned about the lovely limbs of Phryne!

What ecstasies of wild ambition, of longing and desire, thrilled through the minds, and fiery veins of youth,—what sighs of soft regret escaped the lips, as these glowing reminiscences of the once glorious and beautiful, continued to throng through the heated brain! The night was far,—far spent, before each weary eyelid had sunk in sleep, and these visions of a poetic past had converted themselves into the brief, but sweet reality of dreams.

By dawn of the next day, the frigate was in sight of Milo (Melos), the first of the Cyclades, where she took in the pilot who was to steer her through the labyrinth of islands, known to the ancients as the Ægean Sea.

After leaving Milo, we ran almost due north. And, after passing to the westward of Siphanto, Serpho, Paros, Ternia, Syra, Tino, and Andros, and leaving on our left the gulf of Nauplia, sprinkled with rocky islets, we penetrated, just as the sun was setting behind the mountains of Attica, into the canal of Paros,—almost grazing, as we sped by it, the rock of Zea (Coos), which partly masks the entrance into the gulf of Salamino, and the low shores of that of Athens. To the left, and in front of us, arose the towering island of Negropont, its mountain summits still covered with snow.

On the 13th, we entered into the middle basin of the Archipelago, leaving to our left the coasts of Thessaly and Macedonia, but at such a distance, that they were barely discernible,—and, to our right, Scio, Ypsala, noted for a massacre of the Greeks during the last war against the Turks,—the Gulf of Smyrna, Mytilene, whose more low-lying lands seemed better cultivated than those of the other islands—and arrived before dark in sight of Tenedos. Here, the current, occasioned by the precipitation of the waters of the Black Sea through the Bosphorus, the Sea of Marmora, and the Dardanelles, into the Archipelago, begins to be sensibly felt, especially when aided by the north wind, which, during a portion of the year, is so prevalent in these waters.

In fair view of the town and fort of Tenedos, though on the coast of Asia, is the site of ancient Troy. Upon its undulating surface, now covered with woods and undergrowth, may yet be seen a few *tumuli*, which are thought to be the tombs of Achilles and Patroclus. Farther back, the plain is hemmed in by mountains; in rear of which, and looking down upon their jagged summits, stands Mount Ida, with its cap of snow.

The high mountains of Imbro and Lemnos, come next in sight after Tenedos; then, the bay of Besika, where 200 vessels were waiting for a change in the north wind; and, finally, the Dardanelles,—on the right and left of which arose the castles of Europe and Asia, whose cross fire sweeps every foot of the entrance into the strait.

The same wind, which detained so many vessels in the bay of Besika, was driving through the Grecian waters below nearly as many more,—which were returning, after having landed at Gallipoli, their freight of troops, or merchandise.

On either side of the Dardanelles could be distinguished plantations and houses, which gradually increased in number, as we proceeded to the north.

Although it must be acknowledged, that the appearance of the islands, which compose the archipelago of the Ægean sea, is very far from being as unpromising as that of the coasts of the Morea,—yet must one see the whole of this country through the prism of the past, before he can bring himself to recognize in a nature so arid, and apparently so sterile, that rich and beautiful

Greece, of which we have formed so poetical an idea.

But, to what shall we attribute the change which has taken place? To the misfortunes, necessarily resulting from twelve hundred years of successive foreign invasions, and barbarous domination;—to the destructive spirit, which characterizes the Turks;—to the laziness of the modern Greeks;—or, finally, to the sole effects of time, that wonderful necromancer, who changes even the mountains, and again converts into barren rocks the fertile slopes, once densely covered with trees?

The truth is, that it would be, at this day, well-nigh impossible, for any revolution to, replace Greece,—we will not say in her former proud position, but even in a secondary one, more suited to her fallen pretensions. For, the civilization and settlement of all Europe, the discovery of new countries, and the vast impetus given to commerce by the rapidity with which vessels are now propelled at sea, must forever continue to keep modern Greece deprived of the overwhelming advantages which she once possessed, in being then the centre of the civilized world. And without navigable streams or cultivable lands, she can have no hope of winning back, by means of agriculture or manufactures, that of which these causes have successively stripped her.

On the morning of the 14th, the *Montezuma* came to an anchor in the bay of Gallipoli; but in consequence of the heavy sea then running, the regiment was not landed until the 15th.

2

Gallipoli is situated upon the northern side of the tongue of land, which divides the Dardanelles from the Sea of Marmora, and just at the entrance of the latter. Compared with its population, which is of not more than from 11,000 to 12,000 souls, the extent of ground covered by it, is very considerable. Its houses are generally built of wood,—the walls of the upper stories always so; though those of the lower story are occasionally of stone. Their upper stories project over the street in the form of porticos; their roofs, slightly inclined, are constructed of round tiles, of a reddish colour.

The mosques of the town, which are numerous, have each a cemetery attached to them, and are surmounted by a minaret, of which there is but one unvarying pattern throughout all Turkey, and which, more than anything else, resembles a slump (for shading), with only the addition, at the base of its conical extremity, of a globular projection, on which stands the gallery, whence the *muezzins* proclaim the different hours of prayer. Gallipoli, in common with all the other cities in the East, has, when seen from afar, a very picturesque appearance; but its streets are dirty and ill-kept,—whilst, from the material of which its houses are constructed, it is in continual danger of being destroyed by fire.

The environs of the city are under good cultivation, and are planted with fruit-trees to a distance of four kilometres m every direction; beyond that, the earth, for want of labourers, is never touched, and serves only for pasturage. The opposite coast of Asia, near Lamsaki, is both more fertile, and better tilled, than that of Europe.

From Gallipoli, the battalions of the regiment, which successively arrived there on the 14th and 18th of May, were sent to an encampment on Great River, about eight kilometres to the south of the city, and in view of the Dardanelles. The situation of this camp was very agreeable; facing it, on the opposite side of the valley, were cultivated mountains, having a few scattered villages on their flanks, and their summits covered with fine forests. The 3rd Infantry Division of the army of the East, which was to be under the command of Prince Napoleon, was organized at this camp. The 2nd Zouaves, with the regiment of Marines. and the 19th battalion of *Chasseurs à pied,* was assigned to the 1st Brigade, under General de Monet.

On the 22nd of May, the 3rd Division was set to work on the entrenchments, which it was designed to throw across the Thracian peninsula, on a line with Boulaïr,—a large Turkish village, built on the site of the ancient Lysimachus.

On the 31st, the division abandoned its camp at Boulaïr, and took up its line of march, in two separate columns, for Constantinople. That, to which the 2nd Zouaves was attached, proceeded in a northerly direction across the peninsula, so as to strike the head of the gulf of Saros. The country, through which it thus passed, is one of gentle slopes and somewhat undulating character; but it is little cultivated, though its soil is good, and is for the most part covered with brushwood.

The villages are few, and these ill-built, and mostly in ruins. The first bivouac was established at the foot of the chain of hills, which, after partly encircling the gulf of Saros, unites itself on the right with the main range, or dividing ridge of the peninsula. The gulf, itself, is very narrow at its upper part, very shallow, and has a muddy bottom; owing to which, though otherwise admirably situated, it offers no harbour to the mariner.

The column, next, crossed the wooded mountains, which run around the northern shore of the gulf of Saros. Here, are to be seen some slight remains, of those great forests of northern Greece, which the Turks, since their invasion, have laid waste by fire,—in accordance with their settled custom, of converting by this means into pasture lands, those which nature had the most richly endowed for other purposes.

A few live oaks, some wild olive and juniper trees, and a few dwarfed bushes, however,—are all that now remain of the ancient Thracian forests. This country is almost uninhabited; and yet, within a comparatively recent period, it must stilt have been in a very prosperous condition, to judge from the numerous vestiges, which attest the fact,—from the vast cemeteries, seen in the vicinity of fountains of water,—and from the numerous tombstones. It was once traversed by a Roman road; the line of which can still be traced, by the great heaps of ancient ruins with which it is marked—themselves, half-buried under the accumulated ruins of a much later historic period.

At each step, that it advanced, the column was met by mournful evidences of the profound decay, into which had fallen this country,-originally so highly favoured by nature.

On the 2nd and 3rd of June, the 2nd Zouaves, inclining still farther away from the sea of Marmora, plunged more deeply into the interior of the country, until some admirable plains were reached; of which not the tenth part, however, was under cultivation.

The few villages met with, were built alike, of wood, with tile-covered roofs. The Greeks who inhabit them, have regular and handsome features, but stamped with an expression of cunning. They wear, upon the head, a sheepskin cap, lined with its own wool. The Turks are distinguished by a slovenly turban, wound round a greasy cap. A jacket, a pair of brown woollen trousers, with a species of buskins, constitute the dress of the men; the women are clad in a loose black gown, with a white veil over their head and shoulders, which gives them somewhat the appearance of nuns,

These wretched people, a prey to incessant exactions, invariably hid themselves on the approach of the French troops. But they quickly came forth from their hiding-places, on discovering that, far from being ill-used, they, on the contrary, might sell their produce to the soldiers, at ten times the ordinary price; which, for a chicken, is usually one *piastre*, (four *sous*,) and for a goose, two *piastres*; whilst wine is sold at half a *piastre* the *ocke*, (about a pint and a half.)

The column marched through this country, as if it were in Africa,—each man carrying his own rations, and his *tente-abri*[2] whilst, upon *arabas*[3] and mules, were carried the forage and reserve provisions. The 19th Battalion of *Chasseurs à pied*, forming the advanced guard, went some distance ahead of the column, for the purpose of making the road passable for carriages. This battalion amused itself at the same time, by scratching on the stones, on either side of the road, various inscriptions for the benefit of the column behind—some of which were full of French pleasantry, as well of sarcastic allusions to the apathy of the Turks; such as, "*Imperial Railroad, No. 1—An excursion train*

---

2. When are we to have this admirable little tent introduced into our own service?—T.

3. An Eastern cart, which resembles those used in the Basque provinces and in some of the mountainous parts of France. They are narrow, dragged by oxen or buffaloes, and, like the chariots of ancient times, hare, for wheels, usually, a mere round and solid piece of wood.

will leave Paris for Constantinople, touching at Gallipoli, &c."—and

To the memory of Turkish Activity,
Which died in childbirth,
Having been prematurely brought to bed of an unfinished road—
This stone is affectionately dedicated by
The weeping 19th battalion of Chasseurs à pied.

In the neighbourhood of Eginiskian, where the regiment made its bivouac, the soil is rich, and apparently well cultivated by both Turks and Greeks, who inhabit the town in common. Its mosque, surmounted by a large dome, covered over with zinc, is quite a handsome one; being further remarkable for its large granite columns, which must once have belonged to some Greek or Roman temple. A Roman causeway, in very good order still, runs through this town, and reappears, at intervals, along the way, as far as Rodosto, (or Rodosjig,) where it is found in excellent preservation.

On the 5th, the column established its bivouac about four kilometres from Rodosto—a trading and manufacturing place, much larger than Gallipoli, and which has a population, composed of Armenians, Greeks, and Turks, of near 30,000 souls. The houses rise one above an-other, in semicircular form, along the western shore of the sea of Marmora, and at the head of an inlet, which serves as its harbour. Each craft lives by itself, in a, street set apart for it.

These streets, which are sometimes entirely screened from the sun, are very irregularly laid out, and encumbered with heaps of manure, and filth of every imaginable description. The mosques are very numerous, as are also the Greek churches; which last usually are richly decorated. Within the enclosure of the city are several cemeteries. Even in many of the business streets, and perhaps right opposite to a store, one may notice the wails of these cemeteries, pierced, here and there, with apertures; through the gilt gratings of which, are to be discerned rich tombs,—surmounted each by a turban, when that of a Turk,—and shaded usually by trees, or trailing vines, or thickets in odorous bloom.

For, the Turks, like all the Eastern nations, profess a great veneration for their dead, and lavish large sums on the adornment
of their tombs. There are even some houses, in the vestibule of
which the stranger, as he passes through, may see the tombs of
all the ancestors of the family,—there buried, out of a more than
usually reverent feeling for their memories.

On leaving Rodosto, the regiment continued its march towards Silivri, along the western shore of the sea of Marmora,
and always in sight of the high mountains which line its eastern
shore. The halts and bivouacs, however, had to be made at some
distance from the coast, in order to get water which was fit to
drink. The route lay along what remained of the great Græco-
Roman road, which formerly connected the Thracian Cherson-
nesus with Byzantium.

Near all the rivers, down the slopes, and on either side of
the villages, it was paved with large stones, of various shapes;
and, although in ruins, it was still quite passable. All this portion of the country,—with a somewhat rolling surface,—is bare
of woods, almost uninhabited, destitute of water, and but little
cultivated,—although its soil is well adapted to the raising of
cereals.

Only one solitary traveller, was met with by the column;
and that was a venerable *pacha*, riding along in a great, lum-
bering coach, lined with white calico, and attended by a few
horsemen,—of whom one had the honour of bearing the tail,
the badge of his master's authority. But for this tail, no one, certainly, would ever have dreamed of taking the *pacha* for anything
but a comfortable farmer, leisurely promenading through his
grounds.

Before reaching Silivri, the regiment crossed the torrent of
Seräi, near its mouth, over a low bridge of thirty-two arches,
constructed in the time of the Lower Empire. The little town of
Silivri is without a harbour; but its roadstead answers very well
as a shelter for the small coasting vessels, which ply in the sea of
Marmora. Its trade is by no means bad.

The wines grown in the neighbourhood, and which are very much like those of Cyprus, are quite celebrated, and really deserve their reputation: were they only made with a little more care, they would be capital. Silivri, like all the other towns in this part of Turkey in Europe, counts many more Armenians and Greeks in its population, than it does Turks. These last, however, have a very fine mosque, the peristyle of which is supported by huge granite columns, abstracted from some old Greek temple; while, just in front of it, in the midst of a little grove of trees, stands a mysterious fountain, used by them for ablutions.

At the hour of evening prayer this mosque appeared to be filled with devout Musselmen, while, under the peristyle, a few children were playing at dancing dervishes! No doubt, under all religions, and in every country, children are imbued with the same spirit of imitation; yet, in France, they would hardly venture to play at Mass, under the very *portico* of a church!

Silivri is divided into an upper and lower town. The latter, which is the business part, is inhabited by the Turks. The upper, is that where reside the Christians,—the Armenians and Greeks. It is surrounded by ruined walls, successively erected by the Romans, Greeks, and Turks. There still exists on the pediment of one of the northern gates, a long Græco-Roman inscription,—which would puzzle the science of any, but a professed antiquary.

As, however, the *Zouaves* are much more skilled, habitually, in the taste of old wines, than in the inscriptions on old monuments, the regiment passed by this one, with supreme indifference. Our gallant jackals,[4] did not happen to have among them an archaeologist as distinguished, as was that *zephyr* of the 2nd battalion of Africa, who, seeing at Cherchell a whole commission of *savans*, completely at fault before a tombstone from the ancient *Julia Cæsarea*,—on which was this fragmentary inscription, C. . . I. . . POL. E. NO. DE. . . .,—came charitably to their relief, with the following very simple solution:

---

4. The nickname given to the *Zouaves* in Africa.

Celarius Inventavit POLkam Et NOn DEcoravitur![5]

A solution which, though it may not have been unanimously adopted by the commission, at least contributed greatly to its amusement.

One is at once struck, on approaching Silivri, with the evidences of that universal influence, exercised by every great capital, on the country immediately around it. The earth was more carefully tilled; the towns and villages were more numerous, as well as better built; and even the dress of the inhabitants, grew to be more like that of the residents of Northern and Western Europe,—both in its form and colour, as well as in the material, of which it was composed.

Wherever we passed, men, women, and children,—the whole population in fact, turned out to witness the passage of our column. The *Zouaves* especially, with their bronzed complexion and oriental costume, excited, in a high degree, the interest and astonishment of all. The green turbans, worn by these gallant soldiers, were even the occasion of their being, not unfrequently, taken for pilgrims, on their return from Mecca.[6] A queer set of *Marabouts* they, indeed! One may readily conceive, to what jests and pleasantry such mistakes gave rise. The women and young girls were also particularly struck with, the appearance of the *cantinières*, who, somewhat *coquettishly* attired in a costume borrowed from that of both sexes, rode proudly at the head of the regiment, just behind the music. The general conclusion arrived at, in respect to these dashing ladies, was that they must be the women of the Bey's (Colonel's) *harem*: a supposition which, as may be supposed, was of a nature peculiarly gratifying to the legitimate vanity of their real husbands.

3

On leaving Silivri, the 2nd Zouaves directed its march, next,

---

5. Cellarius 'twas, who invented the Polka,—poor devil! Though, he'll never get the cross for it!—T

6. The green turban being, among Mahometans, the distinctive sign of those who have made this pilgrimage. (It is however more especially reserved to the descendants of the Prophet—T.) .

to Budjuk-Tchinedje; a pretty village, standing at the head of a little gulf, of which the upper part is spanned by a magnificent bridge, of twenty-eight arches, and eight hundred metres long. This bridge, of Græco-Roman construction, was thoroughly repaired, and renovated as the inscription on it testifies, by Selim III.

After passing Budjuk-Tchinedje, the column commenced ascending a noble causeway, the first which it had yet seen in the country; and stood, at length, upon the summit of a mountain—whence it was enabled to look down upon the most splendid panorama, whichever it was given to eye to contemplate—and the memory of which, time never will be able to efface from the minds of those who saw it!

The hour was yet a very early one; the dawn had given promise of a stormy day. but the weather, from dark and lowering that it had been, suddenly cleared up, and the unclouded sky became of a soft and radiant blue. Constantinople, at a distance of twenty-four kilometres, lay before us! Above the broad horizon, and fairly glistening beneath the slant beams of the new-risen sun, uprose the thousand domes and needle-like minarets of the great city of the East, standing out, distinct and clear, from amid the thin, vapoury mists, which floated about them.

The soldiers were still too far off, to be able, at such a distance, to make out the walls; and thus all the lower or more earthly portion of the Old Stamboul was shrouded from their sight; but, through the white, transparent veil, which vaguely draped, without concealing it, and which was already beginning to dissolve under the ardour of a June sun, the whole upper portion of the vast city, stood fully revealed to their enraptured gaze, in all its dream-like beauty.

To the left, and as though to frame in the enchanting picture, arose the rounded hills of ancient Hæmus; beyond the minarets, the serrated mountain peaks of Asia; to the right, the sea of Marmora, glowing in the morning light and laving with its smooth flow of waters, the shores of Antigona and the isle of Princes; still further to the right, the coast of Asia, rising abruptly from the sea,—and beyond, the towering form of Mount Olympus, crowned with eternal snows! ... It was a full realization, of one's wildest dreams about the East! ... For a while, the *Zouaves* were lost in a sort of ecstasy; which quickly was succeeded, however, by a feeling of the liveliest gratification at the thought, that they were about to enter Constantinople; as formerly had done the Roman legions—the Crusaders,—the brave Christian knights of their own fair land, who, without the aid of king or Kaiser, had once subjugated this great enterprise,—and finally , the Osmanlis. They were following the same road, which, ages before them, had been trod by a Constantine, a Baudoin, a Mahomet II!

A little while more, they remained mute with admiration, absorbed in the contemplation of the sublime and wondrous scene, which lay spread out in all its loveliness at their feet; then, suddenly turning away and as though seized with a certain sentiment of respect for the vast city of the emperors of the East, all officers as well as soldiers, moved silently down the mountain side, their hearts thrilling with indescribable emotions.

That night, the column bivouacked by the side of a cool rivulet, in the vicinity of a *caravanserai*, named Kharamikhan, and close by a group of oaks, plane trees, and venerable elms, of which some were more than eight metres in circumference.

At dawn of the next morning, it quickly cleared the space, which lay between it and Daoud-Pacha.

The colonel, as soon as he had established his men in the neighbourhood with this huge Eastern barrack, set out, in company of some of his officers, to pay a visit to Constantinople; which was in full sight, and only a few kilometres distant. The young officers were impatient to have a close look at this celebrated city and at its motley population—a population, which it must be confessed, has been painted in colours, a vast deal too warm and rich, by the glowing imagination of the Westerns.

Indeed, when one is brought in close contact with these splendours of the East, so extravagantly lauded on the other side of the Alps, one is often tempted to ask himself,—if the West might not fairly claim for itself, and by a much better title than the other portion of the globe, the palm of imaginative poetry!.

Seen from afar Constantinople undoubtedly offers to the eye a scene of the most romantic beauty; yet, in whatever way he may have approached the city, whether by land or sea, the traveller who would like to preserve his first delighted impressions of it, must carefully abstain from setting foot within its limits! For, the poetic side of Stamboul is but a deceitful mirage; which disappears as one draws nearer to it, until there remains nothing in its place, but the cold, ungracious prose, of a very different sort of reality.

The capital of the Osmanlis may be even likened to an old *coquette*; who, seen at night, by the glare of lamps, and at a certain distance, may still excite no inconsiderable amount of admiration, but whose bleared eyes and faded charms, when viewed by the clear light of day, inspire nothing but disgust.

Built, in the shape of an amphitheatre, along the slopes which descend towards the sea of Marmora, the Golden Horn, and the Bosphorus,—Constantinople is surrounded with cemeteries, and filled with gardens. Trees of different kinds thus mingle their various shades of foliage, with the bold, and yet graceful architecture of its innumerable domes and minarets.

The officers of the 2nd Zouaves entered the city by the suburb, which, extending from the foot of the Castle of the Seven Towers, once constituted the old Stamboul; thence, they passed into the quarter, which is comprised between Santa Sophia, the old Seraglio, and the Golden Horn. This suburb, composed of wretched hovels, between which intervene piles of ruins and heaps of offal, is divided into several different parts, by the wide gaps, resulting from successive conflagrations.

The heart of the city itself, with its tortuous streets, mean buildings, and disgusting filth, would be wholly undeserving of attention, were there not, here and there, though at considerable intervals along its principal thoroughfares, some noble monuments to be met with. These are generally mosques, some of which are of such great size, as, by themselves, to constitute almost a quarter of the town;—there are also the Babylonian palaces of the Seraskier and Minister of Marine; the immense and beautiful mosque of the Sultan Bajazet; and, further on, the celebrated mosque of St, Sophia.

Leaving to their right, the great bazaar, the officers rode down, through narrow streets, to the Golden Horn, which they crossed over a bridge of boats. Putting up their horses at the Hotel d'Europe in Galata, they set out on foot, in the direction of the Golden Horn, and strolled as far as Tophane and the Arsenal. As they were looking at the latter, a slight stir and momentary agitation, visible among the crowds of people in the street, with the turning out of the guards, and the apparition of the *cavas*,[7] gave them warning of the approach of some distinguished personage from the other side of the Bosphorus.

Nor was it long, before a white and slender *caique*, handsomely gilt, and rowed by a crew, uniformly dressed in white linen tunics, shot suddenly into view. The *Sultan*, himself, set foot, the moment after, upon the landing-place just in front of the Arsenal court At the lower end of this court, is an elegant pavilion, which serves as a resting-place for the *Sultan* when, during the Rhamadan, he comes to offer up his devotions at the mosque of Tophane.

Abdul-Medjid, though still young, walked slowly, and with a certain air of gravity. Though pale and thin, he has a look of distinction; his beard is black and silky;—his height, scarce above the medium. He wore, on this occasion, a red *fez* without any ornaments,—a long, loose *caftan* of black cloth,—pantaloons of light green cassimere,—round, silver spurs,—and, for arms, a light, curved sabre. The utmost simplicity prevailed about his person, his dress, and his retinue; there was nothing to indicate the existence of either that moral, or that physical power, which vulgar minds are wont to attribute to the Commander of the Faithful.

As the prince was in the act of quitting the pavilion, on his way to the mosque, he noticed and returned the salute of the

---

7. Policemen.

officers of the *Zouaves*, by a slight inclination of the head; which, however, was paying them an extraordinary compliment, as it is not customary for the *Sultan* ever to return a salute,—and, indeed, his vague and aimless glance is rarely ever known to rest upon any of his own subjects.

After leaving the Arsenal, the officers turned their steps towards the Golden Horn. The streets wore an unusually animated appearance, owing to the feast of the Rhamadan, which was then at its height; they were literally thronged with pious Mussulmen, who were going from mosque to mosque, to offer up their devotions. The officers were just about to cross the bridge over the Golden Horn, which unites Galata with the old Stamboul, when they were accosted by an Armenian, who informed them in French (nearly all the Armenians of Galata and Pera speak French pretty well) that the *Sultanas*, having finished their devotions, would cross here in another moment, on their way back to the palace on the Bosphorus.

A few minutes afterward, in fact, a band of black eunuchs, on foot and horseback, came on, in advance of the procession, to clear the way; which they did with very little ceremony, except when they came to the French officers, to whom they, on the contrary, exhibited the most respectful politeness. The *Sultanas*, to the number of about thirty, were seated in gilt carriages, open on every side, and of a shape not unlike those which were in use in France, toward the latter part of the sixteenth century. The *Sultan's* eldest son, a pretty and graceful boy of about eight years old, was in one of the carriages, seated on the lap of a lady of still youthful appearance.

The *Sultanas* had only the lower part of their face concealed, and that, by a gauze veil so transparently thin, that it was easy to distinguish through it the form of the mouth; which, by the way, is their least handsome feature. Their complexion was of a colourless white; their eyes were brown, almond-shaped, shaded by long lashes, and surmounted by arching eyebrows of the blackest jet; their hair appeared to be very thick and lustrous. Beautiful young girls, all of them,—gay, laughing, and coquettish,—their

103

features were yet wanting in that air of distinction, which is usually inseparable from women of the better class of society in Western Europe.

It was almost impossible to distinguish the outline of their shapes through their heavy and cumbrous garments, which concealed it better than do even the ridiculous skirts, whether crinolines, or chicken coops, with which our own fair country women make it a point of honour to take up all the sidewalk of our cities The women of the East, are rather simple in their dress, pleasing in their appearance, and have, all fine heads, but their movements are slow, as though their bodies were somewhat cramped, by the indolent life which they lead in the *harem*.

About nine in the evening, and after having dined at the Hotel d'Europe, the officers of the 2nd Zouaves set out for Pera, and the promenade of the Franks,—a wide avenue, which runs by the side of an old Turkish cemetery, known by the appropriate name of the *Little Field of the Dead*. Here, as they sipped ices, and listened to the music of an excellent hand, they saw defile before them a host of Armenians,—and women from every part of Europe, all, dressed with the utmost elegance, and according to the latest French fashions.

At midnight, they mounted their horses again, and started from Pera for Galata, accompanied by a *cavas*, who parted from them at the Golden Horn, Alone, and without a guide, in a part of the city which is never lighted, and where the language of the Franks is unknown, they tried almost in vain, to find their way out of the labyrinth of houses and ruins, which surrounded them.

Wandering first into one quarter, then into another,—passing by immense palaces, crossing graveyards,—meeting with no one, save, now and then, before the *cafés*, (which remain open all night long during the Rhamadan,) some cross-legged Turk, silently engaged in smoking his *narguilhé*,—disturbing the dogs, those peaceful guardians of the city,—they were, really, not a little embarrassed. It was a strange scene too; for, while, below, the streets were shrouded in darkness,—above, the sky was red with the glare from a thousand illuminated mosques; each minaret shot upward like a flake of fire, and between them hung wreaths of many-coloured lamps, representing lions, chariots, cannon, and all the various attributes of war.

Yet, the footfall of their horses, alone, awoke the hollow echoes of the night; for, as though the wand of some enchanter had waved over it, the whole, vast city lay steeped in silence. The soft, hushed air, meanwhile, was redolent with a thousand delicious emanations from flower and tree; and, taken altogether, it was as if a scene in fairyland, or as one from the *Arabian Nights!*

Completely lost for some time,—wandering they scarce knew whither,—long years must yet elapse, before the officers of the 2nd Zouaves, will forget that lovely summer's night!

Not before three in the morning, did they reach their camp at Daoud-Pacha. During the week which the regiment pissed in its vicinity, the soldiers visited all the monuments in the city. The regiment being one of the first, which had arrived at Constantinople, the *Zouaves* were naturally an object of great curiosity for its population.

Being constantly taken for Arabs, and not unfrequently even for pilgrims, on the return from Mecca, they had access everywhere, even within the mosques. By simply leaving their shoes at the door, or carrying them along in their hands, they were thus enabled to visit St Sophia,—that vast and costly *basilica*, built by Christians for their own worship, and which, since the downfall of their empire, has served as a model for half the mosques, which have been since erected in their former capital.

This immense mosque, with its courts, bazaars, pavilions, gardens, and fountains, almost constitutes, by itself, a separate quarter of the town. Its dome, which is its most distinguishing feature, has a diameter full twice as great as that of the Pantheon.[8] The general appearance of the building, according to the *Zouaves*, is, for all the world, like that of the upper half of some

---

8. The great Church of St. Genevieve in Paris, so called during the Revolution and the semi-infidel reign of Louis Philippe; but which by Napoleon III. has been restored to the uses of religion.—T.

great ostrich egg; flanked by similar halves of goose, hen, and pigeon eggs. Wide, covered galleries run around the base of the dome, which rests interiorly upon porticos, supported, in their turn, by enormous columns of granite and green porphyry.

The temple is decorated inside, with frescoes and gilt gratings. Suspended from the walls, are large tablets, inscribed, in letters of gold, with verses from the *Koran*. Towards noon, the exterior courts, galleries porticoes, and the interior of the mosque, are filled with Mussulmen; some of whom engage in all sorts of queer transactions; others, again, amuse themselves in walking about; others, standing apart, appear to be chatting of the affairs of this sublunary world, with little thought of those of heaven,—even the heaven of Mahomet; while the greater number, seated in the Turkish fashion, are listening to the sermons of the learned dervishes, who expound and comment for their benefit upon some text, taken from the *Koran*; and others, in fine, stretched out at full length upon the mats, with which the floor is spread, seem to be giving themselves up, heart and soul, to the delights of contemplation,—or of what the Italians perhaps would call, the *dolce far niente*.

A short distance only from St. Sophia, and in the midst of a very populous neighbourhood, are the tombs of several of the *Sultans*; among which, the most remarkable is that of the Sultan Mahmoud, father of the reigning prince.

The coffin, which contains his remains, reposes, under a lofty dome, upon a *catafalque*, partly covered by a sumptuous pall, and inlaid at its base, with mother of pearl, tortoise-shell, and gold,— Mahmoud's *fez*, with its plume of heron feathers studded with diamonds, is lying on the coffin; which is surrounded by several others, all richly ornamented. The dome springs from a series of arches, lined with glass; and between it and the other pavilions, are gardens and clumps of trees.

Near the tomb of this *Sultan*, is a curious museum, in which are preserved patterns of the different costumes worn by every class of the old, Mussulman population.

The castle of the Seven Towers, stands at the extremity of

old Stamboul, near the sea of Marmora, and forms a part of the outer wall of the city. A great, irregular pentagon, with four round, and four square towers,—this sombre fortress has been the prison of more than one dethroned *Sultan*, and of numerous members of the Imperial family; while its vaults have frequently witnessed the assassination of these illustrious personages.

Not far from the castle of the Seven Towers, in a north-westerly direction, is the breach, over which the troops of Mahomet II. forced their way into the city, in 1453. A standing monument of the pride and apathy of the Turks, who have never attempted to repair it,—it remains to this day, the same heap of shapeless ruins, in which the explosion of their mines then left it.

The old Seraglio stands quite near to St. Sophia. Situated upon the point of land, which runs out between the waters of the Golden Horn and those of the sea of Marmora, it consists of several, detached buildings; most of which are of wood, and in a very neglected condition, since the *Sultans* have ceased to make it their residence. They are divided, one from another, by gardens and parks, filled with lofty trees; of their external architecture, it is impossible to say more, than that it has a decided Tartar cast about it.

That in which the *Divan* was held, and which stands at the further end of the court of honour, is a gloomy building, with much more resemblance to a *caravanserai*, than to a hall destined for the reception of ambassadors; and yet the columns, which uphold its dome, are actually incrusted with precious stones. The pavilions by the water's edge have a much more elegant appearance: they look down upon a succession of terraces, and their walls, in-ride, are most delicately sculptured.

The immediate environs of the old city are taken up with vegetable gardens, planted with fruit and flowering trees, and watered by means of wells. Around the city, and at a distance of about four kilometres from it, stand three great barracks,—and an immense military hospital of quadrangular shape, with inner court, oriental towers, minarets at the angles, and pavilions in the centre of each front. Between the gardens and the walls, runs a belt of graveyards,—Greek, Armenian, and Turkish,—planted with trees, chiefly venerable cypresses.

The impressions formed by the European, who penetrates in to. Constantinople for the first time, are not likely to be changed by any subsequent sojourn which he may make there. For, in whatever direction he may turn his steps through this old city, he will invariably meet with the same ruins, the same heaps of filth, and the same wretchedness,—in close juxtaposition with the most sumptuous monuments of marble, granite, and gold.

It is the image of life and death, walking, hand in hand, together. Tombs by the markets, tombs near the bazaars and the public promenades,—vast cities of the dead, in the very heart of the most thickly inhabited parts of the town,—every object met with, serves constantly and forcibly to remind one, of the profound decay, into which has fallen this once great and formidable empire of the Turks; whose fierce spirit and resistless power threatened, during so many centuries of ceaseless warfare, the very existence of Christian Europe!

But, while in the East, the religion of Mahomet, founded on man's natural selfishness, and upon his most brutal passions, has gradually stripped the conquerors of all energy,—in the West, on the contrary, the religion of the God Man,—exalting woman,—teaching man to curb his passions,—to deny himself, occasionally, even gratifications which are lawful,—has thoroughly civilized whole families of barbarians, without robbing them, of their strength, their love of glory, or their scorn for death! This it is which carried the knights of former times under the very walls of Jerusalem; and which has caused the soldiers of modern days to be not unworthy of those brave progenitors, as they have abundantly proved on some of the fiercest and bloodiest battlefields, which the world has ever seen!

4

On its arrival near Constantinople, the regiment had been encamped near the barrack of Daoud-Pacha, about half a league from the western suburb of the city. During its stay here, the

3rd division, to which it belonged, was passed in review by the *Sultan*. The line was formed, with its right close to the village of Eyoub;—the ground chosen, being the immense, fanlike space, opening to the East, which extends between the upper end of the Golden Horn, and the valley of the Sweet Waters of Europe,—that Bois de Boulogne of Constantinople.

The regiments occupied its upper extremity: in front of them, was the vast crowd of those—Franks, Christian Greeks, and Mahometans, but chiefly the former—who had turned out to see the soldiers of the West;—behind this living wall, gay with a thousand flashing colours, appeared Constantinople with its domes, its minarets, and its cypresses;—to the left, the waters of the Golden Horn, with its dark lines of bridges, and the houses which arise from either shore,—next, the tower of Galata,— and, looking down on these, the dwellings of the ambassadors, and the houses of Pera:—finally, beyond the Bosphorus, Scutari, that Stamboul of Asia, and the snow-capped summits of Olympus, closed in, towards the East, one's view of the lovely scene; over which stretched the blue canopy of heaven,—lighted up, at this moment, by a brilliant summer's sun.

The *Sultan*, as he passed before the regiment, was so struck by the martial air and bearing of the *Zouaves*, and by the singularity of their costume, which reminded him of that of the old Osmanlis, that he loudly expressed the admiration which they excited in him.

The day after this review, the division set out by sea for Varna, which had been selected as the point of concentration for the Trench army of the East.

Varna is a rather larger place than Gallipoli, better built, with more resources, and tolerably well fortified. It had the honour, in 1829, of stopping the Russian army during five whole months, and, perhaps, would not have fallen, then, but for the treachery of the *pacha* who commanded it. Its roadstead, open to all the winds from the Black Sea, affords no security to ships. It would cost millions, perhaps, to build even a jetty there.

A part of the English army, the Egyptian contingent, and a

few Turkish regiments, were already assembled in its neighbour-hood. It was a curious spectacle to look on, this assembly of troops, belonging to such various nations,—so opposite in manners, costume, and language,—and yet drawn here from Europe, Asia, and Africa, in defence of a common cause,—and all on such good terms with one another!

For, here, were the men of the north,—English, Irish, and Scotch,—with their fair complexions, blue eyes, and showy costume; the Frenchman, with his open and expressive countenance, smiling and intelligent look, and uniform, made up of whatever he could find prettiest, most convenient, and useful, among those of other nations; the Turk with his grave air, and mien so full of dignity; the Algerian, with his swarthy and angular features; the Egyptian, with crisp hair, withered looks, and gaudy dress; and, finally, the inhabitant of Nubia, with his thick lips, and ebony skin;—and these, crossing and intermingling with one another, in the narrow streets of a Bulgarian town,—a few leagues only from the great river of Europe, and in close proximity to the Russian outposts! Who could have believed it?

After passing a few days, close under the walls of Varna, the 3rd Division was sent two leagues to the north of the town, to a camp, called Yeni-Keuï, where it remained till the end of July. To relieve the dull monotony of a camp life, as well as to escape from the dispiriting effects, produced by the breaking out of a violent cholera epidemic in the army, the 2nd Zouaves went immediately to work, to get up games and pastimes for the general amusement. The front of their camp soon presented an appearance not unlike that of the Champs-Elysées, on a fine day in spring, and served, thus, to call up many a pleasant reminiscence of gay Paris, and the dear homes in sunny France.

All sorts of games were usually going on there: rings, ball, ninepins,—besides two theatres; in one of which, dedicated to the drama, the *Zouaves*, played vaudevilles, and pieces composed by the playwrights among themselves. The other, constructed of branches of trees, and lit up at night by coloured paper lanterns, belonged to a society of Orpheans, who alternated every other evening with the dramatic company.

The Orpheans were in the habit of treating the public to operatic choruses, which they really rendered very well,—as well as to the lighter songs of Nadaud and Levassor. A third theatre, got up in imitation of that of Guignol, had been organized by the buglers of the regiment, under the direction of the *Zouave Zampt*. Here Master Bridou, a rare buffoon, entertained the audience with the productions of his own fertile imagination; which, if occasionally open to criticism, had, at least, the double merit of originality and a most amazing actuality.

It was of all these various actors and musicians, that was subsequently made up the more celebrated company, which used to perform, at what was called the Inkermann theatre, in the Crimea. An idea may he got of the nature and style of the pieces, represented by them, from the following outline, of the plot of one of those performed at the Guignol theatre,—which was to this effect: the Russian army is represented, as in the act of recrossing the Danube in some confusion, after having raised the siege of Silistria.

One of the Russian generals, addressing the troops around him,—who seem worn down by cholera, hunger, and fatigue,—undertakes to prove to them, that the retreat is only a manoeuvre,—and that, as for the epidemic,—why it is nothing more than a trifling indisposition, which is not attended with any danger. But, just at the very moment, when, warming with the subject, he is becoming quite eloquent, the poor devil is suddenly seized with violent cramps! And, after going through a thousand, horrible contortions, and giving vent to the most melancholy reflections, (as it were aside), he suddenly darts away; and, when last seen,—is making rapidly for the side scenes, clutching desperately at his nether garment!

In camp, where a regiment occupies but a few hundred square metres,—and under the thin walls of a tent,—it is no easy matter, to draw an impervious veil over the domestic scene; and, perhaps, nowhere has the old proverb, that *walls have ears*, a more forcible application. There was a *vivandier* in the regiment, named T——, who was, beyond all question, his own best customer, for, from reveille until tattoo, he was incessantly engaged in treating himself to the most copious libations. After the sergeant-major's round in the evening, he was, of course, left to the sole society of his wife, for whom he entertained the most amicable feelings;—but whom he treated just according to the degree of intoxication, in which he happened to find himself,— with tenderness, or impatience, indifference, or brutal violence.

Naturally very talkative, he, under the influence of wine, became, also, quarrelsome, a suspicious, sometimes jealous,—and, then, again, after the most terrible, conjugal row, would perhaps subside into a mood of the most loving fondness, to the enormous scandal of his neighbours! These matrimonial scenes did not escape the vigilant ear of the director of the Guignol theatre, who quickly converted them to his own use; and soon T——, represented under the graceful costume of Punchinello, and the very significant appellation of *Trémoileux*,—ministered to the delight of laughing audiences.

T——, who was very sensitive in matters of *punctilio*, and by no means a person to be trifled with, lost no time in applying to his colonel, for permission to challenge the facetious bugler. The colonel, though he would not refuse him this permission, yet urged him to take advantage of the twenty-four hours, which should intervene between the provocation and the meeting, to go, that very evening, and witness for himself, first, the performance of the objectionable play.—T—— followed his colonel's advice; he even did better,—he took his wife with him to the theatre,—and the two laughed so heartily over the performance, that the laughers passed on their side; and the upshot of the matter was, that T——, a good fellow at heart, finally consented to make peace with Punchinello,—ratifying the same, with many fraternal compotations.

T—— went through the whole subsequent campaign, acquitting himself as a good and brave soldier; and was quite severely wounded, at the attack of the White Works, on the 7th of June. His wife, a courageous and kind-hearted *vivandière*, never failed to accompany the *Zouaves* into action; was several times wounded, and repeatedly recommended for the military medal.

Attracted by these dramatic representations, which, all unskilled and unpretending as they were, nevertheless exercised a most happy influence over the morale of the men, both officers and soldiers, and frequently even the generals of the neighbouring divisions, used to throng to the *Zouave* camp,—sure of finding there the gayety, and liveliness, with many another souvenir of France.

Prince Napoleon not only did his best to encourage and promote these amusements, but frequently, himself, assisted at the play.

During the latter part of July, the 3rd Division left its camp at Yeni-Keuï for a time;—ostensibly, to support the 1st and 2nd Divisions, which had been sent into the Dobrudscha,—but, in reality, rather to escape the ravages of the cholera. It moved northward, as far as Bazardjick-Oglou; a large Bulgarian city, which had been almost totally destroyed during the preceding winter, by the undisciplined bands of the Bachi-Bouzouks. But, on the 2nd of August, after the expeditionary corps had been constrained by a terrible outburst of cholera, to beat a hasty retreat from the Dobrudscha, the 3rd Division broke up its camp at Bazardjick, to return to that at Yeni-Keuï.

It would be difficult,—among all the various examples of towns and cities, which have been laid waste in war,—to meet with an instance of greater desolation, than that presented by the unfortunate city of Bazardjick-Oglou! Whole blocks, nay streets of houses, had been burnt to the ground—its mosques lay in ruins—its tombs were mutilated—its bazaars stood open, and untenanted.

At the beginning of the war, it had rejoiced in a population of no less than 25,000 souls, Christians and Mussulmen:—there barely remained now, three hundred miserable wretches, and they, half dead with hunger and disease. Perhaps, at night, might glimpses be had of a few, ghost-like Bulgarian women, stealing out from amid the shadows of the ruins, and gliding along from street to street, in quest of water, green fruits and roots, in the open country beyond.

But by day, the only living things to be seen, were the storks,—those faithful, but melancholy-looking guests of man, and which in the East are as much respected as in Germany,—which, perched on such of the chimney tops as still remained standing, alone reminded the stranger, passing by, that this wide solitude had, but a short time previously, been alive with the hum of commerce, and teeming with an industrious and thriving population. The country around, exhibited, in a similar manner, the ravaging effects of war; crops, left standing in the fields, ungathered, had been trampled underfoot; fountains and wells, choked with the bodies of dead animals, had been poisoned, or dried up; everywhere, in fact, the ground was strewed with visible traces of the ruin, with which an undisciplined army had marked its passage.

What possible motive could have led to the destruction of so large a city, was a mystery to everyone; but, although these ruins were scarce a few months old,—already they were as silent, and, apparently, as deserted, as those which, centuries old, lie scattered over the lonely plains and mountains of Algeria!

Before setting out, as well as upon the march, the regiments of this division, also, paid a heavy tribute to the cholera; the soldiers of the 2nd Zouaves, however, who had preserved a part of the extra rations, with which they had been supplied at starting, suffered less than the others, and lost only a few men.(*See note following*)

Note:—How much a more generous diet contributes, not only to the contentment, but to the health of the men, is a fact abundantly confirmed by the translator's own experience. He was on one occasion stationed at a post, garrisoned by five companies, and which was cruelly ravaged by on epidemic of yellow fever. The men of the company to which he was attached, were no more acclimated than most of the others, their duty was the same, they were equally exposed,—yet, the proportion of deaths among them was relatively so small, as to excite general remark. there was naturally a cause for this exemption;—which could be ascribed to nothing else, however. than to the superior manner in which—thanks to a large company fund—they were fed and cared for.

The strength of their coffee was doubled, and it was served to them, the first thing in the morning before they were permitted to go out into the morning dews; a small cup of strong coffee was again given to every man after dinner and the men on guard were fortified against the damp vapours of the night, by the some powerful febrifuge, In addition to this, their fare was improved by many little extras; and the sick and convalescent were supplied, from the same fund, with broth, chickens, eggs, gruel, custards, &c. At another time, the scurvy broke out, in the only other company then serving at the post; there were some eight or ten cases of the disease in that company—there was but one in the translator's.—And this one man, a delicate youth, who had been for some time previously in hospital—there, caught the disease from the others, as the doctor himself admitted.

Here, again, the principal difference between the two companies, was, that whilst one had a company fund, from which many little extras were furnished to it, the other had no fund, and was therefore reduced to its ordinary rations; which, whatever may be asserted to the contrary, are not sufficient, in quantity, for a hard-working man, nor of suitable quality, for men exposed to such trying vicissitudes of climate, as the soldiers of our army.—T.

On their return to Yeni-Keuï, the men resumed the interrupted course of their former labours and amusements. But, losing patience at length, like the other corps, they took occasion of a review, one day, to communicate in decided terms to Marshal de St. Arnaud, their burning desire to march upon the enemy. At length, the wished-for-moment came! Towards the middle of August, orders were received to proceed to the Crimea; and the regiment, at once, set gaily about its preparations, for this distant and adventurous expedition.

The effective strength of the regiment was to be reduced for the voyage to 1,250 men; and, consequently, 800 were condemned to await, in Bulgaria, the return of the fleet.

The regrets, which had already been manifested at Oran, on the first formation of the expeditionary battalions, broke out anew and with such violence, on this occasion, that the colonel had need of all his authority, to persuade a portion of his *Zouaves* to remain where they were. A regular detail was made of the officers and non-commissioned officers, according to the rollster of detached service.

It fell, in this way, to the lot of Captain Lavirotte,—the same who had been decorated at the close of the Babors expedition, but who, owing to chronic dysentery, was now greatly reduced in strength, and wholly incapacitated to endure the fatigues of active field service,—to remain in Bulgaria. A brave and brilliant soldier, and a man of noble impulse, he earnestly besought permission to follow his company, vowing that he felt sufficiently sure of himself, to promise that, on no account, would he let himself be reported sick.

The colonel, who both liked and esteemed him, was however obliged, after taking the advice of the surgeon, to refuse his request. On hearing this, Lavirotte immediately repairs to the colonel's tent,—reminds his chief of all the marks of friendship, which he has received from him,—thanks him warmly for them all,—but implores him, to crown these various acts of kindness, by this last and greatest favour, which he asks of him, of allowing him to accompany the expedition to the Crimea. The colonel, however, adheres to his first decision. Then, with tears in his eyes, the gallant fellow confesses to him, that he knows his disease to be mortal, but that he yet entreats him for permission to go, in the hope that he may at least live long enough to be present at the first battle, and getting himself there killed, thus earn for himself a soldier's death.

Deeply affected by this sad, yet noble appeal, the colonel is unable to hold out any longer. Unhappily, fate was less merciful than he; for, not more than two days after the departure of the fleet, the last honours were paid, on board the *Algiers*, to the remains of this brave soldier,—and they were buried in the waters of the Black Sea. Lavirotte was the first of that numerous band of heroic spirits, who, broken down by disease, still refused to report sick or go into hospital, but resolutely awaited death at their posts; thereby giving to all, as example of stern devotion to duty, and unfaltering resignation![9]

On the 2nd of September, the division left its camp for Balt-shik, where it was to embark. The field and staff, and 800 of the 2nd Zouaves, took passage on board the ship of war *Bayard*; 400 more went upon the *Algiers*; and the horses and mules belonging to the regiment, were shipped on board the transport *Due-Fratelli*. Each *Zouave* carried with him twenty-five days' extra rations, which had been purchased at Varna.

Although heavily laden before, the men willingly obeyed this order of their colonel's, being well aware, that the country in which they were going to carry on the war, was destitute of resources, and that for several days after their landing, it would be almost impossible to procure them fresh supplies.

From the 3rd to the 6th of September, the French fleet lay in the bay of Baltshik, waiting for the arrival of the English. On the 6th, the signal to weigh anchor was made, and all sail was made to the northward.

During this time, the cholera had broken out among the crew of the *Bayard*, one of the vessels in which was embarked

---

9. Among these, the translator may be pardoned, perhaps, for mentioning the name of a connection of his own, Louis Coudroy de Lauréal, captain in the 1st Zouaves, who, wounded at the capture of Abd-El-Kader's Smalah, and again distinguished at the storming of Laghouat.—with just enough strength left from a cureless attack of cholera, to drag himself as far as the Crimea,—fell, mortally wounded, at the battle of the Alma, while most gallantly leading on his men to the assault of the Telegraph tower. The cross of honour, which he had richly merited at Laghouat— for he and his *Zouaves*, with General Yusuf, are said to have been, really, the first who penetrated into the town,—together with the announcement of his promotion to be major, were soon on their way from France to him;—but, long before they could reach the Crimea, he was dead.—T.

the 3rd Zouaves; the germ of that terrible infection having been brought by the 19th battalion of *Chasseurs-à-pied*, who were also passengers on this ship. On the 8th of September, the number of the sick had already increased so much, that it became necessary to convert a portion of the first battery into a temporary hospital; within the next few days, nearly all the hospital attendants had taken the disease; and the colonel of the 2nd Zouaves was finally obliged to make an appeal to the humanity of his men, for volunteers who should nurse the sick. His appeal was quickly responded to; and a band of twenty, under the direction of Sergeant Gounneau, was soon organized for this perilous service. They acquitted themselves of it, with great courage, charity, and abnegation.—Sergeant Gounneau, for the share taken in it by him, was, not long afterward, made a Knight of the Legion of Honour; and every man on his detachment, also, was suitably rewarded.

To beguile the tedium of a long voyage, as well as to divert the thoughts of the sailors and soldiers from the lamentable spectacle, which was continually offered to their eyes in the first battery,—the colonel, in concert with Captain Borius, of the *Bayard*, employed himself in getting up a series of amusements. Every evening, accordingly, after supper, the hand of the *Zouaves* struck up, and began playing waltzes, polkas, and quadrilles,— while sailors, sailor boys, and soldiers commenced under the inspiration of this music, a course of the most unheard of saltatory performances. The officers looked on, in crowds, from the quarter deck; the *Zouaves* and *Chasseurs* lined all the rigging and the ladders; and the sailors swarmed about the tops, and along the yards of the main and mizzen masts,—eager and amused spectators, all of them.

When the ball was at an end, a company of singers, under the leadership of the *Zouave* R——, their faces smeared with chalk or charcoal, and most grotesquely attired,—took the places of the dancers, and with their merry, comic songs, never failed to provoke the laughter, even of those who had, up to that moment, remained unaffected by the general hilarity.

This man R—— had been reduced from the rank of corporal, only a few days before the formation at Oran, of the battalions, destined to take part in the expedition to the East. Assigned to the 3rd battalion, which was to remain in Algeria, and recollecting that the colonel had formerly appeared to take some interest in him, he, at a review, one day, petitioned him for a transfer to one of the war battalions—"I shall grant your request," was the colonel's reply to him, "notwithstanding that I had reserved this favour only for good soldiers:—but you must promise me,—bear it in mind,—that you will get yourself killed, at the very first battle in which we are engaged,—and thus forever rid your family of a good for nothing fellow."—R——, unshrinkingly accepts the condition imposed upon him, but at the same time assures his colonel, that, whether he live or die, he is at least resolved upon winning back his confidence and esteem.

Gay, full of wit, and of exceedingly lively spirits, he rendered a real service to the regiment, by organizing the various singing-clubs—among whom he was always the readiest, and most comical, as well as the most versatile performer.—The colonel, in consideration of this, wanted, just before the landing, to promote him to the rank of a first class private. But R—— declined the promotion at that time, preferring to wait until he could earn it in another way.—And, not only did he fairly win it at the battle of the Alma, but, subsequently, he deserved to be made corporal, and then sergeant; and finally gained the military medal, by going one night, at the risk of his life, to reconnoitre the Russian advanced works and the exterior suburbs of Sebastopol.

The officers and crew of the *Bayard*, never ceased during the whole trip to lavish the most kind and sympathetic attentions upon the officers and soldiers who had taken passage on their ship. Not content with sharing, from the beginning with them the best of their own supplies they went so far as at the landing to slip into the officers mess chests and soldiers' knapsacks a quantity of fresh provisions which proved of the utmost service during the first few days, which were passed on

The *Zouaves*, on the other hand, retained a lively recollection

119

of the kindness shown them by the people of the *Bayard*; and, having observed, during the voyage, that the ship's bell was a little cracked, they made off with that of the first Russian village they came across, and, lugging it down by hand, all the way to the beach, which was at least a league distant, they there intrusted it to the master of a cock-boat, to be delivered to the captain of the *Bayard*. Unfortunately, their agent proved unfaithful to his trust, and the bell never reached its destination.

Book 4 - The Crimea

On the 13th of September, the fleet arrived in sight of the coast of the Crimea, during the evening and night of the same day, several of the transport vessels came up; and, on the morning of the next day (14th), the army effected its landing upon the territory of Russia. The first to touch the beach at Old Fort, were four companies of *Zouaves*,—who were not a little astonished, at beholding no signs of an enemy. The beach here, was low, destitute of trees or vegetation, and with, here and there, a shallow pool of brackish water.

In a short time, the whole regiment was assembled, and marched in company with the other troops belonging to the 3rd Division, to occupy a point, about half a league in advance of the landing-place. The 3rd Division, which was commanded by Prince Napoleon, here took its place on the left of the French line, and not far from the English right;—and, in almost the twinkling of an eye, the *Zouaves* had formed their bivouac, and thrown out their grand guards.

The troops rapidly recovered from the fatigues of their voyage, during the short stay which they made at Old Fort; on the very next day which followed their debarkation, there was no longer a single cholera patient in the 2nd regiment of Zouaves,

On that day, the 15th of September, the men, whilst seeking, with those of other regiments, for wood and water, came across a large Russian village, which lay about a league in advance of their outposts. The inhabitants had fled; and, with the exception of the manor-house,—occupied by a few companies of English

Rifles,—the village was entirely deserted. The marauders found here a quantity of fresh provisions, with which they rapidly made off; and, on this being reported to Prince Napoleon, he at once repaired thither, accompanied by the colonel of the 2nd Zouaves and a detachment of his men, for the purpose of placing safe-guards, and posting sentries, in such a way as to protect the village from further depredations.

The manor-house, which was not quite finished yet, belonged to a colonel in the Russian Imperial Guards, who, with his family, had abandoned it during the night, leaving only his steward and a few servants in charge. On the Prince's arrival there, the steward hastened to place the house, and all that it contained, at his, and the disposition of the other French officers. The disorder, in which everything seemed to be, showed plainly how precipitate had been the flight of the master.

Just opposite to a glass door, which opened out upon one of the terraces, a handsome Ehrard piano stood open, its top strewed over with pieces of French and German music,—upon a stand in the middle of the parlour, lay scattered a confused heap of those innumerable little trifles, with which women of elegant tastes so love to surround themselves,—portraits of the colonel and his lady hung suspended from the walls, while, upon a, work-table, in a corner of the room, lay an open volume of Lamartine's poetry,—showing that the fair mistress of the house was busy with thoughts of France, even at the very moment when a French army was disembarking within but a few hundred paces of her lordly residence.

The Prince, before quitting the house, assured the steward, that everything in it should be carefully respected; and, handing him a few gold pieces for distribution among the servants, in requital of the tea, sour wine, and black bread, which they had courteously offered him, he left the poor *major-domo* quite overcome with astonishment, at the discovery that he had been receiving in his master's house, a French Prince, of the far-famed name of Napoleon;—a name no less familiar here, than it is in other parts of the world.

The fellows who had paid this marauding visit to the Russian village, treated their comrades to a rather ludicrous spectacle, on their return. For, they took it into their heads to mate their way back to the bivouac, in a sort of triumphal procession,—escorting one of those little carriages, peculiar to the Crimea, and in which was seated one of their number grotesquely attired—with a magnificent calf by his side which they had tricked out in all the woman's finery they had been able to lay hands on, whilst rummaging the Russian peasants houses. The carriage was afterward sent back to the village; but the calf was turned over to the sick in hospital, who were sadly in want of fresh meat.

The *Zouaves* are much given to such masquerading exploits, and they rarely miss an opportunity of indulging in these, or similar pleasantries,—especially when their marauding expeditions have been attended with more than ordinary success, A few days after the battle of the Alma, and while on the march to Sebastopol, they came upon rich Russian village, just at the crossing of the Belbeck,—and as its gardens were teeming with fruits and vegetables, and the place completely deserted, they enjoyed, that night, a famous supper at their bivouac, for, cabbages turnips, and grapes, were in the utmost abundance—But, in the course of the night, some of them undertook to push then explorations further, and even to pay a visit to a country seat, situated at quite a distance from their camp.

On their return from it, they brought along with them a large and handsome pier-glass, surmounted by a panel on which were painted shepherds and shepherdesses, in the style of Boucher, Hastily erecting a green bower, just in front of their colonel's tent-door, they amused themselves with setting up this glass there—in order, as they afterwards confessed to him, to procure him the satisfaction of completing his toilet,—at least once more during the campaign,—in a *boudoir*, and after a civilized fashion.

Accustomed as they were to the *razzias* of Africa, it was with much difficulty, that the *Zouaves* could be taught to respect the abandoned property of the Russian peasants. This forbearance was all the more difficult for them to practise, too, as they were suffering from an almost total dearth of fresh provisions. But, as the theatre of operations soon became very much restricted, the Tartars,—who, by the way, were remarkably well disposed to the allied armies,—had really little to suffer from them; and for that little, they were afterward abundantly compensated by the money, which they were enabled to make in selling their produce to the soldiers, during the armistice, and by the fabulous bargains they had a chance of making at the time of the embarkation,— when the stores and beasts of burden belonging to the army, were sacrificed to them for a mere song. Upon the whole, they must have retained a very agreeable recollection of the foreign occupation of their country, especially the latter part of it.

On the morning of the 19th September, the army broke up the camp, which it had been occupying in the vicinity of Old Fort, since the 14th of the month, and put itself in march for Sebastopol, by a road running so close to the coast, as to secure it an uninterrupted communication with the sea. In the afternoon of the same day, the troops established their bivouac at a place, called Kermani-Kava-Savia, on the further side of a little, dried-up watercourse,—on a range of low hills, which fronted, at the distance of about a league and a half, the opposite heights of the Alma, on which lay encamped the Russian army.

Prince Mentschikoff, the commander of the Russian forces, sent a few squadrons of cavalry, with a battery or two of horse artillery, to reconnoitre the allied armies, and these troops even exchanged a few cannon-shot with the English, but they contented themselves with examining the French at a distance, and without endeavouring to bring on an engagement with them.—Yet the grand guards were so close to the Russians, that for some time the *Zouaves* fancied, that it was the English who were thus in front of them.

2

In the evening, Prince Napoleon, on his return from general head-quarters, whither he had been to take the orders of the general-in-chief, assembled in his tent the generals and chiefs of corps belonging to his own division; and proceeded to unfold them the plan of the next day's battle, as concerted between the two generals-in-chief. It consisted in turning the right flank of the Russians with the English army, while the 2nd French division, aided by the Turks, should, under General Bosquet, attack the enemy's left, posted upon the precipitous heights which overlook the mouth of the Alma.

The centre, composed of the 1st and 3rd Divisions, in two lines, and of the 4th, held in reserve under the immediate orders of Marshal de St. Arnaud, was to attack the Russian centre; but not until after the wings had become engaged. The two wings were, therefore, to commence the movement first; their orders were to set out between five and six in the morning—the centre, only between seven and eight. Prince Napoleon then issued his detailed orders; after which, drawing the colonel of the 2nd Zouaves aside, "Being acquainted with the known gallantry of your regiment," said he to him, "I mean to give it the post of danger,—but it will be, also, as you well know, the post of glory."

The colonel warmly thanked the prince, in his own, as well as in the name of his regiment, for the flattering distinction thus bestowed upon it, and promised him, that his *Zouaves* would prove themselves every way worthy, of the esteem and confidence thus reposed in them.

As the centre of the army was not to stir, until two hours after the departure of the wings, their *reveille* was not sounded so early; but, long before it did sound, the *Zouaves* were already up, and busy,—some in getting their coffee ready; others in cleaning and reloading their arms.

The colonel then called round him his officers and non-commissioned officers,—and, whilst the soldiers, all ears, as is usual under such circumstances, drew round, and as near as possible,— he gave them his instructions for the coming battle;—then, turning to the men, he addressed them as follows:

Your place in the fight will be between the 1st Zouaves,

your peers in glory, and between the English,—the hereditary foes of France, but now her allies. Let every man among us then, make it a point of honour to let no other get ahead of him.—Remember, that, as sons of that heroic generation, whose valour and conquests shed such an imperishable lustre over the early part of this century, you are called upon to illustrate the second Empire, by new and equally splendid victories.

Pointing with his finger to the Russian army, ranged along the heights of the Alma, he added: "You shall lie placed in the first line;—before reaching the enemy, you will have to cross a river, force your way through dense thickets, and up yonder heights—but recollect, that, when once the battle is fairly begun, it must be fought out *à l'Africaine*: as soon, therefore, as you shall have achieved a first success, charge the Russians with that same invincible impetuosity, which has so often enabled you to dislodge the Kabyles from their formidable positions."

By seven o'clock, the regiment, as it had been ordered, was in full readiness to march. And, being in ignorance of what was passing on other points of the line, the men were totally at a loss how to comprehend the successive delays, which caused the advance of the centre of the army to be put off again and again, until it was eleven o'clock. Their bad humour found vent in a variety of spiteful exclamations and remarks,—not unlike those attributed to the *grognards* of the first Empire, when their hard fate compelled them to assist, as mere lookers-on at a battle, with arms at a support.

The colonel, by way of occupying their attention, had coffee again prepared, and served out to them. Prince Napoleon, entering freely into conversation with them, endeavoured also to soothe their impatience by his kindly words. Finally, Marshal de St. Arnaud came to see them, and on his inviting them to take coffee again, "Our colonel has, already, made us do so," they growled in reply.

"Well, then," said the marshal, "since your colonel has treated you a second time to coffee, I take upon myself to furnish your *pousse café*; but it must be above there, mind you, in the enemy's camp," pointing, as he said so, up to the heights of the Alma.

"Hurrah for the marshal!" thereupon shouted the *Zouaves*.

"Hurrah for those, who will be on their feet tonight," rejoined the marshal.[10]

At length, between eleven o'clock and noon, the regiment moved forward from its bivouac at Kermani-Kava-Savia. Posted on the right of the first line of the 3rd Division, it advanced under cover of two of its companies, thrown out as skirmishers in its front; (the 5th of the 1st Battalion, commanded by Captain Sage, and the 1st of the 2nd Battalion, commanded by Captain Du Lude.)

At half-past twelve, the skirmishers began to make their way through the right of the village of Bourliouck, and the gardens which extend along the right bank of the Alma. Just at this moment, the enemy, whose light troops, armed with long-range rifles, had commenced the engagement, opened fire with his guns. A few round shot came pitching among the troops of the first line:—whereupon the colonel instantly deployed his two battalions, and reinforced his skirmishers with Captain Fernier's 2nd company of the 2nd battalion.

On arriving near the gardens, the men, upon an order given them to that effect, there deposited their knapsacks; by which means, they were both greatly lightened, and acquired more freedom in their movements.[11]

The field of this battle has been so repeatedly and fully described, that we deem it unnecessary to add any topographical description of it here.

The 1st Battalion of the regiment, under Major Malafosse, promptly took up a position in the muddy bed of the river, near the ford whence ascends the road leading over the lofty and precipitous heights of the opposite bank. The 2nd Battalion, under

10. The expression, used by the marshal on this occasion, was infinitely more forcible, than that which we have put in his mouth; it may be found in the Trooper's vocabulary, no doubt, but will be looked for in vain, in the *Dictionnairre de l'Académie*.
11. Each knapsack contained several days' field rations, besides eighteen days' extra rations.

Major Adam, was held back a little to the left and rear, near the gardens.

But it was impossible for the regiment to remain long in this first position for soon the companies, of skirmishers, already hotly engaged amid the tangled cover which lined the other side, would be seriously jeopardized; and it was therefore necessary to come to some positive determination

There were three Russian battalions posted in advance of their line upon a detached hill adjoining, the plateaus, which crown the heights on that side of the river. This hill, a sort of buttress to the opposite bank, jutted obliquely out into the river, and whilst the slopes on its right and left were easily swept by the fire of the enemy, the dip of its summit ridge, on the contrary, was so abrupt, as to make their fire in that direction very uncertain. At the same time the 1st Division was on the point of assaulting the left face of this hill, together with the high bluffs situated in its prolongation towards the sea.

The colonel of the 2nd Zouaves, seeing, at this juncture; the necessity of making a sudden clash at the enemy, asks and obtains permission from his brigade-commander, to assail and carry, with his 1st battalion, the projecting face of the cliff.

At the same moment, one of Prince Napoleon's *aides de camp*, Captain Ferri-Pisani, who had been reconnoitring the bed of the river, brings orders to General de Monet, to take his brigade across the ford, before alluded to, and endeavour to get out of the river bottom, towards his left.

The colonel of the 2nd Zouaves repairs at once to his 1st battalion,—posted, as before said, in the stream, itself. The fire of the enemy's artillery is raking the whole lower part of the valley and the outlet of the ford,—the branches of the great trees, which line the bank, torn away by the round shot, come crashing down in every direction,—shells are bursting over the bank,—and a very hail of shrapnel and canister is poured down every slope.

The *Zouaves*, nevertheless, prepare to climb the opposite bank; the colonel has the "charge" sounded, and putting his horse into a gallop, is followed by the whole of his 1st Battalion. The impulse is given;—but, unable to keep up the road, which is too completely enfiladed by the enemy's fire, the soldiers incline to the right, cross a bend which the river here makes, under a perfect hurricane of iron and lead, and, swinging themselves up the bank, are re-formed at the foot of the hill occupied by the Russian battalions, and where they are in a measure protected by the very steepness of the overhanging ridge.

Making, however, but a brief pause here, the battalion quickly scales the face of the cliff, and hurls itself upon the Russians,— just at the very moment, that the latter are taken in flank by the gallant 1st regiment of Zouaves; and, after a short, sharp struggle, the enemy is, between them, compelled to abandon his formidable position, leaving behind him his wounded, his knapsacks,—and even a quantity of arms.

The 2nd Battalion of the 2nd Zouaves, had followed and supported this movement, on the left; the marine regiment had pushed on immediately after it; and, thus, the whole of General de Monet's brigade was, in a short time, warmly engaged with the Russians.

Masters of the first slopes leading up to the plateaus, the 1st Battalion of the regiment, in spite of a murderous fire, forms itself into a column at half distance, in front of a long line of Russian columns by battalion. Near it, on its right, are the 1st Zouaves, and the 1st and 9th Battalions of *Chasseurs à pied*. The 2nd Battalion of the regiment, which, to effect its movement, has had a much greater distance to pass over, over very rough ground, and under a heavy fire of grape,—forms painfully and slowly on the left of the 1st, which is thrown back *en potence*, so as to form an angle with and protect the left flank of the 1st division, now deploying into line.

Forming at length into column of divisions, at platoon distance, the 2nd Battalion is in readiness to deploy instantly, if necessary, into line of battle, four deep,—to resist a threatened charge of cavalry, which apparently aimed at the left flank of the line, becomes each moment more imminent.

The position taken is, in every way, full of danger; for, under the concentrated fire of several batteries and numerous battalions of the enemy, the regiment is beginning to suffer sorely, and the men are falling thick and fast, under the storm of bullet, ball, and grape shot, rained upon them. On the other hand, to attempt a deployment into line within striking distance of an enemy so strong in numbers and position, seems, at best, but a hazardous manoeuvre.

Yet, from dangerous, the situation may soon become critical; the colonel of the 3rd Zouaves is unable to bear the thought of seeing his splendid regiment cut to pieces—he therefore resolves on one of those desperate attacks which, with French troops, so often prove successful.

The marshal, too, had already exclaimed, as he witnessed the first rush made by the men into battle, "Let them alone 'tis a soldiers' battle!" And the *Zouaves* are still full of ardour. Pointing out to them, then, the unfinished, octagonal tower, intended for a telegraph station, which stands upon the highest point of the enemy's line, the colonel cries out to his gallant fellows, "Follow me, my *Zouaves*,—forward upon that tower!" and, as he spurs his horse in that direction, they all dash after him, at the *pas de course*.

The 1st Zouaves does the same; the two regiments arrive, side by side, at the foot of the tower, and quickly make themselves masters of it,—in spite of the resistance offered by two companies of skirmishers, armed with heavy rifles, who had been placed there to defend it.

But the enemy's reserves,—extended *en èchelon* to the right and left, so as to cross their fire over every inch of the ground lying in front of the tower,—are posted immediately behind, and on either side of it. Between them, the 2nd Zouaves, and the battalion of the first line under the orders of General Canrobert and Colonel Bourbaki,[12] is then begun a close and deadly com-

---

12. Then colonel of the 1st Zouaves, but soon afterward promoted; the same, who saved the English at Inkermann;—one of the most gallant spirits in the French army.—T.

bat; all the more desperately fought, for its being known to both officers and men, that here lies the key to the enemy's position, and the very knot of the battle.

Colonel Cler, who had been the first to reach the foot of the tower, seizes the eagle of his regiment and plants it upon the scaffolding, amid the cries of *Vive l'Empereur!*

Orderly Sergeant Fleury, of the 1st Zouaves, who has managed to get on top of the upper range of scaffolding, sustains the flag in this position, for a moment or two, but soon falls a lifeless corpse, struck down by a grape shot in the head.[13]

The colours of the 1st Zouaves are quickly seen floating side by side with those of the 2nd regiment; and have hardly been raised there, before the colour-staff is cut in two by a shell.

On the arrival of a brigade of the reserve, under command of General d'Aurelles, Lieutenant Poitevin, colour-bearer of the 39th of the line, seeing the glorious place occupied by the colours of the 1st and 2nd Zouaves, rushes forward in advance of his battalion, plants those of his own regiment upon the tower,— and as he presses the colour-staff close to his heart to hold it up, has his breast torn open with a round shot, and pays, with his life, for the performance of this act of generous daring.

The struggle around the tower, is a fierce and sanguinary one—but lasts only a short time. Prince Mentschikoff, seeing the key of his position in the hands of the French, is at length compelled to beat a retreat. The enormous mass of cavalry and infantry, assembled upon this part of the field of battle, accordingly retires in good order under cover of its artillery, which continues to sweep the space around the tower with an unceasing fire. General Canrobert, who during the whole battle, had been in the very midst of his men, is suddenly hit; he is caught, as he falls, in the arms of the *Zouaves*;—but, in a short while, mounts his horse again, and resumes his place in the fight.

Whilst the 2nd Zouaves is forming into line on the left of the telegraph tower, the colonel disposes of the numerous promo-

---

13. This is the moment chosen, by one of our most celebrated historical painters, for the admirable painting, which he has made of this glorious battle.

tions, which he has it in his power to make,—rewarding upon the spot, all those whose conduct in the action had attracted his own notice, or who are recommended to him by their officers. Every *Zouave* of the 2nd class, who being wounded, had continued to fight, is at once raised by him to the 1st class. Prince Napoleon, too, takes this opportunity of expressing to the regiment, the lively satisfaction, which their gallant behaviour has occasioned him; and, warmly pressing the colonel's hands, "I am rejoiced," said he, "my dear colonel, at having it in my power to congratulate you. How proud must you not feel at commanding soldiers such as these!"

Marshal de St. Arnaud rides up soon after, to tender his congratulations to the 3rd Division; and, as he passes down the front of the 2nd Zouaves,—stopping before the eagle, he turns to say to the colonel, "This time, Cler, 'tis the name of the Alma, which shall be embroidered on your colours "[14]

Along their whole line, the French were victorious; but the battle was still raging on the side of the English, On being informed of this, the marshal gives orders to the division of the Prince, to change front forward on its left, and advance immediately to the attack of the Russian right. The order was at once obeyed; but the division had hardly proceeded a few hundred metres in that direction, when news was brought to it of the success of the English and retreat of the Russians, and it was halted. Soon after this, the 2nd Zouaves established its bivouac near the telegraph tower,—upon that very part of the field of battle, where it had helped to shatter and stave in the Russian centre.

3

The series of rapid successes, which had characterized this first battle, had excited the enthusiasm of the army to the highest pitch. None of the wounded, who retained strength enough to keep their feet, would consent to leave their companies until the fight was over; whilst even those, who lay stretched upon

---

14. By the words, this time, the marshal meant to refer to the storming of Laghouat

the field,—instead of asking for help, or requesting to be carried to the rear,—exhorted their comrades, on the contrary, to let them alone, and pursue their success;—and, on any of their chiefs passing by, saluted them with acclamations.

The chief bugler of the regiment, Gesland, was among the number of the wounded; his wrist was shattered by a round shot, which, as it knocked his bugle out of his hands, dashed it with force against his face and breast. He had no sooner had his hand amputated, however, than he quietly returned to the field, and took his place, again, at the head of his buglers. And when, at the evening roll-call, the colonel was unable to conceal his astonishment, at seeing him coming up with the other non-commissioned officers, to make his report, the intrepid fellow replied, "I am quite able to do duty, my colonel, and wished to rejoice with my comrades over the splendid success of the day." [15]

When the colonel went to visit the sick in the evening, he found their *morale* all that he could have wished for,—all those who were less grievously wounded, clamouring for permission to return to their companies,—and those who were mortally so, bowing to their fate with manly resignation.

Among the latter, was Sergeant Sombert, who had received a bullet in the abdomen, and to whom the colonel remarked, that it was his intention to recommend him for the cross of the Legion of Honour.

"Rather bestow it upon some of my comrades," was Sombert's reply, "for as for me, colonel, I am mortally wounded and feel that I have but a few hours longer to live. Yet, be assured that my last prayer shall be that God may forever bless you!"

Out of 165 wounded, there were scarce 20 who failed to recover;—of these last, however, was a very gallant officer, 1st Lieutenant Esmieu.

Unfortunately, the case was very different with the offic-

---

15. Gesland was attended by the surgeon of the regiment; he was sent soon after to the hospital at Constantinople and his wound was completely healed by the end of the month. This brave soldier was made a Knight of the Legion of Honour, a member of the Turkish order of the Midjidie, and subsequently appointed by Prince Napoleon one of the custodians of the Palais Royal.

ers and soldiers, who were suffering from cholera. Among the number of these, was Captain Fernier; who, very much reduced by a chronic dysentery, had yet contrived to drag himself out to the field, and drawing strength from the excitement of the occasion, had set his men an example of the most heroic courage. Although coming out unscathed, from the perils of the battle, he died shortly afterward; as did the Lieutenants Oizan and Delfosse, who had also distinguished themselves by their energy and courage, and like him, perished, victims to this unrelenting disease. The cross, for which Lieutenant Oizan was named in this battle, was sent to his family.

The 21st and 22nd, were spent in burying the dead and attending to the wounded; most of whom were embarked on board the fleet. On the 23rd, the army resumed its march; the 3rd Division being in the first line, along with the 4th. On arriving at the Katcha, the 2nd Zouaves was posted as a rear guard, to cover the passage of the ford.

The Marshal de St. Arnaud, himself, superintended this operation, in spite of his excruciating sufferings. Seated on horseback, near the outlet of the ford, he remained there, until the last man of the long column had passed over. Colonel Cler, aware of his affection for the *Zouaves*, was tempted to try and raise a smile on that wan face, where death seemed to have already set its seal. He, accordingly, gave his orders to the men; and when it came to their turn, at length, to enter the ford,—notwithstanding that the stream ran very swiftly at this spot,—they defiled before the marshal, in regular order, with music in front, just as if marching in review,—while their bugles rang merrily out with the dashing, and now so well known and popular air, of *la casquette du père Bugeaud*.[16]

But, alas! such havoc had disease already wrought in the whole organization of the marshal, that, on his seemingly dead and passionless features, so deeply furrowed with pain, no sign

---

16. Though a very simple, this air is jet a very sincere and affectionate tribute to the memory of one of our best generals;—a man who was as conspicuous among the leaders of our day, for his kind solicitude for his men, as for his good sense and military talents.

of consciousness or interest could now be detected, by the eager soldiers, as they rapidly filed past him. Nor did there fall from his lips any of those playfully kind remarks, which the appearance of the *Zouaves* was usually so sure to elicit from him,—remarks, couched in that rough, bantering, troopers' slang, of which the French soldier is so fond, and which the witty and heroic St. Arnaud knew so well how to use with them,—with his air so full of pleasant malice, yet beaming ever with so much unaffected good nature.

Although he sat his charger firmly, and as if nailed to his seat by the indomitable will, which possessed him, yet the unfortunate marshal had more the look of a galvanized corpse, than of a living and breathing man. It was very painful for the *Zouaves* to see him thus! The warrior was, indeed, dying in his harness,— one might almost say, shrouded in his very victory!

Before crossing the Katcha, the regiment exhibited a very handsome instance of obedience to orders. Its two battalions had been posted, so as to cover the passage of the river, in the immediate vicinity of an extensive vineyard; where the grapes could be seen on every side, hanging in rich, ripe, purple clusters, most tempting to the eye, as well as alluring to the stomach of men, who had been living for so many days, on nothing but salt meat and hard biscuit.

To guard, however, against any possibility of surprise from the Russian scouts, the colonel had given strict orders to his men, to remain in their ranks, and keep out of the vineyard. the order was religiously obeyed. And, to reward them for their obedience, the colonel, so soon as all cause for apprehension was at an end, gave to each battalion in turn, just five minutes to go in and gather the grapes. No more was needed, however,—and, at the end of the time thus fixed, it would have been difficult to find a ripe grape in any part of the vineyard!

On the 24th, the army moved towards the Belbek, in the expectation that, after crossing that river, it would push straight on, and bivouac, that afternoon, on the north side of Sebastopol, and in view of it. It was not until they had reached the river, that the order, given to the columns to incline to the left, excited a suspicion in the soldiers' minds, that the original plan must have been modified, and that the place was to be turned.

That evening was spent by the army in the midst of a wood, without any idea of the whereabouts of the enemy.

On the 25th, the order of march was completely inverted; the English, who had all along been on the left, now took the front. The French divisions made an effort to march on the right of the road; but they were stopped almost at every instant, either by the thickness of the underwood, or by the tail of the English army, which appeared to get on with much difficulty. These divisions remained under arms all day, and, having had a variety of obstacles to contend with, did not arrive at their bivouac on the Mackenzie farm, until about the middle of the night.

The soldiers had suffered greatly from heat and thirst, during the march, and on their arrival here, looked eagerly around for water, but were wholly unsuccessful in obtaining any. They were thus compelled to pass the remainder of the night, without any means, either of allaying their thirst, or even of making a little coffee. Towards morning, a *Zouave* who had had himself let down to the bottom of an almost dried-up well, by means of a string of turbans tied together, was fortunate enough to find a little water, which he hastened to present to his officers. The soldiers bestowed on this dreadful bivouac the appropriate name, of *Thirsty Camp*.

The English, on arriving upon this plateau, had found it occupied by a Russian division, the rear guard of Prince Mentschikoff's army. But with so much precipitation did the Russians retire, on the approach of the English, that they even left behind them a number of wagons, heavily loaded with provisions; and one of their batteries actually overturned its ammunition wagons on the left of the slope, leading down from the Mackenzie farm into the valley of the Tchernaya.

They even dropped the two standards, belonging to one of their batteries, in the confusion of their flight. These were afterward picked up by a *Zouave*, named Rousseau, who brought

136

them to his colonel. The colonel at once appointed him a corporal, and took him with them to Prince Napoleon; who, congratulating him upon his promotion, presented him with several gold pieces, hearing the effigy of the Prince's father; and begged him to preserve them, as a memorial of the day, on which he had won his first grade.[17]

On the 26th, the army moved down from the Mackenzie plateau, by the Balaklava road, towards the valley of the Tchernaya. The 3rd Division had been designated for the extreme rear guard of the army. Just as it was about to commence its movement, the colonel of the 2nd Zouaves perceived a solitary tent, still standing upon the plateau,—and, near it, a covered carriage, which had been captured from the Russians. The tent was that of the Marshal de St. Arnaud, who, only a few hours before, had turned over his command to General Canrobert;—the carriage, was the same which had formerly belonged to Prince Mentschikoff.

The soldiers were still in ignorance of their having a new commander-in-chief.

The marshal had given the *Zouaves* so many repeated proofs of his attachment, that the colonel applied to Prince Napoleon for permission to go and take leave of his former general, and to make him the offer of escorting him with one of his battalions,—under the supposition that there was, as some affirmed, a road leading through the wood, and not far from the Russian positions, by which it was possible to reach Balaclava in less than two hours' journey.

As he approached the marshal's tent, the colonel caught a few, faint moans, proceeding from its interior; and which seemed to be wrung from him who uttered them, as if in spite of himself, and as though he were fairly overmastered by the excess of pain. In the voice of the sufferer, the colonel recognised, with deep

---

17. The moulds, which had once served for the coinage of the gold pieces, issued during the reign of the ex-king of Westphalia, having been recently discovered at the Mint, Prince Jerome had caused a number of these pieces to be struck off for distribution among his friends.

emotion, that of the spirited and lively chief, whom in Africa he had always known so full of wit and gay, good humour. And, as he entered the tent, he found him stretched out upon a carpet on the ground—pale in an agony of pain, and apparently dying.

The marshal thanked the colonel for his visit, by a silent, but expressive look; he even endeavoured to hold out his hand to him,—but his strength failed him, and he fell back exhausted. General Yusuf, who was there, unable to contain himself any longer, dragged the colonel out of the tent, and throwing himself into his arms, exclaimed in a voice half choked with sobs, "My poor Cler, we shall never, never look on him again!"

A moment after, the carriage, before spoken of, drew up in front of the tent. The marshal made a great effort to rise, and, thinking that he might perhaps be seen by the army, he even insisted on walking to the carriage,—or at least on arriving there erect, and upon his feet; in which he partially succeeded,—with the support of his *aides de camp* and physician, who held him up on either side. But the effort was too much for his falling strength, and his foot had hardly touched the carriage-step, before he swooned, and fell over upon the mattress, which had been spread out for him at the bottom of the carriage. It was for a moment thought by all, who stood around, that this exertion had killed him.

This was the last time, that Colonel Cler ever saw the marshal. Nor was he yet aware of the priceless legacy, which the marshal had left; to the three regiments of *Zouaves*, in his report of the battle of Alma;—a legacy, for which these dauntless soldiers have endeavoured to prove themselves grateful, by sealing it with the very best and purest of their blood,

4

Arriving upon the Tchernaya, toward the middle of the day, the division crossed this river, and established its bivouac upon the slopes of the Fedioukine hills, in rear of the canal which conveys the waters of the Tchernaya into Sebastopol.

The next day, the French army came down into the plain of Balaklava, As the officers of the 2nd Zouaves were passing before the house occupied by Lord Raglan and his staff, an *aide de camp* came out to meet the colonel and begged that he would please step inside for a moment, as the general desired to speak with him.

Lord Raglan was very anxious to convey a piece of news, which he had just received, to General Canrobert, to whom it was, indeed, of the utmost importance, that it should be communicated without delay—it being nothing less than the intelligence, brought in by spies, that Prince Mentschikoff, supposed to be on his march to Baktchi-Seraï, was, on the contrary, retracing his steps by the way of the upper Tchernaya, and might, from one moment to another, be expected to *débouch* upon the allied lines. The colonel of the 2nd Zouaves set out at once, with this information, for the bivouac of his general, then established in the gardens of Balaklava.

And he had hardly returned among his *Zouaves*, when orders came for him to turn out his whole regiment, to accompany the general-in-chief and Prince Napoleon, on a reconnaissance which they were about to make, in the direction of, and as far as a lofty eminence; which rose above the hills, that, running parallel with the Fedioukine range, divide in two, the plain of Balaklava.—This eminence constituted the key, which commanded all the approaches into the lower plain of Balaklava, where the allied army now lay encamped.

The 2nd Zouaves was directed to remain here, with two Turkish battalions, and two guns. Their orders were to maintain themselves in this position, no matter at what cost,—and on no account to think of abandoning it. But, as the spies, next morning, brought in the information that Prince Mentschikoff had resumed his movement of retreat to the north, the hill was evacuated: it was afterwards, from this circumstance, known as Canrobert's hill.

On the 29th, the 3rd Division quit its bivouac in the plain of Balaklava, to go and take possession of the plateau of the

Chersonnese; in the evening of the next day, 30th of September, it moved to the ground, which it was to occupy during the siege, and which lay on the right of that occupied by the 4th Division,—in a hollow, overgrown with brambles and vines, and in rear of the house, to which was afterwards given the name of the *Zouaves' House.*

This house, quite a handsome one in appearance, stood on the summit of a little knoll, within camion shot of the place, and was garrisoned by two companies of the regiment, during all the time that the investment of the southern side was going on. The steward of the establishment, who spoke French quite intelligibly, came forward to meet the colonel, on his taking possession of it; and, as he turned it over into his hands, assured him that his master,—the same English engineer who had superintended the construction of the docks of Sebastopol,—would be much pleased to learn that his dwelling was in the hands of French troops.

He added, that the Russians, full of gratitude for the services which his master had rendered them, would certainly respect his house, and be careful not to aim their fire in that direction. Then, drawing the colonel aside, he informed him, that the cellars were full of wine, and he hoped that the *Zouaves* would be allowed to make themselves amends, for the forced abstinence to which they had no doubt been condemned, ever since their landing in the Crimea,

This discovery, though in most respects a very fortunate one, was productive of some uneasiness in the colonel's mind. For, however well assured he might feel of the obedience of his *Zouaves* he could hardly venture, yet, to believe them so virtuous as, in his absence, to resist the temptations, likely to besiege them,—during a whole night, spent in close proximity to full casks of that seductive juice of the grape, for which the soldiers of all nations entertain such a decided partiality.

He, therefore, assembled the detachment, which was to mount guard over the house, that night; and placing it under the command of Captain Blanchet, an energetic and most determined officer, he warned the men, that he had reason to suspect a snare of some kind, in the show of confidence with which the house and its cellars had been given over to him, and that, it was not unlikely that the Russians,—who doubtless had heard of their great fondness for wine,—counted on their getting drunk, in the course of the night, and meant to fall upon them, while in that condition.

The rogues were, however, not at all convinced, by these arguments of their chief; and, at the close of his harangue, broke in upon him with the most dolorous entreaties, that he would at least "let them have just one little quart, each,—only one; they asked for no more,—and he ought to recollect, how long they had now been, without a single drop of any kind!"

"Not one single quart,—no, nor pint even, shall you have tonight," retorted the colonel; "and both officers and soldiers, therefore must make up their minds, to wait patiently until to-morrow, to drink the health of this worthy Russian, who has caused the produce of his vines to be presented to us with so much courtesy."

Though sorely against their will the *Zouaves* had nothing left for it but to obey this cruel order; for, Captain Blanchet was a dangerous man to trifle with, when charged with the execution of any duty. But,—as many of them subsequently acknowledged,—the idea that they were sleeping just overhead a cellar, full of wine, caused them to be ridden by a drunken nightmare, all night long!

The colonel, next day, kept his promise with them; every *Zouave* in the regiment received, at two different issues, a pint, each time, of red or white wine; which, in spite of a pretty marked flavour of essence of rose, was found all the more palatable, for having once belonged to the enemy.

The *Zouaves'* House, although frequently used as a lookout place, was, throughout the whole siege, scrupulously respected by the enemy's fire,—just as had been predicted by the steward.

During the early part of the month of October, the siege *matériel* and supplies for the army were landed, to the south

141

and within two leagues of Sebastopol, near the little village of Kamiesch,—in a deep, land-locked bay, which had been carefully sounded and surveyed by-parties from the French fleet. Still further to the south, was another bay similarly used, and known as that of Kasatch. The two proved of such utility, during the siege, to the French army and navy, that they were called by the soldiers, *the harbours of Providence.*

After the army had been landed on the beach at Old Fort, the colonel of the 2nd Zouaves took advantage of the willingness, manifested by one of his *cantinières*, to send her back to Varna with the fleet,—for the purpose of laying in a stock of extra rations; which she was to pay for, partly out of her own funds, and partly with the money advanced to her for that purpose by the officers of the regiment. The commander of the *Bayard* had kindly consented to bring her and her supplies, back with him to the Crimea, on the first trip which he was to make, with troops, to Kamiesch.

The *Zouaves* hailed with acclamation the arrival of these provisions; which came just in time to supply the place, of those they had brought from Bulgaria with them in their knapsacks.

The service, rendered to the regiment by this worthy *cantinière*, whose name was Dumont, is the more deserving of mention, as, during the poor woman's absence, her husband was wounded at the battle of the Alma, and she, herself, died soon after her return, exhausted by the fatigues of three successive voyages,— combined as they were with incipient cholera, of which she had brought back with her the germ from Varna.

From the 1st to the 9th of October, there were several reconnoissances made in the direction of the city. The battalions of the regiment were constantly employed on this service, as well as on outpost duty in the same direction.

The Russians,—no doubt to deceive us in regard to the distances, which it was difficult to estimate with any accuracy, over such an undulating expanse of ground,—continued for several days, and from the utmost elevation of their pieces, to fire at us enormous projectiles; of which some actually fell within the allied camps.

The 3rd and 4th Divisions, and subsequently the 5th, constituted the besieging force, which was placed under the command of General Forey.

On the evening of the 9th, everything was in readiness for breaking ground; 1,600 men were told off for this important work; among whom were nearly all of the 2nd Zouaves, who happened to be off duty at the time.

Contrary to the general expectation, the Russians made no attempt, either by cannonade or a sortie, to interrupt this critical operation,—usually reputed one of the most thorny and difficult ones, which occur in the course of a siege.

From that time, the regiment continued regularly to furnish its full quota for the various duties, connected with the trenches.

There was little in common, between the kind of warfare in which the *Zouaves* were now engaged, and that to which they had been accustomed in Africa. Instead of attacking an enemy that they could see, on vast battlefields, where there was room for their intelligence to develop itself in aid of their courage, they were now obliged to burrow, foot by foot, in stony or rocky ground,—or coil themselves up in a hole for twenty-four hours at a time, while watching over the workmen or their works,—and to handle the pick-axe, even more than the musket.

Yet this, to them, novel species of fighting,—in which an invisible enemy mowed them down with his ceaseless fire, or took advantage of some dark and dismal night, to fall unawares upon the working and covering parties, frequently all benumbed with cold,—was never able to depress the elastic spirits of the *Zouaves*. They still found means to lighten their rude labours with some droll story, some merry jest or snatch of song, sparkling with the true Gallic spirit, which has never, under any circumstances, yet failed our soldiers,—and has enabled them al ay to support with so much unflinching courage, the many difficult trials to which they have been exposed.

How often, just as the companies were returning from the

trenches, with appetites sharpened by twelve hours' labour, or twenty-four hours' guard, and just as the men were cosily bestowing themselves around the bivouac fire, and, while greedily inhaling the savoury vapour of the *turlutine*[18] preparing themselves to do ample justice to that inviting compound,—how often, just at this provoking moment, have not orders arrived for them, to turn out instantly to the assistance of the threatened working parties, or to repel some sortie of the besieged!

Who can wonder, under such circumstances, at the *Zouaves* sometimes growling a little, after the fashion of a thoroughbred dog, from whom his master has snatched a bone? Surely, it was anything but pleasant to tear one's self away from the 'warm delights of camp, and, with empty stomachs, plunge once more into the underground war of moles! [19] And yet a few cheering words, a jesting remark or two from their chief, were always sufficient to restore their good humour; and they would then obey almost with joyful alacrity.

On the 16th of October, the batteries were all finished and armed, and the generals-in-chief decided to open fire from them the following day. The land batteries were to demolish, if possible, the quarantine fort and the central and flag-staff' bastions; while the ships of war, anchored within cannon-range of the town, should rain death and destruction into all its southern portion.

On the 17th, at half past six in the morning, and at the preconcerted signal,—the discharge of three tombs,—all the French and English batteries commenced playing at once.

The artillery of the place replied immediately, and during a space of four hours, the cannonade was kept up with varying success on either side;—but, the French batteries having become seriously crippled by the enemy's fire, as well as by the explosion of a powder magazine and cartridge chest, orders were given, at a quarter past ten, to cease fire.

---

18. One of the French soldiers' chief dishes, when in the field. It is a sort of ragout of powdered biscuit, rice, and bacon.
19. The name given by the soldiers to the operations of a siege.

Unfortunately, the fleet, from not having been able to take up, in time, a suitable position, had failed to commence its bombardment of the town, simultaneously with the land batteries.

The troops, forming part of the siege corps, had received orders to turn out, that morning, under arms, in front of their camps,—and to be in readiness to march, as soon as notified.

The command of the whole assaulting force had been given, at his request, to Prince Napoleon. A column of 700, made up of 400 *Zouaves*, and 300 picked men from the other regiments of the 3rd division, was placed under the orders of the colonel commanding the 2nd Zouaves, and constituted the first storming party.

All the *Zouaves* in the regiment insisted upon going with this first party; and it therefore became necessary to select them, in the regular order of their seniority, from among those of the first class.

Prince Napoleon, who was aware of the immense risks, which would be run by this column, while crossing so wide a space of open ground by daylight, under the converging fire of so many of the enemy's batteries, authorized Colonel Cler to promise, in his name, to every soldier who should succeed in entering the town, that all the prince's influence should be exerted, to procure for him, either the cross of the Legion, or the military medal.

The men were brimming with enthusiasm; and the little column awaited in feverish, impatience, close by the *Zouaves'* House, the longed-for signal to advance. But, the little effect produced by the fire of the batteries, caused the assault to be postponed. The labours of the siege were resumed; and, each day, the regiment bore its full share, in the duties performed by the working parties and the guards of the trenches.

The engineers commenced laying out the second parallel, on the night of the 22nd of October. This important operation was protected by a covering party of 250 *Zouaves*, and 400 *Chasseurs-à-pied,* under the orders of Captain Banon, In the morning, these men fell back within the trenches, leaving only a few sharp-shooters out, in the rifle-pits, which had been constructed in advance;—the relief of the parallel was already sufficiently high, to afford shelter to the working parties.

On the 26th of October, the colonel had command of all the guards of the trenches, among which was the whole of his 2nd battalion. A strong demonstration had been made, in the course of the day, upon the lines near Balaklava, whilst a numerous sortie had been attempted on the English trenches. Towards evening, the colonel was warned by the general in charge of the trenches, that he might expect to be vigorously attacked during the night; and his command was accordingly reinforced by four battalions.

These battalions were at once disposed in such a way, as to envelop the Russians, so soon as they should have reached the parallel; while the battalion of the 2nd Zouaves was posted, under the immediate orders of its colonel, where it could annoy, and, if occasion served, cut off the enemy's retreat. But the Russians, who may have got wind of the preparations made to receive them, did not attempt to come out that night.

During the twenty-four hours, however, that the 2nd battalion was engaged in this duty at the trenches, it had occasion to deplore the loss of many brave soldiers. For, the Russians, that morning, had unmasked some new batteries in their lines of counter approach, which poured a storm of shot into the French advanced trenches. Bombs were at each minute bursting amid the companies,—while all the avenues of communication were enfiladed with shell and round shot.

Corporal Mouchet had his thigh broken, by the fragment of a bomb;—the colonel, who knew him to be both a good and brave soldier, appointed him a sergeant on the spot, and, pressing his hand, as he exhorted him to keep up his courage, when under the surgeon's hands, promised to send him home to his village, soon, with the cross of the Legion of Honour,

Mouchet bore the amputation very well; he was decorated, according to the colonel's promise, and acknowledged that the hope of gaining this distinction, had had a great deal to do with his cure.

This day's work cost the regiment, also, the life of Captain du Lude. This gallant gentleman and soldier had been wounded in the wrist, at the commencement of the battle of the Alma, but, refusing to quit the head of his company, had continued to command it throughout the day. Unwilling, even then, to report sick, he had remained on duty,—notwithstanding that his wound soon became complicated with both jaundice and dysentery.

On the 26th, in spite of his weakness, and though obliged to carry his arm in a sling, he insisted on accompanying the colonel to the trenches; and, shortly after his arrival there, was struck by a grape-shot, which burst open his temple.

Captain Coupel du Lude was one of the best officers in his regiment; he was universally regretted, and by none more than by his colonel,—his former companion, when at the military school, and who well knew how to appreciate his merit and courage.

During the latter part of October and beginning of November, the companies of the regiment were constantly on duty; and lost a few men killed, from time to time, especially among those *Zouaves*, who volunteered, as gunners, to aid in working the batteries. A great many more were wounded; and among these the surgeon, Gaullet, who received a heavy blow in his side from a sand-bag, knocked out of place by a flying round shot.

The works meantime advanced but slowly,—partly owing to the incessant shower of missiles, which the Russians kept pouring into the head of the French attack, and partly to the hard and rocky nature of the ground, which was such, as frequently to defy all impression from the working tools, and compel a resort to mines. Growing impatient of this slow progress, the commander-in-chief it length resolved upon making a desperate effort,—he, accordingly, charged General Forey to prepare for assaulting the town, on the night of the 5th November.

General Forey selected, for the command of this enterprise, the colonel of the 2nd Zouaves. In company with this officer, he was, on the morning of the 5th, to reconnoitre all that part of the town, lying between the flag-staff bastion, the upper end of the military port and the bottom of the ravine, which formed the boundary line between the French and English trenches.

For this attack, which was to be by escalade, the colonel was to have under his orders, a column composed of *Zouaves*, picked soldiers of the line, sappers of the engineer corps, and sailors from the fleet;—the latter carrying grappling-irons and scaling-ladders, to overcome the obstacles likely to be encountered by the party,—and the sappers, to be provided with bags of powder, petards, and axes, for the purpose of beating down the palisades and gate, known to be in the upper part of the military port.

It had been decided, that the column should take advantage of the darkness of the night, to creep stealthily up to the body of the place, and secure there an entrance for the remainder of the troops. As soon, therefore, as the colonel had made himself master of any one point, he was to send a portion of his force on, in the direction of the theatre, and, with the remainder, make good the passage until the arrival of the reserves,—who were *écheloned* in his rear, and to whom he was, accordingly, to despatch immediate tidings of his first success. But, the cannon of Inkermann, unfortunately broke up this new plan.

Book 5 - The Crimea continued

On the 5th of November, 1854, a day forever memorable in the annals of the French and English armies, the 2nd Zouaves was condemned to take a merely passive part in the great battle which, known as that of Inkermann, was fought partly at Inkermann, and partly in front of their own trenches,—and which so suddenly closed the bright career of the noble, young, and chivalric de Lourmel.[1]

The 3rd Battalion of the regiment was on guard, that morning, under the orders of its major, Adam; and the 1st under Major Malafosse, was just about to felt in with General de Monet's column, to go and relieve the guards of the trenches. The colonel was in camp, with only two of his companies.

Towards seven o'clock, the heavy booming of cannon was heard, off on the right,—but at so great a distance, as to make it altogether unlikely, that it could proceed from the English batteries. Everything, on the contrary, contributed to induce the belief, that the Russians were renewing, upon some other point of their extended line of observation the attempt already made

---

1. A brigadier of Forey's division, and, perhaps, the most youthful general in the army. Admired and beloved by all, and justly regarded as one of the bright, particular stars of the French service, this knightly gentleman was as devout a Catholic, as he was a gallant soldier. He was mortally wounded in the very midst of Sebastopol, while in hot pursuit of the flying Russians; and, had he been supported, would, in all probability, have taken the town.—General Foray's failure to support him, may have been abundantly justified, by the large detachments made from that officer's command, to the assistance of the English on the right, and its consequently weakened condition , but may it not also have been the cause, of that general's subsequent recall,—which was, at the time, so unsatisfactorily explained?—T

at Balaklava.

Nor is it long, in fact, before news is brought, of a terrible fight, that is raging in the very midst of the English camp The Russians have come out, in considerable numbers from Sebastopol, and are attacking our allies! Whilst every preparation is being hastily made to fly to their assistance the colonel of the 2nd Zouaves, who has got permission from Prince Napoleon to march with all that remains of his regiment, organizes a little band of 350 men and sets out for the English camp He soon overtakes the brigade of General de Monet, and his First Battalion, commanded by Major Malafosse. These troops had turned aside from the road leading to the trenches, and were also marching in the direction of the cannonade.

Towards nine o'clock, De Monet's brigade streams over the ridge of Mount Sapoune, on a line with the mill of Inkermann, General Canrobert at once gives it orders, to line the crest of the heights, which overlook the valley of the Tchernaya, and to keep in check the Russian corps which, arrayed upon the slopes of the Fedioukine hills, as well as in the plain extending between the aqueduct and river, threatens momentarily an attack upon that position of our line

General de Monet takes with him the 19th battalion of Chasseurs à pied, the two battalions of the 30th and 22nd Light, and directs Colonel Cler to put himself at the head of the *Zouaves*, and the three companies of Marines.

"Spread out your pants," cries the colonel to his *Zouaves*, "and make as big a show as you can," For, such, indeed, and no other, was the mission of this little troop, consisting of a thousand men at most;—it was to endeavour to impose, by its firm attitude, upon Liprandi's corps;—who was, on his side, charged to effect a diversion upon the extreme left of the Russian attack, and prevent the French, if possible, from coming to the assistance of their allies. De Monet's brigade acquitted itself to perfection of the part assigned to it.—But scarcely as much can be said for Liprandi,—who, contenting himself with parading his cavalry in the little plain of Balaklava, and upon the right bank of the Tchernaya, and with an insignificant cannonade, took no further part in the bloody battle, which was going on to his right.

The French troops of the 2nd Division are, however, beginning to take an active part in the battle. D'Autemarre's brigade is up, in support of Bourbaki's; which is already in the thickest of the fight. The English battalions which, since morning, have resisted with heroic tenacity the efforts of an enemy, who outnumbered them as four to one are beginning to re-form their scattered ranks, near the battery,—which, from that day, was aptly named the *Shambles*.

The general-in-chief has just been wounded, but continues to direct the movements of the army. General de Monet is ordered by him to abandon the crest of Mount Sapoune, and to form, a second line in rear of the English and the troops of the French 2nd Division, on their right,—so as to constitute a sort of reserve to them, whilst at the same time watching over the safety of our artillery, posted on the more elevated portion of the battlefield. Turning then to the colonel of the 2nd Zouaves, "Go, double on behind the Bearskins," said he to him, "but recollect, that you are, at this moment, my only reserve; so try and restrain the ardour of your *Zouaves*, and do not engage without my orders."

The *Zouaves*, hereupon, force their way quickly across the strip of brushwood, which intervenes between them and the English Guards, and, halting a short distance behind our allies, establish themselves in such a way, as, while overlooking the valley of the Tchernaya, to cover, at the same time, the right flank of General de Monet's battalions;—the 50th being on their left.

The *Zouaves* remain here sometime, exposed to the fire of the enemy, with arms at a support, and to all appearance calm,—but, in reality, burning with impatience, to take a more active part in the battle. At one time, their desire seems almost on the point of being gratified; for, their colonel receives orders to move his *échelon* to the front, and, passing rapidly over the battlefield, to pursue the enemy as far as the Tchernaya. But they have hardly advanced twelve hundred metres, when they are overtaken by counter orders, and, returning, take up a position just a short distance in rear of the Shambles battery.

Fortunately for these brave soldiers, the broken nature of the ground permits of their being partially sheltered, from the fire directed upon them from the powerful battery, which the Russians had established on their left, towards the head of the quarry ravine. Yet, notwithstanding the efforts made to find cover for them, there are no less than 80 casualties in General de Monet's small brigade.

At length, perceiving the inutility of their endeavours to break our lines, the Russians begin, shortly after noon, to draw off, and retire in much disorder over the Inkermann bridge. General Bosquet's troops next regain their camps; but General de Monet's brigade remains upon the ground, to assist the English in repelling any fresh attack, which the Russians might have been tempted to make on them, in the course of the evening or night.

The noise of the cannonade had hardly died away before the Duke of Cambridge came up to congratulate the French troops, and to place all the resources of his camp at their disposal. He begged General de Monet to send at once, and get some barrels of rum to distribute among his men, who, being without their *teutes-abris*, would have to bivouac, that night, in the open air. There seemed to be a generous strife, among those of our gallant allies who had survived the perils of the day, to see who should be the first, to press the hands of those, whom they joyfully hailed as their deliverers.

Lord Frederick Paulet, colonel of the Coldstream Guards, whose tent stood close to the bivouac of the *Zouaves*, said to Colonel Cler, as he sorrowfully shook his hand, "No later than last night, there were three fine fellows in it, all three of whom have honourably fallen upon yon bloody field. Tonight, I am all alone;—come, then, and share my tent with me, and let me flatter myself with the hope, that I have at least gained a new friend, in lieu of the three whom I have lost."

Such was the origin of that kindly fellowship, which sprang

up between the *Zouaves* and the English Guards; and which, dating from the battle of Inkermann, and continuing unbroken throughout the whole of the long and severely trying winter, which followed, is strengthened and confirmed, today, by the recollection of so many dangers encountered, and privations endured in common!

The night, which succeeded this sanguinary battle, was fraught with gloom and sadness for all. The soldiers of both nations were employed all night, in seeking out their wounded comrades, from among the heaps of the dying and the dead. It was a dismal sight, to see them wandering in groups, over the corpse-encumbered field, questioning, by the dull and flickering light of their lanterns, the pale faces of the slain! The sky was over cast with clouds,—cold, was the November night,—an icy wind blew in from the sea, and rustled mournfully among the brushwood,—or bore, in sudden gusts, upon its wings, faint clamours from the Russian city, and the sound of tolling church-bells, knelling a requiem for the dead.

One stumbled, at every stop, over the bodies of the slain, or the prostrate forms of the wounded. But it was rare to find among these, any, whose days there seemed to be any chance of saving. The most, of which those who still retained the breath of life, were capable, apparently,—was to turn upon their comrades, as they drew near, long, earnest looks, full of speechless meaning, and evidently intended to convey some last request;—but which there was none, alas! able to interpret, or accomplish!

At break of day, the colonel of the 2nd Zouaves pushed a reconnaissance as far as the top of the hills, that stand over against the ruins of Inkermann and head of the bay. On his return, he went all over the field of battle, in company with Colonel Herbert, chief of staff to the 2nd English Division. The turn of the Russians had come at length, and their numerous wounded were being carried to the rear.

The poor fellows must have passed a night of indescribable agony—a night far more terrible, even, than the day which had preceded it! And, yet, they bore their sufferings with the utmost resignation. Many of them, as they recognized the French uniform, made the sign of the cross, exclaiming, with mild and suppliant voices, as they did so; "*Pardonne, Français Christiane.*"

This interchange of, acts of generous humanity, on the one part, and humble gratitude, on the other,—upon a field of deadly strife,—between two people at war with each other, and differing some little in creed, as well as politics, but whose faith reposed upon a common basis, and sprang from the same original source,—was, after all, a touching tribute paid to the religion of Him, who has taught mankind to practise under all circumstances toward each other, the virtues of charity and forgiveness!

Nearly all of the Russian soldiers, who had been mortally wounded, wore a gentle expression on their features. Those, who had fallen over on their backs, had gently thrust out their hands, either as if to ward off the danger, or entreat for quarter. All of them had medals, or a little copper cases containing images of the saints, suspended around their necks.

There were parts of the field, which were absolutely piled with the bodies of the dead and dying. Broken pieces of wheels and carriages, the blackened fragments of caissons which had exploded, and the heaps of scattered missiles—still marked the spot where had stood the great battery of position, which the Russians had planted on the declivity of the salient eminence that stood in rear of the road leading down to the Tchernaya, as well as that, occupied by the French and English field battery, opposed to it,—on the upper part of the hillside, between the Redan of the Shambles and the road. Numerous carcasses of horses, horribly mutilated,—some ripped open, and with entrails protruding through the ghastly wounds inflicted on them by shot, or bursting shells,—lay in rear of the site of either battery.

The whole hillside was dotted over with thick patches of brush, and in all the open spaces between these,—muskets and bayonets lay strewed, so thickly, as to create a serious impediment to locomotion, especially to those on horseback.

Just as the colonel of the 2nd Zouaves was turning up the road, which runs parallel to the quarry ravine, his attention was caught by some low, confused sounds, apparently of pain, which arose from the depths of the ravine. On going down there, several thousand bodies were found; some dying, but for the most part dead,—lying, pell-mell, upon one another,—a bleeding, melancholy, and most appalling sight! There were arms upraised above this mass of yellowish flesh, as if to implore for pity;—whilst plaintive voices essayed, almost in vain, to articulate a prayer for help, which fell vaguely, and yet as sadly upon the ear, as though it had been the last, despairing wail of utter woe, issuing from some vast charnel house, in which had been entombed the living with the dead!

A number of dead bodies lay, yet, along the line of the English entrenchments, both on the right and left of the road. Whole ranks of these gallant soldiers were here stretched, stark and cold,—in the same places, and in the same regular order, in which they had fallen the day before, while bravely defending the camp of the 2nd English division, against the furious assault of the corps of Soimonoff. In front of the Shambles battery, the glacis was fairly hidden from sight, by the thick layers of the dead, with which its surface was covered.

Large pits, or rather trenches, were being dug towards the foot of the hillside, where the mould was found to be thickest;—and the remains of the allied soldiers were carefully brought down and packed away in these, while the Russians were buried apart. Some 500 of the enemy's corpses were also thrown into the great limekiln, at the foot of the quarry ravine.

Not less than 3,000 Russian dead were counted, in the course of the morning, upon these various parts of the field;—fresh discoveries, which were made the next day, together with the reports of prisoners and deserters, enabled their loss to be approximatively set down, at 12,000 in all, killed, wounded, and prisoners.

There can be little doubt, that many of the unhappy Russian wounded must have escaped the careful search, made for them

155

by our parties; for, to mention a single instance, the colonel of the 2nd Zouaves, while going down to post a picket, near the aqueduct, at the bottom of the quarry ravine, found four of them, still alive, there, no less than twelve days after the battle. The poor fellows were lying under a projecting rock; and, when asked, on what they had contrived to subsist, all this time, they replied by pointing, first, to Heaven, which had sent them water and inspired them with courage,—and, then, to some fragments of mouldy, black bread, which they had found in the pouches of the numerous dead, who lay around them.

No time was lost in transferring them to the French hospital: but, in spite of all the attention they received there, three of them soon died, and the only one who survived, was shortly afterward sent to Constantinople.

The marked difference, which began to show itself, between the Russian dead who had fallen at the Alma, and those who perished on subsequent occasions, was here, for the first time, noticed. At the Alma, they had, all, an appearance of health; their clothing, under clothing, and shoes, were clean and in good condition. At Inkermann, on the contrary, they wore a look of suffering and fatigue. Owing to the cold, indeed, they kept for several days,—some of them were even found, three' months later, near the canal, at the bottom of the spring ravine, in the condition of regular, dried-up mummies.

But, as the siege wore on, it was found, that those who fell between the trenches and the town, entered rapidly into decomposition. At Traktir, and at Malakoff, on the 16th of August, and 8th of September, they turned black and rotted immediately. These observations prove how quickly the rude labours of the siege, and the privations of every kind, to which the Russian troops were subjected, impaired their physical faculties, and undermined the most robust constitutions among them.

2

On the 6th of November, a council of war was held at the English headquarters. Among other things, it was decided that the 2nd Zouaves, and the regiment of Marines belonging to Prince Napoleon's division, together with a battery of artillery, should be placed under the orders of Colonel Cler, and that this little force should be detached from the main body of the French army,—and encamped in the midst of the English troops, near the mill of Inkermann.

Colonel Cler was directed to have an understanding with the English generals, in relation to the measures, to be adopted for the defence of that portion of the lines, extending from Careening Dock ravine and the heights of Mount Sapoune, to Canrobert redoubt. In case of an attack from the Russians, he was to follow his own inspirations and use his own judgment and discretion, until the arrival of Generals Canrobert or Bosquet; from whom he immediately depended, and who were, alone, authorized to give him an order.

The allied troops were posted as follows, along what was called the line of observation. The Light division of the English, in front of Malakoff, with its right overlapping Careening Dock ravine; the 2nd English Division, upon the most elevated part of the recent battlefield, in rear of the line of entrenchments, and with its right resting on the crest of the Tchernaya valley;—between these two divisions, two battalions of English Guards;—on a line with Canrobert redoubt, the battalion of Coldstream Guards. The four battalions of infantry, and battery of artillery, under Colonel Cler's orders, were posted behind the English Guards, a little to the right and rear of the mill of Inkermann.

The order of bivouac of these battalions, was in column by division, at platoon distance;—the *Zouaves* on the right, the Marines on the left: they could thus be most readily formed, to move at any time, and in any direction, in which danger might threaten, the little field hospital attached to the brigade, was placed in the upper part of Careening Dock ravine near the mill The artillery was in rear of the infantry; and, on the same line with them, and to their right, were the engineers.

A few hundred metres to the rear some Turkish battalions were encamped; and there, also was the camp of the artillery and medical staff of the English army Scarcely any change was made in these arrangements during the ensuing winter; except that some time in the month of December the Fusilier and Grenadier Guards came and pitched then tents between the Coldstream Guards and *Zouaves*. It was not before February, however, that any of the line regiments changed their position

Colonel Cler, on assuming command of his little brigade, hastened to have an understanding with Major General Pennefather, commanding the 2nd English Division,—an officer of sound judgment and much experience,—who was entrusted with the defence of all that portion of the line, which lay beyond the field of battle and along the valley slopes, as far as Canrobert redoubt. The outposts of the *Zouaves* were, in consequence of the arrangements thus made, placed where they could command a view of the outlets of the ravines, and of the lower Tchernaya.

The most amicable relations were soon established between the soldiers of the two nations; and they shared, like brothers in arms, between them, the difficult and dangerous duty of the outposts. For the first few nights, the camp was frequently disturbed by false alarms, occasioned by some movement of the enemy. The recollection of the desperate attempt, made by the Russians on the morning of the 6th of November, together with the exaggerated reports of deserters, contributed to keep everybody, for some time, on the *qui vive*.

For fear of a new attack being made on the same ground, the allied troops wore set to work to throw up a chain of redoubts, by which all that part of Mount Sapoune, sloping down to the Tchernaya, was effectually guarded against any such contingency. The one, on the left, having been thrown up by the English, was called by their name. That, on the right, constructed by the French on a hill running parallel to the road, and opposite to the Russian battery near the Inkermann lighthouse, was called *Lighthouse Redoubt*. Those of the Spring and Quarry ravines received parapets, capable of sheltering batteries of field artillery behind them.

The Shambles battery was not armed. But, on the upper part of the field of battle, in front of the lines of the 2nd English Division, another large work was thrown up by the French, and called the Redoubt of the 5th November. And this last was, by way of completing the system, connected with Canrobert redoubt, belonging to the French, by a broken line of parapet and ditch, running along the ridge and upper part of the Tchernaya valley.

The 2nd French Division and Windmill brigade were engaged, for several days, in the construction of these works. And it was whilst they were at work on that of the 5th November, that the Russians, in order to annoy them as much as possible, planted a battery on top of the crags which overhang the right of the Tchernaya valley,—the same which, on account of the feebleness and impotency of its fire, the soldiers contemptuously nicknamed *Gringalet*.[2]

As soon as all these various field-works had been completed and armed,—some of them with ship's guns,—Major de St. Laurent, the chief engineer officer attached to the brigade, set about the construction of a long *place d'armes*, on that part of Mount Sapoune lying between Careening Dock ravine and the upper end of the harbour; which he did, in concert with his English colleague, and with a view of sheltering their working parties from the fire of the batteries, on the right of the Tchernaya, as well as from that of the steamers, which constantly ran up there in aid of these.

This parallel took the name of the Anglo-French *place d'armes*; and, subsequently, served as a base for the operations directed, from that quarter, against the portion of the town lying in the vicinity of Careening Bay,

Up to this time, the weather had been quite endurable; but a sudden change took place during the night of the 13th of November. With daylight, there began to fell such torrents of rain, mixed with hail, that the camp was, in a short time, literally deluged with water;—while at the same time, a raging west

2. A poor, puny, sickly, ghost of a fellow.—T.

wind soon prostrated everything before it. So great was the force of this wind, that the heavy hailstones, instead of felling vertically, or even slantingly, were so borne up and driven before it, as, almost, to seem to skim along the surface of the ground! By nine o'clock in the morning, there was no longer a tent to be seen standing anywhere,—and shreds of canvass, and scattered articles of dress, were caught up in the air, and, in an instant, whirled out of sight.

Such was the fury of the blast, that before its howling gusts, the very men found it impossible to stand up, and had to crouch and cower to the ground, to escape being swept along with it.

The oldest *Zouaves* in the regiment, those who, in the southern part of our African colony, had often witnessed the effects of the fearful sirocco, and of the terrible storms of snow and rain peculiar to those regions, admitted that they had never known a more impetuous wind. Yet, in the midst of all this elemental war, the gayety of the men never for an instant deserted them.

Towards afternoon, they even resolved on lighting fires and preparing their *turlutines*, in defiance of the storm. And, accordingly, forming themselves into groups of companies, they thus opposed to the wind, a living wall, under the lee of which, they were enabled to prepare for themselves a warm repast.

On the day which followed this hurricane, the ground all round the mill of Inkermann, was still so thoroughly saturated with water, that it looked just like the bottom, of some vast pond, suddenly drained of its contents.

During the ensuing month of December, the active battalions of the 2nd Zouaves, were reinforced by 960 men, sent to them, in two drafts, by that portion of the regiment which had been left in Africa. But as these new comers were both younger, and, above all, less seasoned to endurance, than their comrades in the Crimea, they found much more difficulty in supporting the fatigues and exposure of the winter; many of them, accordingly, had to report sick, and some of them were never able to return to duty.

The more veteran portion of the regiment, however, continued to bear up under all its trials, with un-shaken courage. Though but lightly clad,—for only a few of them were yet provided with the *Criméenes* [3] and sheepskin overcoats, of which no general distribution was made to them until after the weather had grown extremely cold,—obliged, during the greater part of the winter, to bivouac, with no better cover than their little *tentes-abris,*—they were, of course, compelled to draw largely on their own intelligence and address, to enable them to supply the many pressing wants, which the administration, with all its zeal and desire to assist them, was not always in a condition to be able to relieve at once.

Turning, then, to a good account, the Russian overcoats, scattered over the field of Inkermann, nor disdaining even to pick up the dead men's clothes, which the English threw away, they lined their tents with the scraps of cloth, thus obtained; and succeeded, also, in interposing a softer and dryer couch, between themselves and the hard, damp earth, on which they lay. Taking advantage also, of the nature of the ground, which consisted of a stratum of friable stone, they excavated it to a sufficient depth below their tents, to obtain, in this way, a not uncomfortable subterranean abode.

There was, usually, no want of provisions. Trained by long experience, too, to habits of frugality, the *Zouaves* always made a sparing use of the extra rations, winch were forwarded to them, by every opportunity from Constantinople, by Lieutenant Réau, an officer of much zeal and intelligence. With the money that they earned in working at the trenches, they were also enabled to purchase, at reasonable prices from the *cantinières,* whose supply of such things was generally very good, both wines and provisions.

It was, of course, not to he expected, that Colonel Cler's brigade should be supplied with as much promptness and regularity, as the other corps in the French army—regard being had to its remote situation, almost at the extremity of the English

---

3. A long, loose overcoat, with collar and hood, which was sent out from France for the use of the soldiers in the Crimea.

camp, and to the difficulty of its communications with the *depôts* at Kamiesch and Balaklava. Nevertheless, it received at different times, and even during the very worst of the winter season, its share of the wine, brandy, cigars, tobacco, and warm clothing, which the emperor had sent out, as presents, to the army in the East.

The days, on which these distributions took place, were, usually, days of high festivity at the bivouac; nor were these supplies, all welcome as they would have been under any circumstances, any the less prized for being evidences of that kind solicitude, which their sovereign donor was so well known to feel for the welfare of an army, battling so far away from the shores of France in the glorious interests of her honour

The commander-in-chief, too, evinced a lively and unremitting interest in the well being of the troops of this brigade He came frequently to visit them, entered readily under their tents, chatted with and spoke cheering words to them, and listened, with great condescension, to the explanations which every *Zouave* among them, thought himself entitled to make, in regard to their mode of life. It so happened, that, in the very dead of winter, and when the snow lay thick about the outposts, the men of this brigade were still without large tents; and it was, necessarily, out of the question for them to think of mounting guard, any longer, with their little *tentes-abris*.

Since, not only would it have been impossible to be taking these down, every morning,—all stiff as they usually were with sleet and snow,—but, moreover, on coming to pitch them again, after a twenty-four hours' tour of duty, the ground on which they before had stood, would, meanwhile, have become thoroughly damp, if not actually running with water. Seeing this. General Canrobert gave directions, that five hundred *tentes-abris* should be immediately carried to the Windmill brigade, for the use of its outposts.

But, unfortunately, all the means of transportation at the disposal of the administration, happened, just at that time, to be engaged in hauling provisions: there was, consequently, no way of complying with the general's requisition. No sooner was that amiable officer apprised of this fact, however, than, unwilling to be balked in the execution of his kindly project, he sent off his own private beasts of burden to Kamiesch, under charge of his orderly officer. Captain de Chard, with instructions to get the five hundred *tentes-abris*, and carry them to the Windmill camp.

He sent word of this to Colonel Cler, and notified him, at the same time, that, as the road was a long and difficult one from general head-quarters to Kamiesch, and thence to the Windmill camp, he would do well to send out his own private sumpter mules, with fatigue parties of the men, to meet the convoy, and assist it into camp.

Yet, notwithstanding the unceasing care and solicitude, thus exhibited for them by their chiefs, the soldiers had some trying moments to go through; especially when, after having already taken upon themselves the charge of the whole line of observation, they were also called upon to labour in the trenches of the Careening Bay attack. Even during the month of January, they had sometimes to spend, as many as twenty-four hours, in the snow, without fire or shelter of any kind.

In February, it is true, the cold moderated, somewhat; but then this milder weather was frequently attended,—towards the close of day, by a warm, drizzling rain, which, as the cold came on again with night, and increased towards morning, froze, in icicles, on their garments.

Amid all this hardship and suffering, the officers and non-commissioned officers continued to set the men an admirable example of obedience and resignation. Even when completely exhausted by the frequency and harassing nature of their duties, joined to the too stimulating nature of their food, they yet persisted in struggling on with sickness, in their tents, so as to be always on hand to march with their companies against the enemy, if necessary,—or, when called upon, perform their tour of duty on grand guards, or in the trenches.

Many of them paid, with their lives, the price of this heroic devotion to duty. Among these, was the Lieutenant Plazolles, an officer of distinguished zeal and energy, who, though very sick, insisted to the last upon doing duty; and, refusing to join a convoy of sick ordered to Constantinople, finally died, about the beginning of winter, carrying with him to his grave the esteem of all his chiefs, and the sincere regrets of his comrades.

Nor, were the private soldiers wanting in the same lofty characteristics; they, too, bore up manfully against the diseases, which sapped their strength and undermined their frames, and endured with invincible fortitude, all the sufferings to which they were exposed. Many of them, too, preferred to await death in camp, rather than go into hospital, or allow themselves to be sent to Constantinople.

Yet, there were one or two, whose courage gave way, under the severity of the tests, to which it was subjected. The *Zouave* B——, for example, a veteran of our African wars, finding that his strength was at last beginning to fail him, remarked to his comrades, one day, as they were returning from a tour of duty in the trenches, "Well, well, . . . I see that my legs won't carry me much longer,—I feel that I'm getting old,—shall be soon cooked;—and, sooner than pass for a shirk, (clampin) I'd rather have done with this world at once."

No great importance was attached to these words by his comrades; but they had scarcely got back to the bivouac, when, hearing the report of a gun, and running to ascertain the cause of it, they found him lying on the floor of his tent, quite dead, and with the toe of his boot still pressed against the trigger of his piece.

Another *Zouave*, A—— D——, who had led a Gil Blas sort of life and was pretty well advanced in years when he entered the service, was since then accustomed to find his chief recreation, when off duty, in enacting,—which he did remarkably well,—the part of the noble father in the camp theatricals. To pass a whole winter,—and such a winter,—without the solace of his favourite divertissement, was apparently beyond his power—and so, one fine night, he disappeared!

His comrades accounted for his disappearance, upon the hypothesis that he must have learned from some Russian deserter, that they were playing high comedy in Sebastopol, and had accordingly gone off to see the manager of the theatre there, with the object of securing an engagement in his troupe. After an absence of eight days, however, he surrendered himself of his own accord to the police at Kamiesch; and was returned to the regiment in a dress having very little in common with the uniform.

He seemed completely cracked, too, and either could not, or would not, give any explanation as to where he had been, or what he had done with himself, during the interval of his desertion. As for his comrades, they remained firmly persuaded of the truth of their original conjecture, that he had in the interim paid a visit to Sebastopol.

"Pshaw," said a wag among them, "he no doubt failed to get into the service of Thalia, and so, while waiting for a better opportunity, he has concluded to resume the mattock, and the musket, in that of Mars."

The positions held by the Russians on the heights of Inkermann, the Mackenzie plateau, at Tchorgoun, and on the Fedioukine hills, were such as to exact the utmost vigilance from the troops, posted along the line of observation, tot guard them against being surprised. So close to each other were the outposts of the two armies, that their advanced sentries frequently got into conversation,—partly with signs and gestures,—and partly with the help of a few French or Russian words.

A hard frost invariably brought about a tacit armistice between them,—during which the sentinels on either side, coming out from their hiding places, tried to warm themselves and restore the suspended circulation of their blood, by briskly moving about, or striking solos and stamping feet together (*battant la semelle*)[4]. But it was more particularly the French and Russians, who were on these terms of amicable understanding with each other.

General Bosquet, who commanded along the whole French

---

4. A winter game common among children in France.—T

line, displayed the most untiring activity; each day, visiting the different points that seemed to require his presence, and, himself, regulating the positions of the outposts, so as to conform to the various changes in those of the enemy. Not content with giving so much of his own personal attention, to ensure the exact and faithful performance of duty by those under his command, he also kept the officers of his staff almost constantly in the saddle, carrying orders and despatches; and there was scarcely an hour in the day, or even night, that he was not receiving the reports, incessantly forwarded to him by his principal subordinates.

It was to this sleepless vigilance, no doubt, that the army of observation owed its continued exemption from attack.

3

The location of Cler's brigade in the midst of the English army, was productive of a very happy effect; for, it led to an intimacy between the troops of the two nations, which nothing short of their daily association could ever have brought about.

For, neither French nor English, in their relations with each other previous to the battle of Inkermann, had overpassed the bounds of a cold and formal politeness. Indeed, considering the very opposite character of the two nations, and the traditionary remembrance of their ancient feuds, it could hardly have been otherwise. The special military education, besides, of our officers, whose delight it was, to be always among their men, and that,—so very different,—of the English officers, who rather affect to keep their profession as much as possible out of sight, were rather calculated to perpetuate this state of things,—even among those belonging to the upper grades.

And so, when, in the harbour of Malta, our ships of war saluted the English forts, or when, in the Dardanelles or on the Bosphorus, the steamers of the two nations ran alongside of each other, their crews exchanged hurrahs, indeed, and the band of one would, to the *Partant pour la Syrie* of the other, as regularly respond with God save the Queen: but that was all,—it was all done by order, and there was no heart in it!

At the camp of Boulaïr in the Thracian Chersonnese, and at that of Varna in Bulgaria, the French and English officers made some attempts to interchange civilities with each other,—and the soldiers of the two nations, when under the excitement of liquor, were not unfrequently seen to fraternize. But even these were rather studied demonstrations:—on the landing of the two armies in the Crimea, they always bivouacked apart;—then, the English made us wait some time for their promised attack on the 20th of September;—and, taken altogether, the intercourse between the regiments of either army was very slight, and confined at best, to a mere exchange of courtesies.

It was not until after the battle of the Alma that the ice began to thaw,—a very little, it is true—for even here, the two armies had fought with a certain interval of distance between them. Still, the feeling of dangers shared and of glory acquired in common and the baptism of fire, which they had received together were of a nature to lessen their estrangement for each other and bring about some little approach to more cordial sentiments for the future. For, as, on the next day they went over the field of their splendid victory and heard of the many spirited episodes, which had distinguished it, it was impossible for either to withhold from the other the well-merited tribute of a sincere esteem.

The French, on their side, could not help but admire the cool, unfaltering courage, with which their ancient foes had marched straight against formidable batteries, and in the teeth of a murderous discharge of grape, not only without a sign of hesitation, but without slackening or even quickening their step, and only pausing, as they went, to close up the bloody rents, which the enemy's shot was, all the while, tearing through their well-dressed lines. The English, on the other hand, had still before their eyes, the rapid and overpowering rush of our brave foot soldiers, which had almost given to their own part of this great battlefield the appearance of a steeple-chase—and which was such, that even the Russians, when speaking of the *Zouaves* declared that "the Africans must that day have either been drunk or crazy."

At the Alma then, both the French and English infantry had had occasion to form a mutually high estimate of each others' good qualities and to acquire at the same time a firm conviction that there was no power on earth capable of resisting their joint attack.

The brilliant charges made at Balaklava soon afterward, induced similar feelings of appreciation between the cavalry forces of the two nations The French cavalry had been spectators of the cold, heroic intrepidity, with which the English rode to an almost certain death, slaves to their duty and to discipline and conscious victims of an unfortunate order. The English horsemen on the other hand had seen our *Chasseurs d'Afrique* on their fleet steeds of the desert falling, sabre in hand, on the Russian squadrons, or cutting down the artillerymen at their guns.

And, yet, before Sebastopol, as at the Alma, there were still two different fields of battle—two distinct centres of action; on one side, the English,—on the other, the French.

But, at length, the thunder of the heavy guns at Inkermann was heard resounding along the plateau, and, for the first time, chance gave to the allied armies a really common battle-field. Io their struggle with the Russians that day, the French soldiers were completely mixed up with the English. From the moment that Bourbaki's headlong battalions,—the 3rd Zouaves, with de Wimpffen's *tirailleurs indigènes*,—came pouring upon the field, and, to the hearty English *Hurrah for the French,* sent up, in reply, their own wild, African war shout,—the troops of the two nations formed but one, single army!

And from that day forth, a true feeling of friendship, and real intimacy, grew up between them. And, certainly, they owed it to each other. We, on our part, were full of admiration for the obstinate valour, with which our worthy rivals in glory had defended themselves, all that morning, under the deadly fire and fierce assaults of the Russians, so much their superiors in numbers. We were witnesses to the stem, unyielding resistance opposed, and to the unquailing front maintained by their thinned and exhausted divisions,—in which the fearful gaps, at each moment opened by the enemy's camion, were as quickly closed again by the mutilated fragments of what, that morning, had been regiments.

On the other hand, all that remained, that evening, of the English army, had seen our battalions, as they came up with the speed and fury of the lightning, fall like so many thunderbolts upon the massive columns of the enemy,—and attacking them both in flank and front with that French *furia*, so world renowned, and so dreaded in all time, compel them at length to cease from their abortive efforts, and to retire in disorder over the Tchernaya bridge, and behind the friendly cover of their city walls.

To mutual esteem, then, had been, that day, added a feeling of gratitude for services rendered;—and to that gratitude, again, were shortly added all those kindly feelings, which are so quickly developed by the unceremonious intercourse of the camp or bivouac, and which so readily spring from a community of labours, hardships, privations, and fatigues, as well as from the mutual interchange of provisions, help, advice, and the various conveniences at the disposal of either.

For, at the Windmill camp, where were the 2nd Zouaves, and French regiment of Marines,—the English Guards and their 2nd Division,—all these things were shared and endured together. And, accordingly, there soon began to prevail among these troops, the most cordial, frank, and unreserved intimacy.

The English soldiers, who were much better off than our own, in respect to pocket-money, but who were generally without sutlers, were much in the habit of frequenting the *Zouaves'* canteens. A great amount of treating and drinking went on there, intermixed with long conversations, carried on, partly, by signs, and partly, by words:—although it must be acknowledged, that the *Zouaves* were generally quite as innocent of English, as the English were of French.

But, our lively Africans are not in the habit of paying much heed, to such trifling obstacles as this; and so, with the help of that *Sabir* tongue, which they employ in their communications with the Arabs, they now carried on with their English friends, such dialogues, or rather monologues, as the following: *Englisch bono, Francis bono, Englisch et Francis semis amis, bibir soua soua, Crimea mackach bono, Arbia bono, chapard beseff,* which signify, that, "the English are good fellows,—so are the French; the French and English are very good friends,—they drink together; the Crimea is a poor sort of place; Africa is worth a dozen of it,— there is any quantity of booty to be made there."

It requires no great stretch of the imagination to conceive, that these horrid barbarisms, which, if repeated to the *Immortals,*[5] would undoubtedly strike them dumb, and set their forty arm-chairs to dancing a witch's *fandango,*—were interspersed with any number of little drinks. Whereupon, the *Zouave,* a very lo-quacious animal by nature, and prone to forget, that his insular friends were unable to comprehend a word of all he said, was wont to narrate to them some of the astounding episodes, which had occurred to him in the course of his African *razzias.*

To these John Bull listened most conscientiously, drinking all the while with mute and solemn gravity, and only inter-rupting himself to rip out, every five minutes or so, some for-midable oath, expressive of his admiration. But, as one story led to another, oath gradually succeeded to oath, and drink to drink, until the little drinks had got to be big drinks, and Bull, succumbing at last under their collective influence, was apt to fall comfortably drunk at the feet of the *Zouave;* who, cutting short his story, to drink one more health in honour of England's queen, addressed himself to the task of conducting his friend home;—happy, when he had not been, himself, overtaken in his libations to the rosy god, for, then, each insisted on carrying the other home;—and did so, of course, after a most original and amusing fashion.

It sometimes so happened, that there were present at the same canteen, some *Zouaves,* who had managed to pick up a few words of English, or, which was less unusual,—a few Eng-

---

5. The members of the French Academy.—T.

lishmen, who were not unacquainted with French. Whenever this was the case, the audience was gratified by long and curious dissertations upon the war itself, and upon the relative valour of the belligerent parties. On this point, as well as in regard to their respective share of the dangers, fatigues, and glory of the war, there was great unanimity of opinion.

"But,"—exclaimed on one of these occasions an individual of the party, present,—"of what earthly use are the *Turre*?[6] Whilst, with a string of *paternosters*, as long as from here to Constantinople, they are quietly boring their prophet Mahomet to death, we've got to do all their fighting, hang them! Faith, they're a jolly set of birds, indeed!"—"Bah, let the *Turres* alone," rejoined another, "the poor devils are just as brave as we—in fact, they're braver; for, all the work our generals give them to do, is just to roll away like sheep,—and they do that without grumbling. You couldn't do half as well, yourself;—so what's the use of sneering at them?"

The last speaker was in the right; the unhappy battalions of *Redifs* (drafted National Guards, who seemed to have been sent to the Crimea for no other purpose under the sun, than to remind the Allies, that there were still a few Turks left in this world), died, literally, like sheep,—without the utterance of a murmur, or complaint. Ill fed, ill lodged, ill taken care of, they seemed actually to melt away, and their cemeteries, each day, grew larger, at the expense of their camps. The French and English officers at the Windmill camp saw a great deal of each other; and whenever those of either camp chanced to receive a fresh supply of coffee, tea, or cigars, the others were certain to be incited to come and partake of them, and were invariably received, and entertained with the utmost cordiality.

The English generals appeared to be quite taken with the *Zouaves*, and never let slip an opportunity of manifesting their partiality for them. Generals Pennefather and Buller, of the 2nd English Division, and Lord Rokeby, commanding the Guards, even went so far as to send them some of the woollen clothing,

6. It was in this way that the soldiers affected to pronounce the name of the Turks.

which they had received for their own troops. Lord Rokeby offered to the officers, a portion of the presents, besides, worked by the fair hands of the English princesses and of Lady Rokeby, which the queen had sent out to the officers of her household troops.

Lord Raglan, also, accompanied by some of his staff, came, shortly after the first of January, to pay Colonel Cler a visit. The English commander-in-chief was pleased, in warm terms, to express the satisfaction with which he beheld the harmony and good understanding reigning between the soldiers of the two nations, and the cordial relations existing among their officers.

The distinctive characteristics of the two people came out, in marked opposition, during their joint occupation of the Windmill camp. The English, so self-possessed and calmly brave in the hour of danger,—at the bivouac seemed to be almost as helpless as children. The *Zouaves*, on the contrary, had all the intelligence and industry of the beaver; and their muskets and knapsacks were hardly put away, before they were at work upon some ingeniously devised contrivance, to make themselves comfortable.

They lined their tents with such scraps of cloth as they could pick up, dug out cosy little dens in the substratum of rock beneath them, and built themselves very serviceable chimneys. The English, admiration at their talents, gladly availed themselves of the help, which the *Zouaves*, for their part always cheerfully disposed to lend them.

Among the *Zouaves*, there was one in particular, a corporal of pioneers,—an obliging, excellent fellow, who had earned for himself quite a reputation, as an architect. He was known at the Windmill camp by the soubriquet of the "*Hoarse 'un*," being indebted, for this appellation, to the effect produced on his voice, by the numerous libations in which he was in the daily habit of indulging. Having been subsequently transferred to the *Zouaves* of the Guard, he was among the first to mount the breach at Malakoff, had his leg smashed there, and remained for twenty-four hours buried under a heap of the dying and the dead, in the ditch of the Russian stronghold;—was even reported dead, and dropped from the rolls of his regiment.

But when his comrades were about to consign him to the grave, he suddenly straightened himself up,—entered a formal protest against any such procedure as that,—went off, limping, to the ambulance,—got himself sent to Constantinople,—refused positively to let his limb be amputated,—and, finally, at the end of six months' time, returned, with his leg in slings, as it were, and, reporting himself for duty to the colonel of the *Zouaves* of the Guard, once more claimed his old place, at the head of the pioneers of the regiment. He is at present living upon a pension in the vicinity of Paris; having, like all the other poor maimed and crippled of the Crimean war, been made sensibly to feel the generous bounty of the Emperor,

4

The French force at the Windmill camp was reinforced, in the early part of February, by the 3rd brigade of the 3rd Division. General de Monet, at the same time, took command of the 1st brigade, and General Mayran, in consequence of the departure of Prince Napoleon, assumed command of the division.

It was about the same time decided, to make, thenceforth, of the Malakoff, the principal object of our attack; our approaches to it were to be carried up on both sides of Careening Bay ravine; and the operations against it were confided, to the 2nd Corps, under the direction of General Bosquet.

The month of February, 1855, was destined to prove a fatal one to the 2nd Zouaves.

On the night of the 12th, 300 men of the regiment were ordered to reconnoitre the Russian posts, near the foot of Mount Sapoune between Careening Bay ravine and the upper end of the harbour—and, if possible, to capture also a few, prisoners The first portion of the order was thoroughly executed, and the men pushed on as far as the edge of the bay; but the Russians retreated so precipitately, that it was impossible to catch one of them. However, upon the information derived from this reconnaissance, it was determined to start our sap, from a point, situated between the Anglo-French *place d'armes* and the parallel which our allies had commenced,—and, while completing the St. Laurent battery, to throw up, along this same parallel, another battery of 15 guns.

From the 12th to the 22nd of the month, the *Zouaves* were actively employed upon the parallels, batteries, and other works of this new attack.

The Russians, whose defence was conducted under the superintendence of an engineer officer of rare ability, wore not long in discerning the importance of an attack, direct, against their commanding position of the Malakoff; and, observing the progress that we were making towards the extremity of the plateau, they, in the course of a single night, that of the 21st February, accomplished the extraordinary feat of throwing up, within a thousand metres of our parallel, counter approaches of an almost incredible development.

We were almost stupefied with amazement, when, on the morning of the 23rd, we saw for the first time, revealed to our gaze, the extent of these works, and noted that their gabionade was already beginning to be covered. As the news flew quickly through the camp a number of the general officers soon collected in the parallel, with the object of examining these new defences,—and of devising, if possible, some means of counteracting them.

The Russian works appeared to be at such a distance from our own, however, as to dispel all hope of our being able to retain them permanently in our possession, even if carried; but it was thought not impossible to wrest them, temporarily, from their occupants, and it was judged advisable to make this attempt,— even if for no other purpose,—at least to teach the enemy, that we were resolved upon destroying every outwork of the sort, which he might endeavour to construct.

So hazardous an enterprise could, of course, only be attempted at night. It required for its execution, too, soldiers who could be implicitly relied on; men who should be as cool and steady, as they were brave,—intelligent, too, so as to understand and punctually execute their orders;—and whom no danger could appal. The 2nd Zouaves was the regiment selected. General Bosquet was directed to make immediate arrangements for the attack, of which General Mayran was to have the general supervision. The command of the troops was entrusted to General de Monet; they were to consist of 900 *Zouaves*, and 450 of the regiment of Marines, with a reserve of two battalions of the 6th and 10th of the Line, under command of Lieutenant Colonel Dubos, who were to remain in the parallel.

Whence it appears, that 1,400 resolute men were to pay a visit, and, if we may say so, leave their cards at an enemy's work,—where many of them were certain to perish—for no other purpose in the world, than that of momentarily disquieting the enemy, and giving him to understand that he would not be permitted to remain there undisturbed. It will be admitted that war has sometimes cruel exigencies!

General de Monet and Colonel Cler were notified, towards evening, to repair at once to General Mayran's tent for their instructions.

The 2nd Zouaves had that day, as many as five companies on duty, either in the trenches, or on grand guard, so that it was unable to furnish to the expedition more than 900 men and 25 officers; and these were organized into two battalions of six platoons, each.

The orders given to General de Monet and Colonel Cler, were to assault the Russian works, known afterward by the name of the *Selinghinsk*, and *Volhynia* redoubts, or, better still, as the *White Works*, and to maintain themselves there, if possible, until they should have completed the demolition of the new outworks;—but to retire before the arrival of the enemy's reinforcements,—and, on a signal which it was left to the commanding officer of the troops engaged, to give whenever he should judge the moment come for it, to fall back rapidly on the French trenches.

It is clear from this, that there were at least a thousand chances to one, offered, of suffering a very heavy loss of life,—without the most remote prospect of achieving any other than, possibly, a short-lived moral result, and, if successful, a very slight, material one. On returning to his camp, Colonel Cler called round him the officers and non-commissioned officers of his splendid regiment, and gave them, in turn, his own instructions for the coming fight.

"Be as silent as the grave," said he to them, "for, the enemy must have no suspicion of our approach. Leave behind you, therefore, the scabbards of your swords, and everything calculated to make a noise. Not even must the war-shout of the *Zouaves* be heard until after the engagement has fairly commenced, or until after the recall has sounded; in the event of your being lost. Let there be no firing; for, at night, 'tis impossible to aim with accuracy, and we should be just as likely to hit friends as foes; the bayonet, and the butts of our muskets, are the arms on which we must rely."

Then, after being satisfied that these general instructions were thoroughly comprehended, the colonel added:

"Letters have been received from France, announcing my promotion to the rank of general; but until the publication of a decree, soon to be issued for the organization of a new division, it will not appear in orders. I see, in this delay, a fresh proof of what you have always believed in,— my good fortune, and favouring stars; for, doubtless, the design of Providence, in permitting me to remain at your head on this occasion, is that I may have the satisfaction of inscribing the name of another glorious combat on your colours."

Never before, had the regiment shown so much ardour and enthusiasm; no one would hear of being left behind; all wanted to go! Those on special duty,—the clerks, the orderlies,—even the sick, smuggled themselves into the ranks, when, at ten o'clock, the battalions were paraded for the purpose of marching to the place of rendezvous, in the Anglo-French *place d'armes*.

At midnight, the little expeditionary band moved from this last point into the second parallel. Here, it was again halted, and the two battalions of *Zouaves* were stationed on either side of the wide openings, which had been made on the right and left of the parapet, for their more convenient egress.

Between them, stood General de Monet, with 450 of the Marines. This last little battalion was to support, and, if necessary, reinforce, whichever of the two battalions of *Zouaves* should happen to require its assistance.

The moon went down at one o'clock. The sky was overcast with heavy masses of gray clouds; and a darkness, so opaque succeeded, that, even at the distance of two steps, it was almost impossible to distinguish an object above the ground. A half-hour later, the two battalions of *Zouaves*, in column of sections, glided noiselessly out of the parallel. The right column was under the direction of Colonel Cler and Major Lacretelle; the other was under the command of Major Darbois. In front of each, and sixty paces ahead of it, went an advanced guard of one company; and in the interval between the remainder of the column and this leading company, followed another, by way of keeping up their connection.

At a given signal, both columns move forward; the right column succeeds in arriving on the line of the rifle-pits, without having drawn a single shot from the enemy; but it has hardly reached that point, when it is saluted, both in flank and front, by a close, sharp, and well-sustained fire of musketry. The Russians, the better to see and aim at their adversaries, light up all the space around the ambuscades, with bombs and fire-balls, which, now blazing brightly up, now burning low again into the gloom of night, cast over the terrible combat which is going on, an uncertain, lurid,—almost spectral glare.

As the hottest fire appears to come from the left of the Russian line, four of the supporting companies of the first column make a dash at that point, and carry the ambuscades, there, at the point of the bayonet;—in a few moments, the whole of the central part of the position, is swept clear of the enemy. The left column, guided by an officer of engineers, has a deep ravine to cross, and is unable, in consequence, to reach the scene of action, until after the first column has become warmly engaged. Its first four companies, however, led on by Major Darbois, come on at the *pas de charge* and such is the darkness of the night, that the two are on the point of charging each other with the bayonet,—each mistaking the other for the enemy. But, Heaven be thanked, the *Zouaves* have religiously obeyed the order, not to fire!

Forcing a way through the line of rifle-pits, the head of the two columns comes suddenly up against the main body of the enemy's force, drawn up, in company squares, along the front and sides of the redoubt. Once satisfied, that it is the Russians they have before them, the *Zouaves* fall impetuously upon them, and breaking through their ranks, engage them in a fierce hand-to-hand encounter, in which the musket butt and the bayonet are mercilessly plied. 'Tis here, that the Lieutenants Baratchard and Bartel are wounded in the midst of their men.

General de Monet, though retarded in his march by the difficulties of the ground over which he has had to pick his way, arrives soon after with the Marines at the outermost rifle-pits. But, being almost immediately wounded in several places, by the enemy's bullets, he is compelled to resign the general command into the hands of Colonel Cler, for whom he accordingly sends;—after which, rallying his strength for a last effort, and pointing to the Russian entrenchments, he cries out to his men: "Follow me,—our way lies over there."

Having got rid of a portion of the troops who were defending the approaches to the work. Colonel Cler gives the direction of the right attack to Major Lacretelle, that of the left to Major Darbois, and, taking with him a few files from each of his own companies, together with some of the Marines, under the command of their Major, Mermier, and of Captain Merle de Beaufonds, he bids the charge sound, and again rushes straight at the entrenchment.

The Russians, strung along the berm and behind the parapet, have just time to deliver one volley, and no more;—the next minute, the screen of gabions, erected on top of the counterscarp, is thrown down;—the wide, but rather shallow ditch, is crossed,—the 1st Battalion of the Selinghinski is overpowered and trampled underfoot,—and the *Zouaves* are upon the parapet!

But this prompt success is bought at a heavy cost of valuable blood; the gallant officers and daring soldiers, who lead the van of the colonel's storming party, fall, like grass, under the mower's scythe, around him.

He, himself, owes his escape, with life, to a lucky fall, which, just as the Russian bayonets were tearing through his uniform, causes him to measure his length on the outside of the parapet. But, quickly re-forming the survivors of his little troop, the colonel instructs them to press close against one another, and to keep under cover of the gabionade, while awaiting the arrival of reinforcements.

A pause, meanwhile, has occurred in the fighting; for, the Russians continue to lie motionless, no doubt by order, at the bottom of the ditch, and the *Zouaves*, as they tramp over them, imagine them to be dead.

But the enemy, who were evidently on the lookout for, and well prepared to receive this attack, are not long in discovering the numerical weakness of their opponents; and, silently closing in upon them from every side, coil round them in deadly folds, which contract and tighten, at each moment, until escape has seemingly become a thing impossible. They come, at length, so near, that the *Zouaves* seeing, and mistaking them for their own reinforcements, cry out to them not to fire!

A short, stern command in Russian, is the only reply;—they find themselves suddenly enveloped in a circle of flashing fire,—there is a sharp report of musketry,—and, instantly, the air grows thick with the driving missiles. Fortunately, very few of them are hurt; the balls pass harmlessly over their heads, and fall among the enemy's own battalions, posted along the *banquette* of the redoubt.[7] A few of the Russian soldiers, more daring than their fellows, then make a rush upon them, but only to die, transfixed, upon their bayonets.

The whole aspect of the scene is something horrible and fantastic. By the light of the signal rockets, by the incessant flashes of the cannon of the town and of the steamers, Sebastopol and the harbour in the background, are every moment brought into view; within the redoubt, a handful of determined soldiers, surrounded on every side, are resolved to sell their lives dearly, and to die, rather than surrender;—stretching away in front is a wide expanse of open ground, all white with gleaming snow, on which, here and there, a few dim specks show, where scattered parties of the French are endeavouring to grope their uncertain way toward the attacking columns;—while, swaying to and fro, beside the ditch, the eye next catches glimpses of a struggling, agitated mass of men, in which the dark overcoats of the Russian soldiers, the red *chechias* of the *Zouaves*, and the black, fur bonnets of the Cossack volunteers, with their flame-coloured streamers, appear mingled in inextricable confusion:—add to all this, the hurried clanging of the alarm bells, the shrieks of the wounded, the sharp, ceaseless rattle of musketry, the thunder of the heavy guns, the dash of steel and frenzied shouts of the combatants,—and one may be able to form some idea of the infernal character

This unequal conflict has been raging for some time, when, all at once, the French bugles are heard sounding the retreat. At this signal, the troops, not surrounded, draw off and retire slowly to the trenches; but the little column within the redoubt cannot make up its mind, yet, to renounce so easily the dear-bought conquest, which has cost the 2nd Zouaves the very flower of its gallant life. The colonel is still in hopes, that a renewed attack may yet be made, which will ensure his victory.

---

7. The Russians, engaged in defending the interior of the redoubt—no doubt for fear of hitting their own men, of the 1st battalion of the Selinghinski, who are fighting with the *Zouaves* in the ditch of the work,—were careful not to fire in that direction.

But, again, the French bugles are heard ringing sharply out from the trenches:—the order must be obeyed! So, gathering around him the few, who remain of his little party, Cler cries out to them: "Let it never be said of us, that we have allowed these Russian dogs to get hold of a colonel of *Zouaves*,—that they may have the satisfaction of parading him through all their villages;—better, a thousand times, death than that!"

Then putting himself at their head, by way of setting the example, he flings himself, head foremost, among the Russian masses, followed closely by the whole of his little band, and is immediately engaged in a close and desperate struggle with the Russians, in which the bayonet, the musket butt, and even the fist, are freely used, and where many a gallant spirit lays down his life, in aiding his comrades to cleave their bloody pathway, through the thick swarming press of the enemy which surrounds them.

'Tis here that fell the brave Captain Sage, and the young 2nd Lieutenant Sevestre, who had joined the regiment but fifteen days before, and who dies, pierced through and through, while in the act of calling round him the *Zouaves* of his platoon, whom he thinks he sees, just on his left.

Captain Banon, too, is, for a moment, struck down, but, rising, follows his colonel, and, for his handsome conduct on this occasion, is promoted, as major, into the 3rd Zouaves; but is killed, just one month later, while repelling a sortie from the Russian lines.

At length, in spite of the numbers and determined opposition of the enemy, this little handful of heroes succeeds in cutting its way out from among them, and, with sadly diminished numbers, makes its way back to the trenches,—over a wide expanse of open ground which intervenes, and which is swept with showers of grape, during the whole of their passage over it.

Just as they are nearing the parallel, Colonel Cler is almost run over by groups of *Zouaves*, who, pouring rapidly out of it, are making off in hot haste towards the enemy. "Whither are you going," he shouts to them, "have you not heard the recall?"

"Ah!—is it you,—our own colonel,"—the daring fellows exultingly cry out, "Why, they told us, sir, that you were a prisoner,—and we were on our way to bring you back;—aye, and we'd have done it, too, colonel, you may believe us,—even if we'd had to follow you into the very heart of Sebastopol, it-self!"

Now, are there any terms of praise, we confidently ask, that can match the recital of these few, noble words, which reveal so clearly the generous courage, and unbounded devotion of those who uttered them!

The loss of the 2nd Zouaves, in this unfortunate night attack, was exceedingly severe. Out of 25 officers engaged, there were no less than 18 killed wounded;—of the rank and file, there were as many as 200 killed and wounded. Of these, 73 fell within the redoubt. Out of all the officers who had been recommended for transfer into the *Zouaves* of the Guard, but one could go,—every one of the others, having been either killed, or disabled.

There can be no doubt, that the Russians were fully-prepared to meet this attack. The fact is apparent, even in General d'Osten-Sacken's report of the affair ;—which we accordingly quote from the *Journal de St. Petersburg's* issue of the 13th of March, and which is as follows:

> Towards evening on the 23rd, the various troops, detailed for the completion of the redoubt, begun the preceding night, were posted as follows:
> The infantry regiment of Selinghinsky, in the redoubt;— the 4th Battalion, constituting the working party for the night ;—the 2nd and 3rd, in the interior of the redoubt;— the 1st in the ditch.
> The battalions of the Volhynia regiment of infantry, were thrown out as covering parties, *viz.*, the 4th in column of companies, in advance of the rifle-pits, constructed in front of the redoubt;—the 1st and 2nd, on the right of the redoubt;—the 3rd, on the left, formed in column of attack.
> The dismounted Cossacks of the Black Sea, Battalion No.

8, were advanced beyond the line of our furthest ambuscades, and there concealed.

So, then, we have here nine battalions[8] carefully posted, and fully prepared,—and who were very probably reinforced, after the opening of the attack, by the reserves from Careening Bay,—to defend a fortified position, supported, on its right, by the batteries of the town between Malakoff and the head of Careening bay,—in rear, by those of the ships of war and those on the right of the harbour,—and on the left, by the plunging fire of the steamers *Vladimir, Chersonnese,* and *Gromonosset,* which were anchored at the upper end of the bay.

And they were attacked, in this formidable position, by 900 *Zouaves,*—issuing from trenches, not yet armed with guns,—and who had to cross an intervening space of from 800 to 900 metres covered with thick brushwood, stones, and snow and cut up with rifle-pits and ravines!

Let us now recite a few examples of courage and devotion, taken at random from among the many, to which the occasion gave birth.

Captain Sage had his thigh broken, and fell close by his colonel, while his comrades were endeavouring to cut their way through the opposing masses of the enemy.

Picked up by the Russians and carried into Sebastopol, he died two days after, in spite of all the care and kind attentions which were lavished on him. He was, as a man, full of life, gayety, and courage, and his premature end was deeply regretted in the regiment. His company was on grand guard, the night of this attack; but he was not with it, being exempted from such details, in virtue of his position of adjutant to the battalion. He insisted, however, on accompanying the colonel as a volunteer, in the assault upon the redoubts, and thus perished, a victim, to his own

8. "The strength of a (Russian) battalion of the line or light infantry, is 1,055 combatants;" that "of a regiment of four battalions, is 4,267" (see p. 65 of McClelland's "*Report of the Military Commission to Europe*")—Without taking into account, then, the Cossacks, steamers, or land batteries, the *Zouaves* would still have had opposed to them a force of 8,534 regular infantry, or, deducting for casualties since the opening of the campaign, of at least 6000.—T.

excess of zeal.

Captain Dequirot is carried away by a round shot, while in the very act of leaping on the parapet of the redoubt. As the insignia of his rank were very heavily embroidered on his tunic, the Russians supposed him to be the colonel of the regiment. (*See note following.*)

> Note—During the armistice, which succeeded the night engagement of the 24th of March, 1355, Colonel Cler, then general, made some inquiries of a young lieutenant belonging to the regiment of Volhynia, as to the fate of the officers and soldiers of the 2nd Zouaves, who were missing since the affair of the 24th of February. In the course of his replies, the Russian officer happened to mention, that the body of the colonel had been found inside of the redoubt,—that all the garrison had thronged there to see it,—and that it had been buried with the very highest honours.
>
> The general, between whom and Captain Dequirot there was some resemblance, entreated the young Russian to give him some description of this supposed colonel of *Zouaves*. In doing so, the lieutenant, among other things, remarked that the colonel was quite bald. "Indeed, dear sir, the colonel of the 2nd Zouaves is not bald yet," interrupted the general, raising his *kepi*, as he made the remark, "just see for yourself, if you please."
>
> "But you,—you are a general," replied the young Russian.
>
> "Yes, I am a general now; but on the night of the 23rd February, I was colonel of the 2nd Zouaves at your service."
>
> "In that case, pray accept of my congratulations, General;—I am rejoiced to hear of your promotion, I do assure you."
>
> "But where may I have had the pleasure of meeting you before, allow me to ask, that you should take each an interest in my success," inquired the General, in some surprise.

"This, General, is now the third time, that I have enjoyed the honour of standing before you; the two first, were at the Alma.—and at the Selinghinsk redoubt," was the Russian officer's rejoinder.

Captain Borel, a man as modest, as he was truly brave, has his thigh broken, and dies from the effects of the amputation. Though lying dangerously ill at the time, in his tent, to which he had been confined for several days, he yet insisted upon rising to take command of his company; and, gallantly leading it on to the left attack, was struck down, just as he was entering the redoubt.

Captain Doux, who falls, mortally wounded, on the parapet, will not allow himself to be raised by the soldiers who hasten to his side; "No, no,"—he tells them, "let me die here, for, I have but a few moments more to live;—go you back into the light, where your help is more needed." The cross of honour, found on the body of this courageous officer, was returned to General Canrobert by the governor of Sebastopol, and was sent by the colonel of the 3rd Zouaves to the captain's aged father. Of such a precious relic, his family may well feel proud! . . .

In spite of a first wound, received while forcing his way through the ambuscades, First Lieutenant Bartel continues to press on, some distance in advance of his company,—when he is again struck, by a musket ball, which shatters his leg. But he waves off the *Zouaves*, who offer to assist him from the field, "Go on, go on," he cries to them, "'tis the best way of proving your friendship for me;" and, a few minutes afterwards, he falls, under the Russian bayonets, to rise no more. He was a most dashing officer in the field, and under fire.

As we have before remarked. Second Lieutenant Sevestre was stabbed through and through, and mortally wounded in the effort to re-form his *Zouaves*, who had just cut their way through the Russian battalions. A graduate of the military school, and having but recently joined the regiment, he had already captivated the affection of all belonging to it, by his many fine qualities: he may be said to have died, in receiving a soldier's baptism.

Sergeants Richard and Breysse, too, greatly distinguished themselves on this occasion. The former, a man of remarkable strength, was killed upon the parapet;—but not before, with his clubbed musket, he had dashed out the brains of not a few of those, who ventured to encounter him. The other, an old soldier, who had grown gray in service, was desperately wounded in the ditch of the redoubt; but declined to let himself be carried off, when the recall was sounded, saying to his comrades; "I'm done for, my friends, and though I thank you for your kindness, had rather you would let me be:—look out for yourselves."

Sergeant Major Lacaze, gravely wounded at the assault of the redoubt, remains in the ditch, where he is made prisoner by the Russians.

The pioneer Pradelle, and the Zouave Thebault, who were orderlies to the colonel, and had been detailed to take care of his tent, begged permission to accompany him, and were allowed to do so. The former, during the affray received a dangerous wound, the latter never, for an instant, lost sight of his chief. These were but a few, however, among the many instances of gallantry, devotion, and manly resignation, which occurred among the rank and file of the *Zouaves*. Fighting, undistinguished, amid the general press, they, naturally, attracted less attention than the officers and non-commissioned officers—whose rank made them necessarily more conspicuous,—and, thus, their names, words, and actions, were more apt to pass unheeded by their comrades.

In a letter, addressed to the commanders-in-chief of the allied armies, two days after the affair of the 23rd of February, General d'Osten-Sacken, the governor of Sebastopol, did ample justice to the conduct of the *Zouaves*. "I avail myself of the first opportunity," he wrote, "to assure you that the bodies of such of your gallant soldiers, as remained inside of our entrenchments on the night of the 23rd were interred in the presence of a part of the garrison, with all the honours due to their exalted intrepidity."

The few wounded *Zouaves*, who fell into the enemy's hands, were treated with so much kindness,—that it was impossible for them not to feel the bitterness of their captivity, in a great measure, alleviated by it.

Nor, were the English slow in testifying their hearty sympathy with the *Zouaves*. One of the first persons, Colonel Cler met with, as he stepped back into the trenches, was the chief of the staff of the 2nd English division, who had just learned with sorrow of his death, and whose delight at beholding him alive and uninjured, was, evidently, as sincere as it was gratifying.

Reaching his tent about five o'clock in the morning. Colonel Cler, who was sorely affected by the heavy loss which his regiment had sustained, at once shut himself up there, with strict orders to his attendants, to allow no one to approach him. Hardly had the day begun to dawn, however, when he heard the voices of several persons outside his tent, who insisted upon seeing him.

They proved to be General Lord Rokeby and his officers, who came, in the name of the English Guards, to compliment him upon the glorious manner in which his regiment, had fought the preceding night, and to assure him of the very true and deep sensations of regret, with which they had heard of the death of so many of their gallant comrades among the *Zouaves*.

"Let me entreat your acceptance of this arm," added Lord Rokeby to the colonel, as he presented him with a revolver, "and promise me that you will not only keep it as a memorial of our friendship, but that you will always take it into battle with you. Someday, perhaps, it may be instrumental in saving a life, which, I assure you, is very dear to us all,"

With what heartfelt emotion, the colonel thanked the English officers, it is scarcely necessary to say.

General Canrobert communicated to the French army, his sense of the distinguished conduct of the *Zouaves* on this occasion, in the following general orders;

Before Sebastopol, February 27. 1855.

Soldiers! in the engagement fought between a portion of the troops of the 2nd corps and the Russians, on the night of the 23rd inst., our object was fully attained, and our arms have acquired a new lustre, for which they are principally indebted to the officers, non-commissioned officers, and *Zouaves* of the 2nd regiment, under the bold and spirited leading of their worthy chief, Colonel Cler, and of his majors, Lacretelle and Darbois.

Brigadier General de Monet, who commanded in person, under the energetic direction of Major General Mayran, the assault upon the Russian outworks, and was the first to penetrate inside of them, was wounded in four different places, and never ceased to set a most brilliant example of courage to all around him. Major Mermier, of the 4th regiment of Marines, First Lieutenant Delafosse of the artillery, and Captain Valesque of the engineers, closely followed the general throughout the whole affair.

Lieutenant General Bosquet, commanding the 2nd corps, has the credit of having planned and superintended the whole operation.

The General-in-chief returns thanks, in the name of France and the emperor, to those who, in this combat, have so nobly upheld the honour of our flag, that our very enemies have been moved to express the admiration, with which such rare courage was so well calculated to inspire them!

Our losses have been very heavy; ninety-four of ours have fallen, almost all belonging to the 2nd Zouaves, whose fiery valour on the occasion was above all praise. Truly may we bewail their loss;—and, yet, we are not without the consolation of knowing, that they died for their country and their emperor, and that their death has been avenged by that of a much larger number of their enemies.

I shall take pleasure in forwarding to the emperor and his minister of war, the names of all who have been recommended to me.

Even as they have set no bounds to their devotion, would I gladly dispense with any in the rewards, which I am authorized to confer upon them. But as limits have been imposed on my powers, in this respect, I must for the present content myself, with only doing justice to the claims of those, who have been designated to me, as having been the bravest among the brave.

The following, is the list of promotions and appointments, made in the 2nd Zouaves, by order of the General-in-chief.

To be Officers of the Legion of Honour: Captain Blanchet; Major Lacretelle.

To be Knights:—First-Lieutenant Baratchard; Second Lieutenant Rambaud; Captain Du Mazel; Captain Lacretelle; Sergeant Fombon; Orderly Sergeant Vignan; Sergeant Aigrot; Sergeant Thyriat.

For the Military Medal:—Pradelle, pioneer; Esmieu, sergeant; Demont, orderly-sergeant; Doridat, sergeant; Faillot, sergeant; Prou, *Zouave*; Derlicque, *Zouave*; Embrée, corporal of buglers; Tailland, corporal; Chazal, *Zouave*; Moreau, *Zouave*; Brand, bugler; Labrut, orderly-sergeant; Mouffard, *Zouave*; Paget, sergeant; Dubois, *Zouave*; Boudet, sergeant; Avrand, corporal; Martinel, *Zouave*.

PROMOTIONS.

To be Major:—Captain Banon.

To be Captains:—First Lieutenants Guillerault and Frasseto.

To be First-Lieutenants:—Second-Lieutenants Dousseau and Villain.

To be Second Lieutenants:—Orderly-Sergeants Sillan and Vincendon; Sergeant-Major Pradier; Orderly-Sergeants, Pepin, Labrune, and Bose; and Sergeant de Cetto.

Colonel Cler may be said to have taken leave of his superb and gallant regiment on the night of the 23rd February; for, in a very few days, he was promoted to be general of brigade, and made his *adieux* to the 2nd Zouaves, in the following orders of the day;

Appointed a, brigadier-general, by imperial decree of the

5th inst., it is, yet, not without a pang of regret, that I see the moment has at length arrived, for breaking off my connection with a regiment so dear to me, and with the companions in arms, whose trials, whose dangers, and whose glory, I have shared, now, for a space of three, consecutive years,

Officers, non-commissioned officers, and *Zouaves* of the 2nd regiment,—on quitting you, I feel bound to thank you, for the cordial co-operation which I have on every occasion received from you, and I beg that you will still continue to preserve me a place in your affectionate remembrance, nor altogether forget my name when, as you gather round your bivouac fires, or, later, round the hearthstones of your homes, in our own dear France, your hearts swell, as your tongues dilate, over the memories of our warlike achievements.

I may not read in the closed book of the future, and, yet, I feel beforehand assured, that it will be difficult, if not impossible, for me to inscribe on the roll of my future services, any names more glorious than those of Laghouat, the Babors,—of Alma and Inkermann,—where, with a feeling of such heartfelt pride and satisfaction, I had the honour of marching at your head.

In bidding you now farewell, my friends, I shall not ask you to practise still the same fortitude, nor to be always as brave;—I have known the *Zouaves* too long for that; and I am too well aware of their habitual patience in suffering, and of their fixed scorn for death. But I will ask you to keep up your excellent *esprit de corps*, and to extend the confidence and affection, with which you have invariably honoured me, to Major Lacretelle, who will this day take command of the regiment, and to the successor, whom it may please the emperor to give you in my place.(*See note following.*)

Note.—The 2nd Zouaves are known to have been very sore on the subject of their repulse on the night of the 23rd

February, 1855; and it is evident from the remarks, with which the narrative of the affair is here introduced, that Colonel Cler shared in this feeling. There was certainly no reason for it; since they really made a splendid fight and covered themselves with glory; while, against such tremendous odds as were opposed to them, it was impossible for any troops in the world to have done more,—for very few to have done as much.

But the *Zouaves* are so unaccustomed to defeat, that they find it hard to stomach any repulse; and so, in the first explosion of their rage and disappointment in this instance, they were unjust to others. With this qualification, and the remark, that the English did no better before the Redan, than the Marines before the Selinghinsk redoubt, I subjoin the very interesting account of the latter affair, reported for the *London Times*, by the able correspondent of that paper in the Crimea, William H. Russell, Esq.

"I was woke up shortly after two o'clock on the morning of the 24th of February by the commencement of one of the most furious cannonades we had then heard since the siege began. The whole line of the Russian batteries from our left opened with inconceivable force and noise, and the Inkermann batteries began playing on our light; the weight of this most terrible fire, which shook the very earth, and lighted up the skies with incessant lightning flashes for an hour and a half, was directed against the French.

"The cannonade lasted from a quarter-past two to half-past three, a.m. When first I heard it, I thought it was a sortie, and up I started and rode into the moonlight towards the fire; but ere I could get over the ground to Inkermann, the horrid tumult ceased, and it was only next morning that we found out the cause of such a tremendous exhibition of power. It appeared that the activity of the French in making their approaches against the Malakoff, had rendered the Russians so uneasy, that they began to make

191

counter-approaches and pushed out trenches to rifle pits placed on the Mamelon and on the head of Careening Creek ravine. These were observed by the French, and General Bosquet, acting by order of General Canrobert, directed General de Monet and General Mayran to attack these works with 1000 2nd Zouaves, a battalion of the Fifth of the line, a battalion of the 10th of the line, and a strong body of Marines; and that operation was effected about two a.m. The Russians offered a very vigorous resistance, and the *Zouaves* were not properly supported by the marines or the troops of the line. De Monet was badly wounded. In the desperate conflict, the *Zouaves* lost three officers killed, thirteen wounded, one missing, 69 men killed, and 159 wounded.

"The Russian riflemen showed in front with uncommon boldness, and in great numbers. The *Zouaves* were exceedingly irritated against the Marine infantry, whom they threatened in detail with exceedingly unpleasant "quarters of an hour" at some time to come, for their alleged retreat on the morning of the 24th. The poor fellows came in for hard language, for the *Zouaves* had got it into their head, not only that the Marines bolted, but that they fired into those before them, who were the *Zouaves* aforesaid. In their excessive anger and energy, they were as unjust to their comrades, perhaps, as they were complimentary to ourselves, and I heard two of them exclaim 'Ah, if we had had a few hundred of your English, we should have done the trick; but these Marines—bah!'"—T.

Book 6 - The Crimea conclusion

1

General Cler was succeeded as colonel of the 2nd Zouaves, by Colonel Saurin, an officer of much experience, and who had served a long time in Algeria, both in the foreign legion, and in the 2nd Battalion of Africa.

The 3rd Division of the 2nd Corps, to which the 2nd Zouaves was still attached, was, in the reorganization of the army, which took place about this time, assigned to the duty of guarding and extending our approaches in the direction of Careening bay; and, consequently, remained in its old camp, at the mill of Inkermann.

On account of the severity of the winter and of the little leisure left them by their army arduous and important duties, the *Zouaves* were, during the whole of that season, compelled to forego their ordinary diversions. But with the first glimpses of returning spring, they began to long for their favourite pastimes, and were soon busily engaged in preparations to renew them. Gardens were laid out around the tents, and a theatre was quickly erected in front of the line of the encampment, on the site formerly occupied by the English Guards, now removed to Balaklava.

The thespian company was reorganized under the direction of Lieutenant Petibeau, and the theatre of *Inkermann*, soon commenced a series of representations, for the benefit of the prisoners and wounded of the regiment. Lithographed playbills, announcing the pieces to be performed, and the distribution of the several parts, were circulated through all the corps of the army. They were surrounded with a vignette border, made up of caricatured representations of the principal events of the war, and of snatches of life behind the scenes. The undertaking was crowned with success and, from the very start, the performances drew crowded houses,—in spite of the fire of the *Gringalet* battery, which, showering shot and shell incessantly upon the Inkermann plateau, succeeded, now and then, in occasioning some little annoyance to the managers, but never interrupting the course of the play

Sometimes just as the curtain should have risen, (for there as a veritable curtain and the theatre was a real *bona fide* theatre) the manager would step in front of the stage to announce to the assembled audience that as the regiment had received orders for the performance of some martial duty the play would have to be postponed until the following evening. And it rarely happened, in such cases that it was not again necessary to apologize, the succeeding evening, for the non-appearance of some of the actors, absent, unfortunately, for the best of reasons;—since the bayonets and the fire of the Russians were apt to make but small distinction between the artists and their audiences.

Towards the close of winter and beginning of spring, the regiment lost several men by scurvy, and a few by fever. Among those carried off by the latter disease, was First Lieutenant Guillon, who, being very sick, had been sent to Constantinople for a change of air, and better nursing than he could receive in the field-hospitals of the Crimea. He had hardly spent a few days in that city, however, when he was induced by an excess of zeal, and before he was entirely cured, to return to the Crimea.

The consequence was a relapse, from which he soon died. An officer full of zeal and courage. Lieutenant Guillon had had the honour of bearing the colours of the regiment, both at the storming of Laghouat, and at the battle of the Alma.

The works thrown up by the Russians on the Mamelon Vert, in advance of Careening bay, and by them called, the Kamchatka, Selinghinsk, and Volhynia redoubts,—by us, the redoubt of the

Mamelon Vert, and the White Works,—had gradually attained a formidable development. Armed with guns of a very heavy calibre, and covered in front by a screen of ambuscades, connected together by curtains, *caponieres*, and trenches, they were not only in the way of our own approaches, but, by their close fire, inflicted a very heavy loss on us every day.

It was at length decided between General Pélissier and the commander-in-chief of the English army, after a council of war held on the 6th of June, that these works should be at once carried by assault. The attempt was to be made the next day, and the arrangements for it were left to General Bosquet. The 3rd division of the 2nd Corps, in which was the 2nd Zouaves, was particularly selected for the attack of the White Works (the Selinghinsk and Volhynia redoubts).

On the afternoon of the 7th, General Bosquet assembled the troops, composing the attacking force, and gave them his instructions;—which he closed with the remark, that "of the successful issue of the assault, he entertained not the slightest doubt;—what he wished to impress upon them, was that the works, when taken, must be retained in our possession, no matter at what cost,—as they were of indispensable importance to our ulterior operations,"

The general's remarks were received with acclamation, but nowhere was the enthusiasm greater than in the 2nd Zouaves. For they were going, this time, to light by daylight,—they would see their enemy face to face,—would fight, moreover, on ground already illustrated by the courage of the regiment, and profusely watered by the blood of so many of their brave companions, whose death they had not yet ceased to deplore,—and they wanted nothing more. They avowed a perfect confidence in their ability, not only to take, but to keep fast hold of the redoubts in question,—asserting that if these had slipped from their grasp on the night of the 23rd of February, it was less owing to the numerical superiority of the Russians, than to the darkness of the night, and their own ignorance of the localities.

The troops of the 3rd Division were disposed for the assault as follows;—General de Lavarande's brigade, to which the regiment belonged, on the right, in front of the Selinghinsk redoubt;—it was to carry the work, itself, and the curtains on either side, which connected the Selinghinsk, with the Volhynia redoubt, on the right, and, on the left, with a little work, over-looking the harbour. General de Failly's brigade, stationed on the left, in the French parallel, was to make itself master of the Volhynia, and of the trenches by which that redoubt communi-cated with Careening bay.

The 2nd Zouaves was posted as follows:—its 1st Battalion, under the direction of Colonel Saurin and Major Lacretelle, opposite to the left salient, and its 2nd Battalion, under Major Darbois, opposite to the right salient of the redoubt. And the 1st Battalion was to be preceded by Captain Lescop's company, deployed as skirmishers.

Alongside of its 2nd Battalion, the 4th regiment of Marine Infantry was to attack and carry the principal curtain, and the little redoubt near the harbour.

The signal is given, by rockets, at 6 o'clock, p. m. General de Wimpffen's brigade at once rushes to the assault of the Mamelon Vert,—General Mayran's to that of the White Works. The 2nd Zouaves pours out of the trenches, leaps over the parapet, and while Captain Lescop's skirmishers are making on the full run for the ditch, the 1st and 2nd Battalions bear rapidly down upon the two salients of the Selinghinsk redoubt. In an instant, the ditch is crossed, and, clambering up on the berm, the *Zouaves* exchange a volley with the defenders of the work,—who heap every species of missile upon them, even to stones and dirt.

Colonel Saurin, standing on the top of the counter-scarp, endeavours to re-form the regiment; but, finding that his men, under the combined cross-fire and enfilading fire of the Russian batteries, are strewing the ground like autumn leaves around him, he flings himself into the ditch, which is also swept from one end to the other, by the carronades of the fleet,—makes his way thence, up on the berm, is there closely followed by all of his gallant fellows, and, scaling the parapet, they burst together into the redoubt. Both battalions attacking simultaneously, they carry the work after a brief, sharp combat with the bayonet; and not a Russian escapes,—all whom the steel has spared, falling into the hands of the French as prisoners.

The rush upon the redoubt, its assault, and capture, succeeded one another with such rapidity,—such was the impetuosity with which, they were made,—that it was impossible to note all the acts of individual daring which distinguished them.

One of the first to arrive upon the parapet, where he received a mortal wound, was Captain Pruvost, adjutant to one of the battalions; collecting all his strength for the effort, he faced round once more to his company,—waved them on to the attack with his sword,—then sank a lifeless corpse. The young Captain Perrot, struck down just as, at the head of his company, he had arrived on top of the scarp, shouts with his last breath: "On 2nd Zouaves, on!"

Captains Doré, de la Vaissière, and de Lignerolle, are killed, all three, while bravely fighting at the head of their men. Many of the *Zouaves*, themselves, having got upon the parapet, continue fearlessly fighting in that exposed position, disdaining all cover and utterly braving the enemy, to the wonder and admiration even of the latter, themselves.

No sooner had General de Lavarande made himself master of the enemy's works, than, turning their own cannon upon them, he took such measures to strengthen himself in his new position, as to defy any attempt at recapturing it.

But the fiery and impetuous spirit of Captain Lescop will not suffer him to stop here; at the head of a few hundred men, he follows in hot pursuit of the flying Russians, enters pell-mell with them into the battery of the 12th of May, situated between the White Works and the town, and is finally killed, just in front of the revolving bridge, (*pont tournant*,) which crosses the lower extremity of Careening Bay.

Lieutenant Michelin, whilst pressing closely after him, is killed hard by the same battery; the guns of the battery are spiked; and then, though with great reluctance, the *Zouaves* retrace their steps to the redoubts, where they had left their companions.

During the assault delivered by the 2nd Zouaves, the 4th regiment of Marines, and the brigade of General de Failly have carried the works allotted to them; and, thus, the whole of the White Works are in our possession.

Apprehending that the Russians would make an effort to re-capture them, in the course of the night. General de Lavarande, towards nightfall, stationed the *Gendarmes* of the Guard, who had been given to him as a reserve, inside of the redoubt; and threw out the 2nd Zouaves, in skirmishing order, to the front, in such a way as to cover all the approaches to the work.

At daybreak, a portion of the troops was permitted to return to camp, and the defence of the captured works was entrusted to the *Gendarmes* of the Guard; the *Zouaves* and Marines, remaining in the ditch to aid them.

The 2nd Zouaves continued on guard, here, until 11 o'clock, a. m., of the 10th of June, when it was relieved by fresh troops.

The loss, sustained by the regiment in the affair of the 7th of June, was very considerable:—seven officers killed, twenty-one wounded or contused, and about 650 non-commissioned offic-ers and *Zouaves*, smitten by the fire or steel of the enemy, show how large was the part taken, by the 2nd Zouaves, in the glori-ous combat of that day.

On the 8th of June, the army had to bewail the loss of the young and dashing General de Lavarande. Seated on the *ban-quette*, where he was completely sheltered from the direct fire of the enemy, he was engaged in dictating a report to his *aide de camp*, and orderly officer, when a ricochet shot came bounding over the parapet, and shattering his head and all the upper part of his body, stretched him lifeless on the ground.

Let us now be indulged in a brief word or two about the of-ficers of the 2nd Zouaves, who were killed on this occasion.

Captain Pruvost, one of the adjutants of the regiment, an of-ficer of much zeal, great modesty, and thoroughly versed in his profession,—who had been decorated for his handsome con-duct at the battle of the Alma,—had been so ill, at the beginning of the winter, as to have to be sent to Constantinople, and thence to France. But, declining to avail himself of the sick leave tendered to him, he soon tore himself away from the arms of his mother; and returned to share, with his companions-in-arms, their toils and dangers,—and to die a soldier's death, while setting the example of a soldier's courage.

Recklessly brave, insensible to fatigue, and filled with a passionate thirst of glory, Captain Lescop was a thorough soldier; and, for his gallant conduct at the battle of the Alma, he, too, had been rewarded with the cross of the Legion of Honour. Like the Knight of Malta, in Charles Quint's army, who, riding up to the very walls of Algiers, drove his dagger into the gate, called Bab-Azoun, he, too, under the impulse of his boiling courage, would fain have left his mark upon the battlements of Sebastopol;— equally brave, but not so fortunate as his chivalrous countryman, the Knight of the Frankish tongue,—he threw away his life, in the bold, but desperate attempt!

Captain Perrot, a very young officer, and full of promise for the future, had already, on several occasions, given proofs of his intrepidity.

Replete with zeal, and a very slave to his duties, Captain Doré had always, and everywhere, freely exposed his person to danger. Of a poor, hut respectable family, he had also, like a good son, frequently shared his meagre pittance with his parents.

Just arrived from Algeria, where he had already been decorated for his gallantry, Captain de Lignerolle had been but a few days in the Crimea, when he received his mortal wound, while rushing among the foremost, to the assault of the enemy's entrenchments.

Captain de Lignerolle had been, a brilliant officer, had already made himself remarked for his cool courage and indomitable resolution. He fell, while fighting gloriously at the head of his *Zouaves*.

A man of rare modesty, and of calm, unshrinking courage. First Lieutenant Michelin was much beloved among his comrades, and by his men.

The following are those, who were specially noticed for their gallantry on the 7th, in the general orders of the 15th of June, *viz.*: Captains Pruvost, Doré, Perrot, Lescop, and de la Vaissière; Second Lieutenants Beysser and de Cetto; Sergeants Susini and Vuamet; and Corporal Voirin.

The following were, at the same time, appointed Knights in the Legion of Honour, *viz.*: Captains Lauer, Pouyanne, and Javary; Orderly Sergeant Vasseur; and Sergeant Coutery.

2

In the interval, which succeeded the capture of the White Works, (known subsequently by the name of the Lavarande redoubts,) the 2nd Zouaves continued to take an active part in the construction of our new batteries and approaches. The line of picket stations, both for night and day, was established on the canal, which, connecting with the aqueduct over Careening Bay, conveyed the waters of the Tchernaya into Sebastopol. And the fire of the batteries, which were here thrown up, soon compelled the Russian steamers to seek a refuge in the sheltered creeks, which indented the northern shore of the bay.

Even in a material point of view, the results derived from the capture of the White Works and Mamelon Vert, were of immense importance. For, by becoming masters of positions of such commanding strength, and which, in addition to four months of incessant labour, had cost the enemy such a heavy expenditure in men and material of war,—not only were the besiegers enabled to sweep the harbour with a direct and, to some extent even with a reverse fire, but they were also brought within only a few hundred metres, of the Malakoff that Gordian knot of the whole defence.

But the moral effect, thus produced, was immeasurably greater. In the short space of a single day, the besieging army had made a giant stride toward the attainment of its object. It was now quite clear to everyone that Sebastopol was struggling in the last throes of her death agony and must soon fall. Already, the Russians seemed busy with the thought of retreat, and with preparations for effecting it. Else, why the bridge of boats, which they were so assiduously engaged in throwing over that portion of the harbour, comprised between the military port and the forts on the northern side?

On the other hand, this prompt and brilliant success had exalted to the highest pitch of confidence the spirit of the French army. And when, on the 16th and 17th of June, their fire opened on the enemy with redoubled fury and intensity, its marked preponderance over that of the Russians, was beyond the possibility of question.

It was, doubtless, in consideration of these motives,—which were probably deemed of sufficient weight to justify a departure from the well-established principles of the military art,—that it was decided to anticipate the moment, indicated by the latter, as the proper one, for assaulting such a formidable position, as that of the Malakoff.

Accordingly, on the evening of the 17th, orders were sent to several divisions of the French army, and also, to a part of the English army, to hold themselves in readiness for a general assault, upon that part of the town lying between the Karabelnaïa ravine and greater harbour.

Each corps received its particular instructions for the attack to be made on the 18th, and, between the hours of one and two in the morning, moved silently down to the position assigned to it. The 3rd Division, commanded by General Mayran, was ranged along the left shore of Careening Bay, in the following order;

The 1st Battalion of the 2nd Zouaves, under Major Lacretelle, near the aqueduct; the 2nd, under Major Darbois, next to the 1st; next to that, and on its left, the Marines and 19th *Chasseurs à pied*;—and then, General de Failly's brigade.

Since General de Lavarande's death, the 1st Brigade of the 3rd Division was commanded by Colonel Saurin. Posted as has been just explained, it was to operate against the Point and Black batteries, and the *Maison en croix*, and thus cover the right of the main attack, which was directed against the Malakoff.

The signal for the assault, was to be given by the simultane-ous discharge of three rockets from the Victoria redoubt.[1]

General Mayran having sent orders to Colonel Saurin to be-gin the attack, the 2nd *Zouaves* at once quitted its position, and advanced upon the town. Before it, lay a wide, intervening space of ground, covered with thorn-bushes and brushwood, which greatly impeded its march. No break in the ground, concealed its advance;—and the fast dawning day, already shed a sufficient light over the surrounding scene, to make objects visible, even at a certain distance.

Permitting them, therefore, to approach to within 300 metres, the Russians within the works, all at once opened upon them with tremendous discharges of grape and musketry, in front, while the steamers in the harbour, assailed them with a reverse fire of every species of projectile. For, the Russians had been expecting an assault, and had made every preparation to repel it. Their parapets were lined with a triple rank of men, who kept up a murderous file-fire upon our defenceless columns, while the batteries on the left of the town, and the heavy guns of the steamers, swept, with an incessant storm of grape, every foot of the ground over which they had to pass.

Just at this critical moment, too, Colonel Saurin received a grape shot through his leg,—Major Darbois a musket ball through the cheek; and both, being too badly wounded to be of any further service to their men, were compelled to leave the field. So heavy were the losses of the regiment on this morning, in addition to those which it had sustained on the 7th of the month, that it was left almost destitute of officers; and when the wasted fragments of its two battalions, were re-formed by Major Lacretelle, behind a little swell of ground, they were found to present a total strength, of not more than 400 effective men.

Wishing, however, to make another attempt, Major Lacre-telle inclined to the left, and, with his little handful of brave fel-

1. As is well known to all familiar with the history of the siege, General Mayran, misled by the unintentional discharge of a rocket from some other port of the works, made a premature attack, which, unfortunately, caused the failure of the whole plan.—T.

lows, moved down in the direction of the *Maison en croix*, until he came up with General de Failly's brigade; which he found halted in a quarry, distant about 200 metres from the place,—and which had been as severely maltreated by the enemy, as his own troops.

Here, he was, however, obliged to stop. For, to advance in the teeth of such a terrible cross-fire, as that with which the enemy raked all the ground in front of their works, seemed downright madness. The soldiers evidently hesitated to make the attempt. A few intrepid officers did all in their power to stimulate them to it, and freely exposed their own persons, out in the open ground in advance of the quarries, by way of setting an example; but the effort only provoked their destruction. Major Lacretelle, already wounded in the leg at the commencement of the action, is again struck by a grape shot, which lacerates his breast. Second Lieutenant Escourrou, a young officer full of ardour and devotion to his profession, falls seriously wounded. Colonel de Cendrecourt, of the Marines, and General Mayran, both dangerously wounded, have to be carried off the field.

All hope of taking the town is at an end; yet no one thinks of retreat. Brought to a dead stop by the hurricane of shot and shell, which opposes an impassable barrier to their further advance, the troops stand sullenly at bay, within a short distance of the Russians, and seem, by their very presence, to defy the latter to come out. But the cautious enemy is prudently unwilling to run any risk of compromising the success already gained, by making a sortie under such circumstances; he prefers to wait, in calm security, behind his formidable entrenchments, either until another rash attack should put us completely in his power, or until such time as our bugles should call us off. At length, the recall sounds, however, and our troops fall slowly back upon their lines.

The losses of the regiment on this day, were the more sensibly felt, from their following so closely in the train of the cruel losses, sustained on the 7th of the month, and by which the effective strength of the regiment had already been so sadly diminished. Again had several officers been killed;—the three highest in rank in the regiment, together with eight of lesser rank, had been wounded, and among the latter, two had fallen into the enemy's hands;—while, at the same time, more than 300 non-commissioned officers and *Zouaves*, had been either killed or wounded.

Captain Pouyanne, who was reported missing, but who had been in reality killed, was an officer of much natural vigour, both of mind and body,—who had just been rewarded for his gallantry on the 7th of June, by the cross of the Legion of Honour. Modest, zealous, and devoted to his duties, he was universally regretted by all who knew him.

The young Captain Frasseto, who was also reported missing,—an officer of much promise, and already distinguished for his merit,—received his death-wound, while gallantly leading on his *Zouaves* in their exposed and dangerous march upon the town. Although very ill during all the winter, he yet had refused to quit his company, and, though scarce able to walk, had insisted upon accompanying it, on every expedition against the enemy or service of danger, for which it was turned

First Lieutenant de Vermondans, mortally wounded, while marching, at the head of his *Zouaves*, to the assault of the town, was an officer who, to great energy of character, united a gay and sprightly disposition, which had made him a general favourite among the officers and soldiers of his regiment. He had been already wounded at the battle of the Alma, where he had made himself remarked for his daring, and though very young, he had been decorated, and was, now, just on the point of being made captain, when death came thus suddenly to rob him of his promotion.

Second Lieutenant Gabalda was another of the officers mortally wounded, on this occasion. After having already performed a tour of service in Africa, as orderly sergeant in a regiment of the Line, he had voluntarily resigned his grade, for the privilege of entering the *Zouaves* as a private. But his good conduct and courage had not only quickly won him back his former grade,—they had carried him, as is seen, much higher.

In general orders of the 25th of June, the general-in-chief made the following promotions and appointments;

To be an officer of the Legion of Honour,—Colonel Saurin.

To be Knights,—First Lieutenant Fayout; Sergeants Carlin, Deleuze, Liotard; Corporal Guignot; and the *Zouaves* Castaingts, Chouanard, and Nicolod.

Major Lacretelle was promoted into the 19th of the Line, as lieutenant-colonel.

We have already had occasion, in our relation of the campaign in the Babors, to speak of Colonel de La Tour du Pin, of the staff. And, from the sketch then given of his character, it may be readily conceived, that this eccentric officer,—whose passion for danger and glory was pushed to such a remarkable extreme,—was little likely to see the *Zouaves* starting off for the East, without being strongly tempted to follow them.

Accordingly, Colonel Cler's jackals had been but a short time in the Crimea, when their friend, *the colonel with the frying-pan*, turned up there, too,—as rash, as reckless, and imprudent as ever;—and whenever he made his appearance in their camp, knowing what such visits usually portended, they could again repeat, with the same, confident assurance, as in the past, "*Ha,! ha! there'll be tobacco to smoke, soon!*"

And, in fact, their previsions were seldom disappointed; for, all infirm as he was, and cut off by his infirmity, from taking any more active part in the scenes, in which his soul delighted, than that of a simple volunteer, yet this poor, gallant officer never let slip any occasion of exposing himself to ball or bullet, provided he could thereby secure a nearer and better view of a battle, or skirmish. He almost seemed, to be present, on these occasions, as a judge of the lists, or, at least, as the second for both parties in their colossal duel;—and it was difficult for one who saw him there, so cool, and calm, and imperturbable, under the hottest fire and amid the bloodiest carnage, not to fancy him endowed, like Achilles, with the quality of perfect invulnerability,—even to his heel!

Having, on the 26th of October, learned that the Colonel of the 2nd Zouaves was on trench duty, on the extreme left of our Left Attack, and that new approaches were to have been commenced during the night, de La Tour du Pin hastened to join his friend at his perilous post. Already, several of the batteries in the Russian counter-approaches had been unmasked, and were beginning to rain death into the French trenches,—while the line of the parallel was barely more than traced, along the ground,— yet this was precisely the moment chosen by de La Tour du Pin, to seat himself quietly, there, by the side of his friend, and begin a conversation upon the future character, and probable results of the siege operations.

Colonel Cler tried to point out to him, the danger to which he was exposing himself, and the impropriety and uselessness of thus risking his life, when there was no obligation of duty for him to do so. Whereon, de La Tour du Pin branched off into a discussion of the merits of the Russian fire, maintaining, for his own part, its utter inefficacy. It so happened that, just at that moment, and as if to expose the fallacy of his opinion, a Russian round shot, knocking over the sand-bag behind them, passed right between the two friends;—while the dead and wounded, who lay around them, together with the many scattered fragments of exploded bombs and shells, seemed to afford pretty convincing evidence, that the Russians were anything but in the habit, of wasting their powder!

Yet in spite of all these proofs to the contrary, de La Tour du Pin clung pertinaciously to his opinion; and the colonel of the 2nd Zouaves was reduced, at length, to the necessity of employing almost as much force as persuasion, to induce his friend to quit the place.

Soon after, occurred the battle of Inkermann, and, as may well be supposed, he took good care, not to lose such a glorious opportunity of gratifying his favourite passion. And, although he accompanied General Bosquet's battalions into the thickest of the fight, and never left them while it lasted, he had the good fortune to come off with no more serious injury, than a trifling scratch in the face.

When the weight of our attack was turned against Malakoff, de La Tour du Pin seized every opportunity of studying the town from that quarter, and, especially, of watching what went on in the harbour; he, to this end, paid repeated visits to the camp of the mill of Inkermann. One day, he came and besought his friend for permission to visit the furthest outposts. Captain de la Vaissière, one of the adjutants of the regiment, offered to guide him out, as far as one of our rifle-pits, which, though occupied at night, was abandoned during the day, on account of its too great exposure to the enemy's fire;—and they accordingly started off together.

On arriving there, de La Tour du Pin took leave of his companion, who returned to his duties, and nestling quietly down into the most comfortable position he could find, with no other company than his spy-glass, began leisurely to reconnoitre the Point battery and upper end of the harbour. When he had completed, to his satisfaction, his prolonged and searching examination of these points, he got up to go; and following, as he supposed, the path by which he had come, tried to make his way back to the nearest grand guard.

But, unfortunately, the path was not very distinctly marked out,—the ground being very stony and covered with brambles, besides being cut up with ravines, and of a very uneven surface,—and being, moreover, extremely near-sighted, he gradually took a wrong direction, and soon became completely lost. After wandering about for some time, without the slightest idea of where he was,—but noticing that the holes, ploughed in the ground by round shot, and the traces of their passage on the surrounding rocks, were becoming much more frequent, and that little columns of dust were incessantly being knocked up all round him,—he finally came to the conclusion, that he must be approaching the town,—and, meanwhile, was serving as a target for the Russian sharpshooters!

He then faced about;—indeed, it was quite time for him to do so,—and trusting to Providence, set off in the opposite direction;—succeeding, finally, after perambulating round for an hour or so, in getting safely hack to the French outposts,—more confirmed, than ever, in his contemptuous opinion of the Russian marksmanship

On the 18th of June, the fearless colonel set out with the leading columns, and was present, as an amateur, at the whole of the terrible combat, in which were engaged the divisions of Generals Brunet and Mayran And when the bleeding remnants of these two divisions were obliged to fall back, over the open space where they had already suffered so severely, *the colonel with the frying-pan* seated himself gravely upon the ground, there where he was, in the very centre of the battlefield, and quietly retained his position, until after the last soldier had filed past him, before he rose to resume the unruffled tenor of his own solitary course, back into the trenches!

Yet here, again, he escaped unscathed! But, just as the last bloody act of the great drama was about to be played out,—on the 8th. of September, the day of the capture of the Malakoff,— he was struck by the fragment of a shell, while following the rush of General de MacMahon's columns to the assault,—and his leg was laid open by it, to the bone. Transferred to Marseille, he died there;—a victim, at length, to the singular passion, which, while he lived, had impelled him upon every battlefield in Europe.

The name of the intrepid and unfortunate Colonel de La Tour du Pin, is still held in affectionate remembrance among our soldiers;—it will never be effaced from the hearts of those, who served with him in Africa and the Crimea. For long years yet to come, as they gather round their bivouac fires, will the Zouaves of the 2nd regiment, especially, relate to one another the daring exploits, and amusing adventures, of their friend, *the colonel with the frying-pan.* And when the memory of other actors in the same scenes, has wholly passed away, no doubt his romantic history will still form the theme, of some thrilling legend of the camps.

The 2nd Zouaves was much too seriously crippled after the bloody affair of the 18th of June, to be capable of taking any further part in the labours of the siege. It was, in fact, reduced to a perfect skeleton,—the strength of its companies was wasted away almost to nothing; and, besides the number of its wounded, who filled the hospitals, it had a large number of others, who were taken care of in its camp.

During the month of July, then, it was relieved from further duty at the Right Attack, by the 7th of the line, and, with the rest of the 3rd Division, to which it belonged, was transferred to the army of observation on the Tchernaya. The position assigned to it, on the lowest of the three Fedioukine hills, to the right of the Traktir gorge, speedily procured it the opportunity of taking a glorious part, in the battle fought, the 16th of August, on. the banks of the Tchernaya River.

Before entering into any account of that splendid victory, in which the 2nd Zouaves had so large and honourable a share, it is necessary, in order to a proper understanding of the evolutions of the two armies, to furnish some description of the ground, over which they manoeuvred.

The Tchernaya River, after issuing from the mountain gorges near Tchorgoun, flows, at first, through a narrow valley—which, gradually expanding opposite the Fedioukine heights, again contracts, about the ruins of Inkermann, just above where the river loses itself in Sebastopol Bay. Near the gorges of Tchorgoun, a canal receives the waters of the Tchernaya and of its affluent on the right, the Tchouliou, and, crossing the former stream over an aqueduct, conveys them, after a long and devious course, into the interior of Sebastopol.

This canal, which is everywhere deep, but narrow, and in most places lined with a steep embankment, skirts the foot of the Fedioukine hills,—inclines, again, toward the Tchernaya,— passes under a little bridge, about a 100 metres in rear of the Traktir bridge,—flows through a reservoir, scooped out of the hollow space, which lies between the Fedioukine hills and

Mount Sapoune,—winds around the base of the latter,—and finally enters Sebastopol, by an aqueduct thrown across Careening Bay.

The valley of the Tchouliou is shut in, on the right, by a range of heights, which, crowned with lofty plateaux of difficult access, constitute the dividing ridge between it and the Tchernaya valley. The direction of this ridge is oblique to the course of the Tchernaya; and it abruptly terminates, at the point where that stream emerges from the deep *cañon*, through which it has worked its way, down, from the little plain above Tchorgoun.

It is just at this point, that the aqueduct crosses the Tchernaya, approaching it through a narrow defile, lined with almost perpendicular walls of rock,—where it so blocks up the way, that, with the help of a few earth-works, the Piedmontese have made themselves completely masters of the passage. To the left, beyond the aqueduct, the ground slopes gently up to the little village of Kamara,—situated at the foot of one of the projecting spurs, of the chain of mountains extending from Balaklava to the valley of Baidar.

The Fedioukine hills, which occupy a somewhat isolated position, being divided, by two considerable openings, from the other heights of that side of the Tchernaya valley, consist of three separate, but contiguous hillocks, rising one above the other. Commanding, as they do, the plain lying to the north of them, through which the river flows,—and, to the south, the little plain of Balaklava,—they constitute an excellent defensive position. The one on the right, and which was, at the same time, the lowest and most accessible of the three, commanded the left of the Traktir gorge,—through which passed the road, leading from Balaklava up to the Mackenzie plateau. And It was on top of this one, that were encamped the 2nd Zouaves and the 19th battalion of *Chasseurs-à-pied*.

On the 15th of August, the eve of the battle of the Tchernaya, the allied army was distributed as follows:

1° On the extreme left, below the heights of Mount Sapoune, and between the telegraph and Canrobert redoubt, was encamped the 1st Brigade of Herbillon's division, consisting of the 14th Battalion of *Chasseurs*, and of the 47th and 52nd of the Line,

2° On the highest of the Fedioukine hills, was a portion of Camou's division,—that is to say, the regiment of *Tirailleurs Indigènes*, the 6th and 82nd of the Line, and a battery of the 13th Artillery.

3° From the centre hill streamed the pennon of General Herbillon, indicating that, there, were his head-quarters, and near him, and a little to his left and front, were the 50th of the Line and 3rd Zouaves, belonging to General de Wimpffen's brigade,—the 95th and 97th of the Line, belonging to General de Failly's,—and three batteries of the 2nd Artillery,

4° Further to the right, the lowest of the three hills was, as before remarked, occupied by the 2nd Zouaves and 19th battalion of *Chasseurs-à-pied*, belonging to the 1st brigade of General Faucheux's division.

5° In rear of General Herbillon, was the reserve of the French army on the Tchernaya, commanded by General Cler,—consisting of the 62nd and 73rd of the Line, and of five batteries of artillery,—of which two belonged to the Imperial Guard,—under the direction of Colonel Forgeot.

6° The division of cavalry, principally made up of the regiments of *Chasseurs d'Afrique*, and commanded by General Morris, had its bivouac in the little plain of Balaklava, to the right, and a little to the rear of the Fedioukine hills.

7° On the right of the French, the whole of the Piedmontese army lay extended along the slopes, which, falling gradually away from the village of Kamara, terminate in a steep escarpment over the *cañon* of the Tchernaya,—or, with easier fall, stretch gently away to the little river Kreuzen, which, rising near Varnoutka, empties into the Tchernaya, opposite Tchorgoun.

Outposts had been pushed forward, across these streams, on the heights overlooking the village of Tchorgoun; and they were covered by *épaulements*, thrown up between them and the enemy.

The little Piedmontese army, so perfectly organized under the superintendence of its brave and skilful commander, General Alphonse de la Marmora, had established its camps on both sides of the Woronzoff road; and, by means of batteries and earthworks, its position had been rendered very formidable.

The utmost harmony prevailed between the soldiers of the two nations;—especially between our own and those of the brigade of Savoy, commanded by General Mollard, between whom there reigned a cordial intimacy, growing out of the uniformity of language, character, and appearance, which made them almost as one people. They fairly burned for an opportunity to fight in the same cause, on the same field, and side by side with us, as their fathers had done before them.

8° The Turkish contingent lay to the right of the Piedmontese, in the forests, which covered the summits of the lofty group of mountains, extending from Balaklava to the valley of Varnoutka.

9° Finally, some English corps, composed almost entirely of cavalry and artillery, occupied the plain and hillsides between us and Balaklava.

Towards evening, on the 15th of August, General Herbillon, commander of the army of observation, received from General d'Allonville, who was in command of a mixed division of cavalry and infantry, in the valley of Baidar, a telegraphic despatch—of which, though interrupted by the gathering darkness, enough was transmitted, to apprise him that the Russian, army had been in movement all day, and that, at that very moment. General d'Allonville's left was threatened by heavy masses of their troops, who seemed bent on turning his flank, in that direction.

Expecting, in consequence, to be attacked that night, or the next morning, General Herbillon sent to put his lieutenants on their guard, and completed the instructions, which he had already given them for their direction, in the event of an attack, by fresh ones, more particularly designed to meet the present emergency.

During the night of the 15th of August, six divisions of Russian infantry, three of cavalry, and a numerous artillery, moved down from the Mackenzie heights, along the road and mountain ridges, which overhang the Tchernaya near Tchorgoun. Three of their Infantry divisions, the 7th, 6th, and 12th, under the orders of General Read, were to attack the French; the rest, under Liprandi, were to fall upon the Piedmontese.

The cavalry was to support both attacks; and the artillery, ranged along the heights of the opposite side,—from the redoubt, which commanded the Mackenzie road, just below Bilboquet, up as far as the Piedmontese entrenchments,—was, while the battle lasted, to keep up an incessant fire, both direct and oblique, upon the right of the Fedioukine hills, and the entrance to the gorge of Traktir.

A little after four, a.m., accordingly, the advanced guard of General Liprandi's corps drove in the Sardinian outposts, upon the heights between Tchorgoun and the Tchernaya, and forced them back across the river. Immediately after this, the heavy Russian artillery on the opposite heights, and their field artillery, posted halfway down the side of the valley, near the redoubt recently thrown up just under Bilboquet, opened a brisk fire upon all the ambuscades on our side of the Tchernaya. The three divisions of Read's corps, poured down at the same time, upon the river;—the 7th inclining to the right across the plain,—the 5th and 12th making straight for the bridge.

3

At the first sound of the cannon, the French divisions fall in, under arms, and are hurried away to the positions, beforehand assigned to them. A dense fog hangs low over the Tchernaya, and, shrouding the smoke of the enemy's gun, makes it impossible to conjecture, on which point of our line, he is bearing down in most force. However, the sharpshooters in the ambuscades, aided by strong supports, obstinately defend all the approaches to the aqueduct, and the whole line of the riverbank.

But, as we are only writing the history of the 2nd Zouaves,

it may be well to premise, that we do not intend to enter into any account of the attacks, directed against other points of our line; both the plan and the limits of this narrative are opposed to such an attempt. We shall confine ourselves to a simple description of that part of the battle, fought on the lowest of the three Fedioukine hills,—to the left of the bridge,—and in the Traktir gorge.

The Russian fire, then, has scarcely opened, when, snatching up their arms, and cheerfully abandoning their coffee, which they have been just on the point of taking, the *Zouaves* of the 2nd regiment hasten down to meet the enemy. Major Darbois, although barely recovered from the wound he had received on the 18th of June, is in command of the regiment. Orders are sent to him by General Faucheux to move his two battalions[2] down, on the left of the plateaux, to support, and, if necessary, reinforce the line of our advanced skirmishers, extending above the bridge. Major Alpy's battalion, accordingly, descends as far as the aqueduct; while that under the immediate direction of Major Darbois, remains in reserve, further up the hill.

But our skirmishers along the Tchernaya, overpowered by the heavy masses which the enemy has brought to bear upon them, are at length compelled to retire upon the aqueduct. Quickly following, the enemy swarms across the river, upon light, portable bridges. Major Alpy resolutely holds his ground;—but soon, mortally wounded, has to be carried off the field. Major Darbois then comes down with the rest of the regiment, to the support of his other battalion; and assuming the offensive, forces the Russians back, and again clears the ground, lying between the river and the canal.

But, gathering up their supports, the Russians again advance, and, by means of planks and ladders, thrown from one bank over to the other, cross the aqueduct, and reach the foot of the hill. Against such overwhelming odds, the *Zouaves*, though stub-

---

2. The regiment was reduced to less than 1200 men, since the bloody affairs of the 24th February and the 7th and 18th of June, in which it had no less than 65 officers and 1100 men killed, wounded, or disabled.

bornly resisting, can make no lead. Yet, supported by the fire of Captain de Sailly's field battery, posted in rear of them, near the gorge, they still oppose a steady front to the enemy, and retire slowly, disputing every inch they yield, and making desperate stands, behind every little patch of brushwood,—each slight wave in the ground.

Their chief, Major Darbois, performs prodigies of valour; on horseback, had always in front, with his cap raised high on the point of his gleaming sword, he serves, both as a continual mark for the enemy's fire, and as a rallying point for his men. However, in spite of its losses,—which, being instantly repaired, it does not feel,—the heavy Russian column continues to advance;—it has, at length almost reached the top of the hill. While, on the other hand, the regiment, with no supports in sight,—is, every moment, losing some of its best officers, some of its most intrepid *Zouaves*.

Major Darbois receives his death-wound, by a bullet which strikes him in the abdomen. Second Lieutenant Bosc, the colour-bearer of his battalion, is hit by another, full in the chest. But, as he falls, his colours are instantly caught up by some non-commissioned officers, who are near him;—who, raising them high above their heads, flaunt them in proud defiance, right in the very faces of the enemy!

Still, the *Zouaves* keep closing up their ranks, which the Russian fire is so cruelly thinning, and, though they have scarcely any officers left to direct them, they continue to retire in unbroken order. But, at length, even the friendly support of Captain de Sailly's battery fails them; for, becoming masked by their line, his guns have to be limbered up and moved to the rear.[3]

---

3. At this stage of the battle the 1st brigade of the 3rd Division, constituting the first line,—having lost the regiment of Marines, which had been recently detached, part to Kertch, and a part to Eupatoria,—scarcely mustered a thousand men. Every officer of rank was down.—General Manèque, its commander, had received three dangerous wounds in the affair of the 18th of June;—Colonel Saurin, seriously wounded at the same attack, had been sent down to Constantinople; Major Alpy and Darbois had just been mortally wounded, and the commanding officer of the 19th Chasseurs had, the night before been suddenly taken with cholera, and was then in hospital.

At this critical moment, General Cler,—who, at the commencement of the battle, had moved with three of the battalions belonging to his brigade, to the right of Faucheux's division, to form there a second line and a reserve,—comes suddenly into view, with his three battalions already deployed into line. The smoke of the cannonade and the undulating character of this part of the plateau, by concealing his movements, had permitted him to steal this march upon the enemy.

Quickly informing himself of what has taken place on the hill before his arrival, he gives immediate orders to Colonel de Pérussis, of the 62nd of the Line, to advance with his two battalions, and attack the ponderous Russian column on its front and left flank, while he sends his *aide-de-camp*. Captain Caffarelle, to guide his remaining battalions round upon the enemy's right. Then, spurring forward his horse to meet the *Zouaves*, "Why, which way are you going, 2nd Zouaves?"—he cries to them,—"that is not your way:—to the front, my friends to the front!"

The *Zouaves* who have just recognized their old colonel, in the general who has brought them these welcome reinforcements, send up a cheer, which fairly makes the welkin ring—then, facing instantly about, and while, loud above the roar of battle, is heard once more the blast of their bugles sounding the regimental march, they, with levelled bayonets, and the impetus of a falling avalanche,—hurl themselves upon the foe! The latter, taken all aback by the unexpected fire of General Cler's battalions, and the fiery and resistless onset of the *Zouaves*, begin to waver,—soon, give way,—and, the next moment, are trampled underfoot, and rolled headlong down the slopes, into the canal.

Attacked with equal spirit and energy by General de Failly, on the slopes to the left, and at the bottom of the gorge, the whole mass of Russians is borne back, in refluent disorder, over the bridge and across the stream. Saving the wounded and the dead, not a man of their 5th and 12th Divisions remain on this side of the Tchernaya. On the extreme right of their line, their 7th Division, which, in the beginning of the day, had assailed the French left, is, at the same time, vigorously repulsed by the brigade of General de Wimpffen.

Perceiving the failure of his first attempt upon our lines, but resolved to make another, the Russian general-in-chief calls down the reserves, which he has on the heights of the Tchouliou, and, giving them, as a support, to the divisions already engaged, sends down the whole to a fresh attack. The huge mass is again put in motion,—and again makes straight at the French centre.

To cover its advance, the Russian artillery,—in battery, all along the heights and midway down the sides of the valley, from below Bilboquet, up as high as the ruined redoubt, and the entrenchments of the Piedmontese outposts—sweeps, with a hail of fire, the sides and lower plateaus of the Fedioukine hills. Even the camp of the 2nd Zouaves, on top of the hill, is reached by it, and the ground about the camp, is literally ploughed up with round shot. The seven French batteries engaged,—two of which, those of Captains de Sailly and Armand, are stationed on the lowest of the three hills, and therefore exposed to the full force of this terrible cannonade,—instead of making any reply to it, turn the whole weight of their fire upon the advancing infantry. And they are aided in this, by the field and heavy batteries of the Piedmontese artillery on their right.

Meanwhile, the Russian infantry again attempts to pass the river:—the remains of their 12th and 5th Divisions are already pouring over the Traktir bridge. But they are met by the troops of General de Failly, who rush down, at the *pas de charge*, upon the bridge and the river bank below, while the 2nd Zouaves, supported by the battalions of General Cler, contests the passage of the river above. There is a fierce shock of bayonets,—a brief, sharp struggle,—during which the enemy's round shot, respecting neither friend nor foe, cut long and bloody lanes through the solid mass of human flesh; and that of the French, aimed high over the heads of their own battalions, fall with crushing weight, on the tail of the enemy's columns, and throw them into disorder.

The Russians are at length beaten back, and, leaving the little valley strewed with the bodies of their dead, they retire under cover of their artillery, to the foot of the hills on the other side, and are there re-formed.

Seeing how useless are his efforts to force across the Traktir bridge, the Russian general is to make an attempt in another direction, and selects for this purpose, that part of our line, comprised between the French right and Piedmontese left. For, at this point, the receding hills leave a wide opening, close to the Tchernaya and the aqueduct, and these two water-courses are, here, everywhere fordable.

Accordingly, the 17th Division, which, up to this time, had only been employed as a reserve, is, in conjunction with the regiment of Odessa, directed against that point. Crossing the river and the canal, and pushing rapidly across the plain, towards the French right, for which it reserves the full force of its blow, it begins to make its way up the hill under the friendly cover of a ravine, which extends down the right side of the lowest of the three Fedioukine hills. But General Faucheux at once orders down upon this point a half battery of artillery, and some companies of the 14th Battalion of *Chasseurs-à-pied*, in aid of the battalion of the 62nd of the Line, under Major de Lavoyrie, which General Cler had already sent down there to oppose the ascent of the Russian column.

The Piedmontese throw forward their left wing, at the same time, to counteract this movement of the enemy; and while one of their battalions of Bersaglieri inclines over to the French right, and takes post in rear of the threatened slope, their artillery and the division of General Trotti suddenly deploy on the left flank of the Russian column A few volleys of musketry are exchanged, and Major de Lavoyrie falls, mortally wounded , but, before being carried off the field, he enjoys the consolation,— so great in the eyes of such a gallant soldier,—of first seeing the enemy in full retreat towards the aqueduct.

Obliged, thus, to renounce all hope of forcing the allied centre, and with no alternative, if they would retreat any further in the same direction, but to run the gauntlet of the Piedmontese fire, as they retraced their steps across the open space, to the right of the French position,—the Russians re-form their broken ranks, at the foot of the slopes occupied by our troops, and, for some lime, content themselves with keeping up a steady fire on our extreme right. Fortunately, their bullets, owing to the elevation at which they are necessarily fired, only pass over our heads, without doing us any mischief.

At length, seeming to have made up their minds, and forming themselves into a massive column, with the Odessa regiment in front, they again begin to ascend the hill, on the side, where Armand's battery is posted, on the verge of the upper plateau.

Divining at once, the object of this, the enemy's last and crowning effort. General Cler disposes two of his battalions,—the 2nd of the 62nd, under Colonel de Pérussis and Major Cottat, and the 1st of the 73rd, under Major Deparfouru,—in rear of the battery, with directions to its commander to be prepared to fire every gun in it, at the instant of hearing the "charge;"—and, leaving a single company of the 2nd Zouaves, commanded by Lieutenant Vial de Sabligny, in front, where it can be seen by the advancing column,—he quietly awaits the latter's approach. Without any suspicion of the snare thus set for it, the Russian column continues its toilsome ascent up the bill, stopping only to align its platoons, every now and then, upon the little marker's flags, borne by some of its non-commissioned officers.

The *Zouaves* fall slowly back before it, gradually unmasking the battery behind; and, increasing, the confidence of the enemy, as well by their retrograde movement, as by the paucity of their numbers, encourage him to come on. At length, the head of the Russian column succeeds in reaching the edge of the plateau—and is there received by a last, general discharge of all the guns of the battery—and, while the drums are hurriedly beating the "charge," the guns are instantly run back, by hand, to the rear, so as to leave a clear field for the operations of the infantry, and the two battalions, rushing forward from their concealed position, charge down upon the head and flanks of the ascending column, with such suddenness and impetuosity,—that, staggered, taken by surprise, and reeling under the shock, the latter offers but a feeble resistance,—is soon completely routed,—and, hotly pursued by the battalion of Major Cottat and by the *Zouaves*, is driven down the hill upon the aqueduct, and thence across the river;—leaving a large number of prisoners in our hands, and the field strewed with the bodies of its dead and wounded, as well as with drums, markers' staffs, and arms of every description.

With this, the battle was at an end;—we had won another signal victory; and the 2nd Zouaves, which had contributed so large and distinguished a part towards its attainment, was fairly entitled to inscribe the name of Tchernaya on its colours, alongside of the glorious names of the Alma and of Inkermann. For, no less than four times had it repulsed the successive assaults of the Russian columns; while three hundred of its number, among them eleven officers, had freely shed their blood to achieve this splendid result.

Major Darbois, who was mortally wounded, while commanding the regiment in this battle, had come to the Crimea with the 1st regiment of Zouaves, but promoted, soon after, as major, into the 2nd regiment, he proved himself every way worthy of his new epaulettes, by the bold and effective manner in which he led his battalion to the assault of the White Works, on the night of the 23rd of February. Cited in the orders of the army for his conspicuous gallantry on that occasion, he soon made himself again remarked, in the affair of the 7th June—and again, in that of the 18th of the same month—when he was wounded in the face.

Scarcely recovered from this wound, when he assumed command of the regiment, he, nevertheless, guided it with consummate ability and energy, at the battle of the Tchernaya. And for this, his last deed of arms, he had the consolation of receiving, before he expired, the cross of an Officer in the Legion of Honour.

Major Alpy, who was also desperately wounded in the very beginning of the battle, had been only two days with the regiment, having last served with the *Chasseurs* of the Imperial Guard. He was, however, much regretted by the *Zouaves*; who, even in this brief time, had learned to appreciate his many valuable qualities as an officer.

Modest as well as brave, and devoted to his duty, Second Lieutenant Bosc, who bore the eagle of the regiment in this battle, had already signalized himself at the storming of Laghouat, by the unshrinking courage with which he several times ventured into the hottest of the Arab fire, as bearer of orders to the different companies of his battalion. He was, then, only commissary sergeant. For his handsome conduct on the night of the 23rd of February, he had been appointed second lieutenant; and, again distinguishing himself at the battle of the Tchernaya, where the colours in his hand were absolutely riddled with bullet-holes, was there mortally wounded, and died soon afterward;—but not before he had had the satisfaction of receiving the Knight's cross of the Legion, which was awarded to him in consideration of his courage.

Captain Arnaud, an extremely dashing officer, whose promotion as first lieutenant dated from the storming of Laghouat, where he had greatly distinguished himself, and who had been again honourably mentioned for his conduct in the affair of the 7th of June, was another of those mortally wounded in this battle; where, as usual, he had set his men an example of the most daring courage.

Second Lieutenant Berger, who was killed just as the regiment was in the act of resuming the offensive, had originally joined the 2nd Zouaves as a non-commissioned officer, but was made a second lieutenant for his gallant behaviour in the affairs of the 7th and 13th of June.

In addition to those we have just named, Captain Réau and Sergeant Girardot received the decoration of the Legion, and several of the soldiers, the military medal;—while numerous promotions were made throughout the regiment.

The battle of the Tchernaya was the last of the engagements of the Crimean war, in which the 2nd Zouaves was called upon to display its well-known bravery and soldier-like devotion. So much had this gallant regiment been reduced by its successive losses, within the past few months, that it was no longer in any condition to take part in the arduous labours of the siege. Being left, for this reason, with the army of observation on the Tchernaya, it continued with it until after the capture of the city in October, when it moved its camp, for a short time, in rear of the Col de Balaklava; and thence, in the latter part of the same month, to the heights of Mount Sapoune, between Telegraph hill and Canrobert redoubt;—where it still was, when peace was proclaimed.

In. the month of June, 1856, the 2nd Zouaves, or what remained of it, set sail for Algeria—thus for ever taking leave of these shores, which it had so profusely watered with its blood, and of the noble dead belonging to it, who, after so gallantly sacrificing their lives for the honour of France, lay sleeping their long, last sleep, there, under the green Crimean sod.

The regiment returned to Oran,—where it found both the garrison and the inhabitants ready to vie with each other, in giving it that triumphal welcome, to which it had so signally entitled itself, by the services which it had rendered,—the blood it had spilt,—and by the eminent examples of courage, fortitude, and devotion, with which, since its departure, it had enriched the glorious annals of France.

www.ingramcontent.com/pod-product-compliance
Lightning Source LLC
Chambersburg PA
CBHW032032090426
42733CB00029B/260